MY
USUAL
GAME

ADVENTURES IN GOLF

VILLARD BOOKS · NEW YORK · 1995

MY

USUAL

GAME

DAVID OWEN

Portions of this work were originally published in different form in
The Atlantic Monthly, Condé Nast Traveler, Esquire,
Golf Digest, M, and *The New Yorker.*

Library of Congress Cataloging-in-Publication Data

Owen, David
My usual game: adventures in golf / by David Owen
p.   cm.
ISBN 0-679-41487-8
1. Owen, David. 2. Golfers—United States—Biography.
I. Title.
GV964.094A3   1995   796.352′092—dc20 [B]   94-44003

Manufactured in the United States of America on acid-free paper

9 8 7 6 5 4 3 2

Book design by JoAnne Metsch

For Ann,
in spite of everything

"Just once, I wish I would play my usual game."

—Traditional golfing lament

CONTENTS

MY
USUAL
GAME

1

MY USUAL GAME

I PLAYED GOLF WHEN I WAS TWELVE AND THIRTEEN, BUT then I stopped. For one thing, I was terrible. For another, it was 1969. Richard Nixon played golf, and Jerry Garcia didn't, and the war in Vietnam seemed not entirely un-golf-related, and so forth. At the age of thirty-six, though, I took it up again. My friend Martha invited me to play one day, and on a whim I went. I shot a humiliating score, but something clicked in my head. The next day, I joined the little nine-hole golf club in the small Connecticut town where I live. I bought shoes, a bag, a glove, and a lot of other stuff. I already had some clubs, an old set that my brother, a good golfer, had abandoned. For a few years, those clubs had been behind a chair in my office, and I had gradually begun to enjoy thinking of myself as the sort of person who just has a bunch of golf stuff lying around. Now, I started playing as often as I could, usually several times a week, a practice I have continued to this day.

I like to start off as soon as it's light enough to see. At that time of day, I am almost always the only person on the course, except for the greenkeeper, who lives in a small house just behind the pro shop. He has maintained the course for twenty-five years, and he has become a part of its fabric. Even when I don't see him, I find his spoor: the meandering tracks of his golf cart, his footprints near the sprinkler controls, a pocket of his cigar smoke trapped in the damp air under the trees behind the fourth green. Visible or not, he makes me nervous. He has the third lowest handicap in the club, and he always seems to turn up just before I have to hit a difficult shot. Sitting stiffly in his cart, he looks like an alarmed librarian watching a reader bend back the pages of a book. Sometimes, though, he nods, or makes a slight waving motion with a hose, or offers a curt observation about the weather. One morning, I came within a few inches of sinking a tricky thirty-five-foot putt on the fifth green, near a patch of burned-up grass that he was watering by hand. "That was a good putt, that," he said without taking the cigar from his mouth, a comment I view as my highest achievement in the game to date.

When I play early in the morning, the greens are so wet that from a distance they look almost white. A rolling ball kicks up a plume of spray, like a car driving through a flooded parking lot. Greens that in the afternoon will be as hard and fast as bowling lanes are so slow now that I have to muscle the ball to get it near the hole. When I am finished, I can look at the ground and see an exact diagram of my putts preserved in the dew. When I have badly misread a putt, I will sometimes walk back over the line to conceal the evidence with footprints. The diagrams last until the green-keeper's sleepy teenage assistants arrive with their mowers and their Walkmans. Eyes half-closed, with steps as slow as elephants', they erase the sad history of my putting one broad stripe at a time, clearing my account, resetting the course to zero.

One of the things I like best about golf is the sense of infinite possibility. Even a lousy golfer will accidentally hit a great shot once or twice in a round. Every so often, I'll sink a long chip, or drop my tee shot three feet from the pin on number three, or hit a gently drawing seven-iron into the green on number six. Other sports are different; I could swing at major-league pitches for the rest of my life and never come close to hitting a home run. But in golf there is always the chance that the next shot, or the one after that, will be terrific. And if it can happen once, why not again? Golf is addicting because it is whimsical. Like a pigeon pecking at a colored disk in a psychology experiment, I keep playing because every so often I am rewarded.

Golf is appealing for other reasons as well. Although a typical round of golf, like a typical baseball game, consists primarily of inactivity, the inactivity is punctuated by moments of tantalizing violence. A golf ball is a big, sleek, slow-motion bullet that you can see, and with the surprising strength of your own body you can send it whizzing perhaps a sixth of a mile away. A golfer is a sniper. Studying a difficult pin placement and selecting the right club from his bag, he is a sharpshooter coolly preparing to pick off the madman who is holding the first grade hostage on the fourteenth green.

Murderous instincts aside, I am a sucker for any activity involving equipment that you have to buy. If I had not become a writer, I could have been happy as an office manager, avidly purchasing case after case of felt-tip pens, correction fluid, paper clips, and staples. I feel the same way about power tools, which have a sleek and titillating loveliness that is distinct from any function. And I feel the same way about golf stuff. I like to buy balls four or five dozen at a time and stack the individual sleeves in neat columns on a shelf in my office directly across from my desk, so that I can look at them while I work. I like to carry a few tees and ball markers in my pocket at all times, even in winter. I like to clean the heads of my clubs with steel wool, a toothbrush, and toothpicks. I like to assemble and arrange my equipment the night before an important match, like an Apache warrior straightening the feathers on his arrows on the eve of battle.

Nongolfers tend not to understand the compulsiveness of those who play compulsively. A friend once asked me, "When you say you love golf, do you mean you love being outside on a nice day, or do you actually love the game?" I said I did enjoy being outside, but that it was really the game that got my juices going. He said he couldn't understand that. How could anyone get excited about just hitting a ball? He had played golf a few times, he said, and he had liked it well enough, but he could take it or leave it. Soon after our conversation he married a golfer and began to play frequently. A couple of months later, he called me and said, "Now I understand what you mean." He had improved to the point where he was able to hit a good shot every once in awhile. When he finished a round now, he said, he found himself thinking anxiously (even compulsively) about when he might be able to begin another.

When I am unable to play golf, I try to find substitutes. On the hill behind my house is a grove of enormous white pines and blue spruces. The trees shield my house from the road and block the winds that blow over the hill. Not long after I began playing, I realized that the trees are virtually impenetrable to golf balls. I can take a full swing with a seven-iron from forty yards away and be confident that the ball will never, or almost never, reach the street. Sometimes it will even squirt back into the yard, saving me the trouble of looking for it. Before I realized that my trees could be a backstop, I had to content myself with hitting soft wedge shots from just in front of the front door to just in front of an old stone wall, a distance of about sixty yards, and then from just in front of the stone wall down to the narrow isthmus of grass between the back door and some big weeds. The return shot requires great concentration. Pulling the ball slightly will send it clattering across the roof or bouncing off the clapboards; the faintest push will bury it in heather and poison ivy. Any iciness of nerve that I have as a golfer has arisen from repeatedly forcing myself to negotiate these twin perils.

Like most compulsive golfers, I practice my swing at every opportunity. I once tried on a pair of pants before buying them at Penney's even though I already knew they were the right size; I wanted to check my pivot in the big triple mirrors in the dressing room. When practicing a full swing is socially unacceptable (for example, when I am talking to an old lady at a wedding reception), I will sometimes practice shifting my weight from my right foot to my left. The movement is so subtle that no one would ever suspect—except my children, who almost always catch me, saying, "Daddy, are you practicing your swing?" (In order to condition my children to approve of my playing lots and lots of golf, I always give them any money I win on the course. I sometimes give them money even if I have lost.) When I am driving my car, I hold the steering wheel as though I were gripping a golf club, with a little extra pressure in the last three fingers of my left hand. When I am raking leaves in my yard, I try to pivot on each stroke exactly as I would if I were swinging my pitching wedge. I am deeply envious of my brother, whose bedroom has high ceilings and a large closet with mirror-covered folding doors. The bedroom is so large and the ceiling so high that he can stand in front of the mirrors and take a full swing with a driver. In addition, he can arrange the closet doors in such a way that he sees the same view of himself that an observer standing in front of him would see, rather than a mirror-reversed simulation.

During my first couple of weeks as a born-again golfer, I was embarrassed to swing a club in public. On the first tee one day, I hit my ball sideways, nearly killing a man on the putting green. I hit so many balls into the woods that I seldom had trouble finding at least one of my own when I went into the woods to look for the one I had just hit. I clawed enormous divots from the fairways. I launched putts in improbable directions and wildly miscalculated distances. But the more I played, the more I realized that I wasn't all that much worse than most of the other golfers I saw. Even after just a couple of weeks, I found that I could keep up with my friends, or at least play along beside them without infuriating them. In fact, they scarcely seemed to notice me at all, so absorbed were they in their own struggles. As my friend Jim told me, "Nobody ever gave a shit about how anybody else played golf."

Now that I have gotten my game into reasonable shape, I am unashamed to play anywhere. In a little over three years, I have worked my handicap down from forty or so to a single digit, and I hope to keep chipping away at it over the next decade or so, until age and stiff muscles begin to nudge it back up again. I am a member of two golf clubs, a small one in my own town and a big one a couple of towns away. I own six pairs of golf shoes. I buy spikes in boxes of one hundred and change them frequently. I have four golf bags, two of which I use only to store clubs that I don't use anymore. I can happily spend half an hour scouring the pages of a golf-equipment catalog. My front-hall closet is crowded with swing-training devices. I own two virtually identical sets of clubs, and I have them both regripped twice a year. My entanglement with golf has progressed to the point where I even dream about playing. Curiously, virtually all my dreams are quite mundane. In them I am usually playing an ordinary round on my local course, hitting some shots well and others poorly, missing and making short putts at my usual frequency. My golf dreams remind me of a dream I once had in which I played a full game of solitaire, patiently flipping card after card, then shuffled the deck and began to play again. When I told my friend Jim about my golf dreams, I said, "You'd think that I could at least dream about playing someplace exotic, like St. Andrews or Pebble Beach." Jim said, "Yeah. After all, it's free."*

For the first time in my life, furthermore, I can understand why a person might move to Florida. I am afraid of old age, but I console myself by thinking that when I am twenty-five years older than I am now, I will at least be able to live in one of those golf-course

---

*I've had only one golf dream that was surreally anxiety-ridden in the standard dreamlike way. In it I was getting ready to tee off on a 193-yard par-three on a fancy country-club course that I knew nothing about. The first player to hit used a nine-iron. His ball cut low between two big maple trees, threaded its way through a partly opened wrought-iron gate in a high stone wall, and landed pin-high on a green the size of a mattress. There were some cars parked near the green, and in fact, the green sometimes seemed to be situated in an empty parking space on a crowded city street. It was now my turn to hit, and I felt embarrassed that I was going to have to use a three-iron after the first player, whom I didn't seem to know, had used a nine. I had a great deal of trouble finding a place to tee my ball, because half a dozen golfers were sitting in large armchairs arranged haphazardly on the tee. They were laughing and talking loudly and paying no attention to me. As I moved anxiously among them, I was also somehow crawling near the green, and I found several balls hidden in some thick rough. I seemed to know that one of these balls belonged to the first player, and I believed that by studying it closely I would learn something that might help me with my own shot. I was having trouble concentrating, because I was worried about something the first player had done before teeing off. He had teed his ball three club lengths behind the tee markers, a distance he had measured with his club, and while I crawled among the big chairs I tried to decide whether I should inform him that the rules of golf permit teeing the ball no more than two club lengths behind the tee markers. I was worried that my concern about his violation of the rules would affect my ability to hit my own shot. My struggle seemed to go on for a very long time. Before I got around to hitting my ball, I woke up.

condominiums, wear golf clothes all the time, and drive to the grocery store in a cart. And I'll still be able to watch golf on TV. And even if I no longer have the strength to lift a golf club to my shoulder, I will still be able to chip. Or, at the very least, to putt.

One of the hardest things about becoming a golfer, for me, has been finding a way to conceive of the game as something more than just a pastime for people who have more leisure than they deserve. For an American of a certain age, cultural outlook, and political inclination, a love of golf is more than faintly embarrassing. Is there any sound more evocative of grody Republican smugness than the sound of golf spikes on brick? In my mind I am seventeen years old and smoking hashish at a Janis Joplin concert. In actual fact I am virtually middle-aged and telling a joke about women golfers while waiting for my tee time at a three-day member-guest tournament.* When I exchange pleasantries with the guy who carries my bag from the storage room to the first tee, I hear myself using the same tone of condescending familiarity that my father uses with the guy who carries his.

The inescapable truth is that, at least in this country, golf carries a heavy freight of ugliness. Golf in America is conceptually inseparable from the country club, one of our most repellent native institutions. To play golf at all is to endorse, at least in some symbolic sense, the inherent unseemliness of American society. The fact that golf is played by people of all incomes and races and religions is encouraging but doesn't make up for everything. Golf is still a game of exclusion.

As a result, golf occupies such shaky moral ground that nonplayers feel entitled to abhor it as a matter of course. The assumption is that a golfer has no defense. "I didn't marry a golfer," my wife said menacingly, a remark perhaps not unrelated to her discovery that I had broken her car's windshield with a slightly misdirected pitch

---

*Here's the joke: How do you teach your wife to play golf? With a bucket of balls, a one-iron, and a downhill lie. You say, "We'll take things easy at first, starting with the number-one club, and we'll put the ball on a little down slope, to make it easier to hit. Now, just relax, and let the club do the work."

shot that I had been aiming at an outdoor lamp. (My wife refers to herself not as a golf widow but as a golf divorcée.) Fortunately, her antagonism does not diminish my enjoyment of the game. In fact, it may enhance it. Still, there are times when I find myself wishing that she would learn to like golf—not to the point of taking it up herself, of course, but perhaps to the point of joining me some afternoon for a few happy hours spent watching videotapes of my swing.

Even if one disregards the moral dimension, a love for golf is problematic. Golf is to sports what dentistry is to medicine. In the eyes of other athletes, a golfer is a slacker. He's the guy who is too fat, or too slow, or too short to make it in any sport where people have to breathe hard. Golf, furthermore, is the only professional sport in which one is likely to see a competitor smoking a cigar while competing. It's the only sport in which the contestants hire other people to carry their equipment, the winning score can be a negative number, and players can wear more or less whatever they want, including black socks, flared pants, and cowboy hats. At the country-club level, the game is even more absurd. A typical five-hour match consists of perhaps ten minutes of mild physical exertion accompanied by four hours and fifty minutes of standing still or driving around in a miniature electric car. Golf is the only sport in which a participant will routinely pause midway through an important contest to eat a hot dog. Off the course, golfers are perhaps the most tedious conversationalists in all of sport. There are not ten golfers in the world who have not at some time imperiled the mental health of someone they love with a stroke-by-stroke recounting of some unremarkable recent round.

Nonetheless, golf does have some objective virtues. I will list them, so that the thoughtful golfer can refer to them easily, perhaps while arguing with his wife.

1. Golf is just a game. Games don't do anything to solve the world's problems, but they don't do very much to make most of them worse, either. That is more than can be said about a lot of the things that a lot of people spend a lot of their time doing.

2. Golf is founded on honesty. It is the only professional sport in

which players are expected to—and often actually do—call penalties on themselves. In the National Football League, a running back would be considered negligent if he did not try to steal a few extra inches by surreptitiously nudging the ball forward after being tackled. A golfer, in contrast, is expected to call a penalty on himself if, for example, his ball moves slightly all by itself after he has addressed it.

On the other hand, there is probably more routine cheating in golf than there is in any other sport. There's an old joke about the golfer who is so accustomed to fudging his score that when he one day shoots a hole in one, he marks it on his card as a zero. Most amateur golfers play the game according to absurdly generous rules of their own devising. There are even well-known professionals who are notorious among their peers for not calling penalties on themselves, and even for improving their lies when no one is looking. Still, intentions count for something, and golf intends to be a game of honor.

3. Playing eighteen holes with someone is a good way to take his or her measure. The game has a way of magnifying character flaws—whininess, explosiveness, dishonesty, lack of charity, self-delusion—that may be less readily detectable in nongolfing situations. You can know a guy for twenty years and not realize he's a jerk until you've played a round of golf with him. The much-derided male custom of conducting business on the golf course actually has a certain validity. Would you really want to invest your life's savings with somebody who had just toed his ball into a better lie when he thought you weren't looking? (No. But you might want to retain him as your lawyer.)

4. Golf is a sociable game. There is so much downtime during a typical round that golfing partners can actually carry on real conversations between shots. I have met many nice people while playing golf, and I have turned many acquaintances into friendships. On more than a few occasions while playing in other cities, I have eagerly invited my new friends to visit me in my hometown, join me for a round or two on my local course, and come over to my house for a big dinner that my wife will cook. Although on further reflec-

tion I hope my new friends never take me up on any of this, I still have warm feelings about them, and I hope I run into them again, perhaps while I am traveling on business in a distant city.

At the same time, virtually all of the conversing that takes place during golf is (especially among serious players) about golf. I used to belong to a weekly poker group. When I would come home from a poker game, my wife would ask me if I had picked up any gossip. "No," I would say. "We just played cards." She was appalled by the idea that half a dozen friends could sit around a table for four or five hours and never say anything to one another more interesting than "I'm out" or "More beer?" More recently, my wife asked me what an old friend and I had talked about during a long day together at the golf course. "Our swings," I said truthfully. The only serious golfers I know who don't talk about golf while playing golf are those who have decided that not talking about golf while playing will improve their games.

5. Its sociability notwithstanding, golf is unusual among competitive sports in that it can be played alone. Teeing off by oneself as the sun is coming up is an intoxicating experience and a good way to charge one's mental batteries for the day ahead. Nine holes alone on an uncrowded course in the early evening is as good as a martini at expunging one's daily store of disappointment and despair. Even fifteen minutes on a driving range can transform one's outlook— occasionally for the better.

Whether played alone or in a crowd, golf is a solitary contest. Its essence is, in the words of the wonderful golf writer Herbert Warren Wind, "man's battle against himself." One learns to play better primarily by learning to get out of one's own way. Maddeningly, many of the problems that plague poor golfers are exacerbated by their efforts to prevent them. Aiming farther to the left makes the ball fly farther to the right; flexing one's arm muscles while swinging makes one's drives weaker, not stronger; trying to swing harder makes the clubhead move more slowly. The paradox of the golf swing is that one begins to gain control of it only by seeming to let it go.

6. Golf, when properly used, promotes a healthy sense of play.

Most grownups don't play enough, in the kid sense. In fact, most of what passes for play in the adult world is just work by other means. Virtually all golfers treat golf not as a game but as a job they wish they had the guts to quit. But it doesn't have to be that way. Golf is ideally suited to pretending.

Like most adults, I have watched my childhood powers of fantasy atrophy into powers of self-delusion. When I was eight years old, it was easy for me to pretend that the monthly meetings of my Cub Scout pack were the conferences of a secret international intelligence organization whose members happened to wear blue shorts, yellow neckerchiefs, and beanies. Nowadays, I mostly accept reality for what it is: no more slow-motion touchdown receptions, very little air guitar. On a golf course, however, I occasionally find myself playing in the old way—for example, pretending that my club's three-day member-guest is the Walker Cup. Of course, doing this often requires a positively herculean suspension of disbelief. Not many world-class amateurs follow a sliced drive with a shanked approach, a sculled pitch, a chunked chip, and three feeble putts. But there are occasional moments of transcendence.

7. Because of golf's handicapping system, competitive matches can be played by players of greatly different levels of skill. If Tom Watson, for some reason, could find no one else to play with, he could play with me and, after spotting me the necessary strokes, still hope to have an interesting contest. Golf is the only sport I can think of in which direct competition between pros and amateurs, men and women, adults and children, young women and old men, or old women and touring professionals is routinely feasible. The use of different tees makes it possible to adapt the course to the abilities of the players, and the handicapping system allows further adjustments. As a result, you can play golf on an equal footing not only with your wife but also with your kids. Thus, golf simultaneously enhances sexual parity (important to liberals) and traditional family values (ditto to conservatives).

The same sort of leveling is not possible in, for example, tennis. There is nothing that Ivan Lendl could do, short of blindfolding himself and holding his racket in his armpit, to make a match with me come out anywhere close to even.* Incidentally, Lendl is a good golfer and a fierce though good-natured competitor. He lives in Connecticut and belongs to a nearby nine-hole club that for close to fifty years has played an annual two-day grudge match with mine. Last year, Lendl played as the number three man on the other club's team—I played as the number eight man on ours—and on the first day he was paired with a friend of his at our club named Spencer. The night after the first match, Spencer's phone rang, and an accented voice said, "I just wanted to say that I enjoyed kicking your ass today," and hung up. The next day, Spencer slipped Lendl's putter out of his bag when he wasn't looking and put a condom on the grip. "Is this new, I hope?" Lendl asked when he discovered the trick. As usual, our team won.

8. Golf is a literate game. The list of golf's distinguished chroniclers is impressively long: Bernard Darwin, P. G. Wodehouse, Henry Longhurst, Grantland Rice, Herbert Warren Wind, Peter Dobereiner, Dan Jenkins, George Plimpton, John Updike, among many others. The game lends itself to metaphor and reflection, and it has the great distinction among professional sports of being both played and covered by people who, by and large, went to college. Football is more fun to watch than to read about; baseball is more fun to read about than to watch. Golf, in contrast to both, is equally interesting in fact and on paper, and it has the further advantage of being a game that is actually played by its fans. Indeed, one reason golf writing in general is so good is that many of the people who cover the game are themselves avid players. Golf pros, golf writers, and golf fans share a huge body of common experience and knowl-

*Further evidence of the superiority of golf over tennis—as if any were needed—is the fact that there are no tennis jokes. Actually, there's one: "Distraught wife: 'You love golf more than you love me.' Husband: 'That's true. But I love you more than I love tennis.'" This is not to suggest that golf jokes are funny; they are not. But the scarcity of tennis-based humor of any kind indicates how superficial the game is. Jack Nicklaus once said that tennis is a "better" sport than golf. Quite obviously, he meant only that playing tennis is better exercise—a point already universally conceded. In every other way, however, golf is better than tennis. Tennis is to golf as checkers is to chess.

edge. The only thing I find disappointing is that virtually all of them voted for George Bush.

9. Golf provides an organizing principle for travel. Mere idle globe-trotting holds no appeal for me; I like a trip to have a purpose. For this reason, I enjoy traveling with children. Having kids along forces you to do the things that you really enjoy (buying crappy souvenirs, going to Disney World, eating at Wendy's) and to skip the things you really don't (going to plays, touring the wine country, looking at art). Keeping your kids from slitting one another's throats compels you to find activities that are actually interesting, as opposed to merely sounding like the kinds of activities people engage in when they are on vacation. When children are not available, golf can serve a similar function. Rather than tramping aimlessly around Scotland in the hope of being moved by differences between it and America, one tramps around Scotland checking off names on one's life list of British Open courses, with an occasional castle thrown in to appease one's wife.

10. Although golf is expensive in absolute terms, on an hourly basis (especially on crowded public courses) it isn't that much costlier than bowling. A perfectly serviceable set of new clubs can be had for a couple of hundred dollars, and decent used clubs can often be had for considerably less. An hour or two spent poking through the bushes on virtually any course will turn up a month's supply of balls. Sneakers can often be substituted for spikes. Public courses are often very good. I know hunters and fishermen who spend far more on their favorite form of recreation than I do on mine.

11. If you walk and play fairly quickly, golf provides a certain amount of exercise. Not aerobic exercise, of course, but a mildly elevated level of metabolic activity. I've lost a few pounds since taking up golf, if only because time that I spend on the golf course is time that I cannot also spend sitting at my desk eating coffee ice cream and drinking Yoo-Hoo. Mark Twain once dismissed golf as "a good walk spoiled," but I think he got it exactly wrong. In my view, golf is a walk improved, since golf, unlike mere walking,

gives you something challenging to think about, as well as something interesting to do with your hands. Golf is a walk with a purpose. Unfortunately, those golfers who have the most to gain from walking usually insist on taking carts. Indeed, too many American golfers are such miserable physical specimens that they are capable of exhausting themselves to the verge of collapse simply by climbing in and out of a golf cart sixty or seventy times in the space of four or five hours.

12. Golf confers no particular advantage on extreme youth. The average major-tournament winner is somewhere on the lower slopes of middle age. Masters champions tend to be in their early or middle thirties, a time of life by which professional football players, for example, are viewed either as has-beens or as medical anomalies. It is not at all unheard-of for golfers in their forties and fifties to compete successfully day in and day out with golfers half their age. Raymond Floyd, now in his fifties, at one time seemed to be capable of simultaneously dominating both the regular and the senior professional tours. Youth means so little because golf is as much a mental game as a physical one. It rewards experience, poise, and strategic resourcefulness, just as life does. Unlike major-league baseball, professional tennis, and the city of Los Angeles, it is not dominated by adolescent thugs.

13. Golf is continually challenging. I frequently play with a low-handicap player and longtime student of the game named Art. One day when Art was struggling a little off the tee, he said to me in exasperation, "I can't remember how I take the club back." Every golfer is familiar with this situation. One day, your swing is there; the next day (or hole), it's not. No matter how good your game may seem at some particular moment, there's always some part in need of tinkering. Furthermore, you always know that the parts that now seem sound may suddenly disintegrate. This prospect of arbitrary, undeserved disaster causes thoughtful golfers to engage in strange behavior. Nick Faldo doesn't trim his fingernails once a tournament begins, for fear of throwing his swing out of whack. Tom Watson always carries an odd number of coins.

Because the golf swing is so volatile, it requires special treatment.

My own theory is that you should always be changing something about your game, even when you're playing well. Your swing won't sit still, so you mustn't either. Your only chance of keeping up is to try to stay a step ahead. Maybe strengthen your grip slightly, or open your stance a bit, or think a little harder about the position of your chin—anything to distract the game-destroying gremlins that are always standing on your shoulders, waiting for you to become complacent. Once when I was playing especially well, I decided suddenly to change the type of ball I had been playing. I wasn't unhappy with my old type of ball; I just needed something different to think about. And if my game suddenly went south the following week, I wanted something silly to blame it on.

14. Golf is a game of good and bad luck. It is played on purpose under circumstances that ensure superior skill alone will not always determine the victor. A ball sliced out of bounds may hit a tree and ricochet back to the middle of the fairway. A perfectly struck drive may land on a sprinkler head and carom out of bounds. In an attractively thought-provoking way, golf is frequently unfair. The player who drains a sixty-foot putt to close out a match knows that his victorious stroke was the sum of a thousand offsetting errors and accidents that could easily have added up in a different way. Perhaps as a result, golfers tend to be more gracious in defeat and less pompous in victory than other athletes. (I've heard this, anyway.)

15. Golf satisfies many of the same testosterone-based male yearnings that hunting does, but without bloodshed. For a lot of men, in fact, golf gradually becomes a more or less acceptable substitute for sex. (Bobby Locke once said that golf is similar to sex in that one can enjoy it without being good at it.) Basic golf terminology has a lascivious cast: balls, shafts, heads, etc. A number of common golfing expressions are vaguely suggestive: A driver is a "big stick"; scrambling for par is "getting up and down"; to hit a ball straight at the pin is to knock it "stiff"; feeble putters are invariably reminded that never to be up is never to be in. Golf courses themselves have an erotic quality, with provocatively contoured fairways and well-guarded holes. Playing a course for the first time is comparable to having a fling with a new lover; playing one's home

course year after year is roughly analogous to taking one's spouse to a movie and falling asleep in one's seat.

The element of sublimation in golf may help to account for the seemingly reflexive resentment of many nongolfing spouses. If golf is, in part, a game of spouse-avoidance, should one wonder that spouses don't like it? Or perhaps they really do like it, and their apparent disapproval is merely a clever, if unconscious, masquerade. Knowing at some level that their hostility will encourage their mates to persist at an obviously impossible pastime that keeps them out of the house for extended periods, they affect to dislike golf. Thus is peace between the sexes maintained.

16. In addition to being a substitute for sex, golf can provide an agreeable alternative to marriage. The members of any club tend to pair off over time, forming stable on-course relationships that are the equivalent of matrimony. The same guys play together week after week, gradually coming to seem less like individual golfers than like the joined halves of some improbable but delicately balanced machine. (Incidentally, a typical foursome is not a relationship among four players, as is commonly assumed, but rather an opportunistic alliance between two discrete golf marriages.) Some golfing relationships are based on the domination of a weak player by a strong one; others resemble something like a union of equals; still others are entirely inscrutable. In every case, the members of a golfing pair evolve defining eccentricities that eventually make them unsuited to playing with anyone else. The very rhythm of their swings can be thrown off by the absence of their habitual partners or by the presence of outsiders who have unfamiliar putting strokes, tell odd jokes, walk at an unaccustomed pace, play for unusual stakes, praise or fail to praise certain shots, and so forth.

It is sadly not possible to discuss golf marriage without also mentioning golf divorce. Recently at my local club, a golf marriage of many years' standing came abruptly to an end. One day, the relationship seemed to be happily intact; the next day, one of the members turned up at the first tee with a different partner and never looked back. The scorned player stayed away from the club for a while, then returned with a succession of new partners—some younger, some older, all unsatisfactory. One day, my friend (and devoted golf spouse) Jim spotted the interloper on an adjacent fairway and shouted, "Home-wrecker!"

17. Golf keeps you interested in being alive. The great British golfer Harry Vardon once wrote, "I have sometimes heard good golfers sigh regretfully, after holing out on the eighteenth green, that in the best of circumstances as to health and duration of life they cannot hope for more than another twenty, or thirty, or forty years of golf, and they are then very likely inclined to be a little bitter about the good years of their youth that they 'wasted' at some other less fascinating sport." You don't hear people talking like that about their jobs, except, perhaps, inversely.

Whenever I play a round with a good older golfer, I mentally subtract my age from his or hers and figure that, with a little luck, I will perhaps be able to play decently at least as long as that. The only reason I don't regret not having played golf through my adolescence and young adulthood is that if I had done so I would have been miserable during the eight years my wife and I lived in New York City, where playing golf is essentially impossible. I now judge all illnesses and injuries solely according to their probable impact on my game. I drive my car more slowly than I once did, because even a minor car accident would clearly be golf-threatening. When I see a man on crutches or in a wheelchair, I think, "Gee, I bet he can't hit it more than about a hundred yards." I used to think that if I suffered some terrible injury to my hands, I would have the surgeon fuse my fingers so that they would fit on the home keys of a typewriter keyboard; I now know that I would have them fused in a slightly strong overlapping golf grip.

18. Golf reminds you of your mortality. Like life, a round of golf begins in easy optimism, progresses through a lengthy middle period in which hope and despair are mingled, deteriorates into regret, confusion, and resignation, and comes abruptly to an end. Teeing off on the tenth hole, I usually find myself feeling pretty much the way I did when I turned thirty-five: Hey, what happened to the first nine? Then: Oh, well, maybe I'll birdie in. Being reminded of one's mortality is good for one's game. If you knew you

were going to live forever, how hard do you think you would work on your putting?

Still, what is finally fascinating and appealing about golf is not its similarity to life but its differences from it. Unlike life, golf has rules, an internationally recognized governing body, and a clearly defined purpose. When people say that golf is like life—or, in some extreme cases, that golf *is* life—what they really mean is that they wish life were more golflike than it actually is. Golf is life simplified and improved. Golf would truly be like life only if, as John Updike has written, "some players were using tennis rackets and hockey pucks, some were teeing off backward from the green to the tee, and some thought the object of the game was to spear other players with the flagsticks." In the end, the game is really just a game. Its tragedies are ephemeral, its victories are artificial, and the pro overcharges for balls.

Hmmm. Like life after all.

In northwestern Connecticut, where I live, the golf season ends around Thanksgiving and doesn't start up again until income tax time. During that four-and-a-half-month hiatus, my friends and I try to keep our swings alive by hacking around our snow-covered golf course with seven-irons and orange balls. When the sun is bright and the snow is deep, we track our shots by sound as much as by sight. Someone aims into the glare while everyone else stands still with one ear pointed down the fairway, waiting for a muffled thump. Then we trudge off in what we hope is the right direction, being careful not to confuse the trail by making too many new footprints. The orange balls glow eerily from the bottoms of their burrows, like domes of magma rising through the ocean floor. We dig them out, stamp down a teeing area, and hit again.

I was introduced to glacier golf by four men who at the time ranged in age from sixty-five to eighty. They called themselves the Fuckheads, after their customary term of endearment. One of them later moved away, mainly because his wife had finally decided that she had had enough of New England winters. Two of the remaining three were once crack golfers with low single-digit handicaps. They've watched their swings erode over the decades, but they still turn out at eight o'clock on most Saturdays and Sundays from December through February. When they were younger, they used to end their winter rounds by lighting a fire in the unheated cabin that serves as a clubhouse and drinking scotch while frost formed on the insides of the windows. One bitterly cold January morning long ago, the liquor froze in a glass that one of them had left on a table a few paces from the fire. Nowadays, they usually play just nine holes, and they're happy if two out of three show up. They don't seem to mind it when I join them. Indeed, there are times when I feel a little bit like a Fuckhead myself.*

Playing golf in the snow is good for a golf swing. Snow dissipates the energy stored in a clubhead even more than sand or dirt does, so you have to keep your head still and swing smoothly. Each of us carries only a single club, a limitation that inspires inventiveness in shot making. It was while playing winter golf that I learned what must be the first principle of the golf swing: that the key to achieving power is not effort but ease. Facing a hundred-yard shot and having only a seven-iron with which to hit it, I swung easily and gracefully and launched my ball on a high, gorgeous, left-bending arc that ended deep within the woods behind the green.

In early spring, when the course is too wet to walk on, the Fuckheads prowl the edges of the fairways, looking for old balls that have popped up through the thawing ground like corpses of gangsters rising in the Hudson River. As the temperature climbs, the compressed snow at the bottom of their footprints melts last, making what looks like dance diagrams or the work of a sewing machine gone wild. The course becomes green again in splotches. New buds and then small leaves incrementally obliterate the open winter views. Water trickles audibly but unseen in the curtain drains

---

*According to the United States Golf Association, playing golf in the snow was invented by Rudyard Kipling, who used to paint balls red and hit them into tin cans buried in snow in the vast front yard of his house in Dummerston, Vermont. Rudyard Kipling—the original Fuckhead.

beneath the fairways. Antsy members drive hopefully into the parking lot, spot the COURSE CLOSED sign still dangling from the gate by the first tee, and drive away.

My local course is always one of the very last in the area to reopen. The greenkeeper is exacting, and he is impervious to the scowls of members. The other club that I belong to has better drainage and always opens a week or two earlier, and there's a public course nearby that always opens a week or two before that. As March draws to an end, my friends and I begin to hit the telephones, calling the most likely prospects each morning to ask for an update. "Not today," the pro will say. "Maybe on Tuesday, if the rain stops." Someone hears a rumor that a municipal course three towns away is already open, but the rumor turns out to be false. "Try again on Friday." The Weather Channel gloomily persists in predicting rain. One night, the temperature plunges into the twenties, and in the morning the frost is so heavy that you could almost believe the ground was covered with snow. Finally, though, the sun comes out for two days in a row, and the phone at the nearest public course is tantalizingly busy. "Eight o'clock tomorrow," a bored voice says when I finally get through. Summer always seems to end almost before it begins, but winter lasts for years.

In early spring, the courses in my area are often fogbound. I have sometimes played when the women's tees were invisible from the men's. Dense fog isn't necessarily bad for a golf swing. You can't see the trees or the ponds or the boundary walls. You force yourself to imagine the fairway, and then you swing. In fog you always seem to be alone on the course—even when, as is often the case, you really are. Then the fog lifts and the spring winds begin to blow. A strong wind is good camouflage for a creaky early-season swing. When drive after drive leaks feebly to the right, who's to say that it isn't the fault of the breeze, even if it's blowing the other way?

My local course stays mostly empty until Memorial Day, regardless of the weather. Most of the older members are obedient creatures of the calendar. They put away their clubs after the first weekend in September, and they don't bring them out again until the last weekend in May. After that, the course begins to seem uncomfortably crowded on nice weekends. With luck, I've found my swing by then and can begin the gradual annual process of losing it.

In the dead of summer, the hot air loosens stiff muscles, a well-hit ball seems to float forever, the fairways and greens get hard. At last, you can put away your turtlenecks and begin the idiotically enjoyable task of deciding which souvenir golf shirt is most likely to bring good luck today, and which you should save for tomorrow. The sun seems never to go down. In July, you can rise at dawn and squeeze in eighteen holes before work, or you can tee off after an early dinner and squeeze in eighteen holes before tucking your children into bed, or you can do both. There's a club tournament of some kind almost every weekend. The grass burns up on the practice tee. A doe and her fawns pause in mid-chew to watch you miss a short putt for bogey on the eighth. A father lets his six-year-old daughter drive the golf cart as soon as they're out of sight of the pro shop, hoping to keep her occupied for a few more holes.

Gradually, the mornings and evenings grow cooler. The sun's arc shortens and drifts lower in the sky. The autumn light makes the course look breathtaking, but now even balls hit into the fairway are sometimes difficult to find. The drone of gasoline-powered leaf blowers replaces the drone of cicadas. In the trees behind the fourth green, the air smells vaguely of bourbon; it is the smell of wet earth and decaying leaves. The course seems to smolder as you stand on the first tee, impatiently drinking coffee and waiting for the first frost of the late season to burn away. The greenkeeper moves all the pins forward and leaves them there so that they will be easier to retrieve when the first hard freeze comes. You tee off at three-thirty but pack it in after sixteen, no longer able to see. Golf bags begin to disappear from the bag room. Golf balls go on sale. The pro runs out of spikes and doesn't bother to restock. The guy with the big compressor comes to blow water out of the sprinkler lines. Acorns falling on the clubhouse porch sound like errant golf balls. Against a sky the color of sheet metal, half a dozen crows chase a hawk in tight circles above the seventh green, nipping at its wings. Leaves fill the cups, and you have to scoop them out before you can

putt. At last, you can put away your golf shirts and begin the idiotically enjoyable task of deciding which souvenir golf sweater is most
likely to bring good luck today and which you should save for
tomorrow.

On the first day of December a couple of years ago, my friend Jim
and I played our final round of the season. The temperature was in
the low fifties, but there were heavy clouds moving in from the
north. The rain was supposed to begin that afternoon, and it was
supposed to turn to sleet the following day, and the temperature was
supposed to drop below freezing and stay there. It was the last real
golf day we would have for at least four and a half months; ahead lay
nothing but icy winds and Fuckheads. Jim and I had the course
entirely to ourselves, and we both played well. I hit almost every
fairway, and Jim sank two chips. After eighteen holes we were even.

The temperature was dropping, but the rain hadn't come yet, so
we decided to go around again. One down after eight, I birdied
nine and pulled back to level. The wind was picking up. We decided to stop there.

I felt sad that the golf year was over, but not terribly sad. My
swing felt solid, and I figured it would keep until spring. Jim and I
stood on the first tee for quite a while, just looking at the course. "A
good finish to a good season," Jim said, and I agreed. Reluctant to
leave, I dug a few old balls out of my bag, and we hit them into the
woods. We cleaned our stuff out of the bag room. I found an old hat
of mine in the lost-and-found box. Then Jim and I shook hands, and
we went home.

The rain came down so hard that night it woke me. A couple of
hours later, my son, who was three, woke me again. He had had a
bad dream. As I got him a drink of water and put him back to bed, I
noticed that the rain had stopped. There was still no rain at six, when
the kids and I got up for good. We had breakfast, and I read them
some books. As I did, I kept glancing out the window. The sky was
very gray, and the clouds were churning. The temperature was in the
low forties, but there was no rain and no frost. At nine, I called Jim.

Ten minutes later, we were back on the first tee. "The first round
of the new season," Jim said. And we teed off.

2

GOING TO CAMP

MY REINTRODUCTION TO GOLF FOLLOWED THE USUAL BE-
ginner's pattern. My game improved dramatically during the first
month or two, since I had started essentially at zero, but it quickly
reached a rather low plateau and seldom rose above it. My drives
gradually ceased to threaten the lives of my playing partners, but
even when they looked fairly decent, they didn't go very far. I
developed a booming slice that began to seem indestructible, and
to compensate for it I started setting up virtually perpendicular to
the direction of the fairway. (A slice is a shot that, for a right-handed
golfer, curves sharply to the right; a hook is one that curves to the
left.) In fact, I began aiming so far to the left that I sometimes
appeared to be playing an adjacent hole. My occasional good shots
were almost invariably followed by whiffs, or twenty-yard skulls, or
snap hooks out of bounds. My elbows ached from repeatedly hitting the big ball instead of the small one—wiseacre golf talk for
smacking one's club into the earth. My putting stroke remained a
sort of random, tentative stab. I took lessons fairly often, but thirty
minutes never seemed like enough time to learn very much, and
almost everything I did learn evaporated as I made my way back to

the course. Each time I developed a new swing flaw, my teacher would show me a trick that would neutralize it—move your right foot back, move your left hand to the right, take your club back inside—and the trick would work for as long as the lesson lasted but no longer. I never seemed to get anywhere. I found myself wishing that I had studied golf in college, instead of wasting my physical peak on beer and *The Norton Anthology of English Literature.*

Only once during that first season did my game seem to fall into place. It was about a month after I had started playing. My friend Bill and I had made a date to go out late in the afternoon, after he got home from work. It looked like rain all day, and I felt anxious and depressed, figuring that we wouldn't get to play. But then, suddenly, the sun broke through the clouds, and the threatening skies turned benign. The golf course was empty when we got there. It was suffused with an eerie but soothing light. As we played, I wasn't thinking about anything in particular. I was just enjoying the evening and feeling pleasantly surprised that the sky was clearing. At some point, though, I noticed that I was making an unusual number of pars. (Any number of pars was unusual for me then.) I was also hitting my drives a long way, and I was making the ball go where I wanted it to go. On the last hole, a short par-four, I nearly put my drive on the green, then chipped to within four or five feet, and just missed my birdie putt. My par gave me a thirty-nine for nine holes. I had never come close to a score like that before, and it would be months before I would come close to it again, but my memory of that round will keep me playing for the rest of my life.

That afternoon will always mystify me. I suppose that what happened was that for a couple of hours my numerous swing flaws magically fell into alignment and canceled one another out, enabling me to pull off a convincing imitation of a decent player. Whatever it was, the spell didn't last very long. Bill and I had been planning to play only nine holes, but I naturally insisted on finishing the round—I wanted to notch my first score in the seventies, or at the very least my first score in the eighties.

Sad to say, I had trouble keeping my score in the nineties. On the second nine I scored a far more typical fifty-eight, for a total of ninety-seven (or "three under," as my father and his friends would say). By the following weekend, when we played eighteen holes with a couple of friends, I had reverted totally to my old self. As I sprayed the ball at random within a compact radius of my feet, Bill kept saying, "Gee, you should have seen him the other night."

That thirty-nine was flukey and wonderful. It also seemed like a kind of challenge. Far more than the isolated good shot, the isolated good round makes golf seem enticingly approachable. My thirty-nine sat there smoldering, a teeny ember in the middle of my head. I didn't seem to be able to repeat the experience, but I couldn't put it out of my mind, either.

Then, one day as I sat in my office pretending to work, I found myself gazing dreamily at an advertisement in the back pages of a golf magazine. The advertisement was for a golf school. I immediately realized that what I needed more than anything in the world was to do what struggling tour pros do when their games go south: place myself in the hands of a highly skilled teacher, who would help me build a new swing from scratch. I bought a paperback book called *The Guide to Golf Schools & Camps* and spent several days thumbing through it. It listed golf schools for children, women, left-handers, families, old people, high handicappers, low handicappers, people with disabilities, people interested in working only on their short game, and others. The schools were in places such as Florida, California, Hawaii, Mexico, Jamaica, the Bahamas, Spain, the Canary Islands, the Dominican Republic, and Kansas.

In the end, the listing I found most appealing was that for *Golf Digest* Instruction Schools, a sister company to the magazine. (At that time, I had no connection to *Golf Digest;* I am now a contributing editor.) *Golf Digest* conducts roughly 150 three-day and five-day schools each year at resorts and golf clubs all over the country. Among the sites are the Innisbrook Resort and Golf Club, in Tarpon Springs, Florida; the Ocean Edge Resort, in Brewster, Massachusetts; and Troon North Golf Club, in North Scottsdale, Arizona. After several days of happy deliberation, I settled on a mid-November session at the Sea Island Golf Club, in Georgia, where *Golf Digest* had recently opened a state-of-the-art teaching facility called the Learning Center. The Learning Center has a high-tech video studio, an enormous, amphitheaterlike driving range with target greens and fairways, covered hitting stalls that enable you to practice in the pouring rain, and a staff of experienced teachers. It is situated on the grounds of the thirty-six-hole Sea Island Golf Club, one of the best resort courses in the country. A three-day, four-night session would come to a little over twenty-three hundred dollars, including hotel room, green fees, and all meals (the price has since gone up). I sent in my deposit and made airplane reservations.

When I told my friends that I was going to golf camp, some raised their eyebrows, some expressed envy, and some became apocalyptic. "I knew a guy who went to golf school," a friend told me. "When he came back, his handicap was ten strokes higher, and it took him six months to get his game back to where it had been before." I heard dire warnings often enough to make me worry slightly. But I figured that my game was already so lousy that the downside risk was low.

During the weeks before my departure, the mail brought several packages from *Golf Digest*. One contained special scorecards that I was supposed to fill out and send in for computer analysis. (I eagerly did.) Another warned me not to wear bifocals during my lessons. (I might not be able to tell which ball I was supposed to hit.) Another contained a list of the names, occupations, addresses, and handicaps of my eleven fellow students. (My handicap at the time, twenty-four, placed me roughly in the middle of the class.) Another contained a questionnaire concerning my goals as a golfer. (I said I wanted to become "consistent.") I packed my suitcase two days early. I scrubbed the heads of my golf clubs with steel wool and dishwashing detergent, and I cleaned the grooves with toothpicks. I filled the ball pocket of my golf bag with balls that cost twice as much as the kind I usually played with. The night before I left, I lay awake for hours, waiting for my alarm to go off. I felt as excited as if I were fifteen years old and on my way to screwing school.

.   .   .

Sea Island was founded a little over sixty years ago by a group of investors led by Howard Coffin, the designer of the first Hudson automobile. Coffin envisioned a secluded coastal enclave for non-Jewish rich people that would prosper as the nation's primitive network of paved roads grew. The resort opened in 1928. Its low, tile-roofed hotel, called the Cloister, was designed by Addison Mizner, who had made his name designing fancy houses in Palm Beach. George and Barbara Bush spent their honeymoon at the Cloister, in 1945, when it was still a fastness of leisurely anti-Semitism. They made a second visit shortly before my trip to golf camp, and the president had his leaky, right-bending swing analyzed in the video room at the Learning Center. Today, Sea Island is still a confederate stronghold, but any bigotry is no longer a matter of official policy, and the resort welcomes anyone who can cough up the hard currency; plastic is not accepted. The resort's golf courses are a ten-minute drive away, on St. Simon's Island, which sits between Sea Island and the mainland. The Sea Island Golf Club has four nine-hole courses, each with a fairly distinct personality (one runs along the ocean, one skirts the edges of a ball-hungry marsh, and so forth). They share a single clubhouse, and they can be played in different combinations. According to local legend, Bobby Jones once said they were among the finest courses he had ever played. Davis Love III lives near the tee of a long par-five on the course called Retreat, and he uses the fairway as a personal driving range.

Waiting in my room when I arrived at the Cloister was a class schedule, a group assignment, and a green binder in which I was to take notes during class. My golf bag had been whisked off to some hidden storage cavern the moment I arrived, so I had to practice my swing with an umbrella that I found in my closet. While I swung my umbrella, I watched what was then called the Kapalua International golf tournament on TV. That evening, I met my fellow students and our instructors over cocktails and dinner in the main building. The class consisted of ten men and two women. Nearly all were in their thirties or forties, and none was interested in talking about anything except golf. The instructors were Jack Lumpkin and Scott Davenport. Jack was in his fifties and looked like the good kind of high school football coach. He had the sort of gentle Georgia accent that should be required equipment for anyone in the business of imparting athletic skills. He also had a compact build and reddish blond hair, and there was a sort of impish twinkle in his eyes that was probably the remnant of a once fierce competitive fire. He played on the PGA Tour in 1958 and part of 1959, but there wasn't much money on the tour in those days, and he and his wife had a tiny baby, so he turned to teaching. Over the years, he held head-professional jobs at several well-known country clubs, including Oak Hill, in Rochester, New York, where the United States Open was played during his tenure, in 1968 (and where the Ryder Cup will be played in 1995). He has worked with a number of touring pros, most notably Donna Andrews, Beth Daniel, and Davis Love III. Davis III's father was Jack's best friend. (Davis, Jr., helped conceive the Learning Center; he and two other *Golf Digest* instructors died in an airplane crash in 1988.) Davenport, who was in his mid-thirties, had never played on the tour, although he had the look: blond, skinny as a finger, permanently tanned. He had been with *Golf Digest* since 1981, and he lived near Sea Island with his wife and their two young children. He has worked with Tom Kite, Tom Purtzer, and several other prominent touring pros. Scott and Jack also both contribute regularly to *Golf Digest*. Indeed, the faces of both were familiar to me from the hours of feverish study I had devoted to that magazine. (The last time I read more than a few pages of any text that had nothing to do with golf was April of 1991.)

Class began the following morning, at eight-thirty, after a gargantuan buffet breakfast—fresh raspberries, smoked salmon, waffles, omelettes, bacon, sausage—in the dining room at the Cloister. Our golf bags had materialized on the driving range some time before, and each was leaning in its own stand beside a folding chair that had a towel draped over its back and a white *Golf Digest* hat sitting on its seat. Hanging from the handle of my bag was a *Golf Digest* tag with my name on it, and pinned to my sweater was a *Golf Digest* pin. With so many potent charms affixed to myself and my equipment, how could I help but improve?

Jack told us to warm up by hitting a few short irons. I selected my eight-iron and, quite naturally, used it to hit a succession of anemic shanks. I felt mortified but also perversely pleased, in the way one does when one's child vomits in the waiting room of the pediatrician. Then Jack summoned me to the far end of the tee to be videotaped from two angles while hitting two shots with my five-iron and two shots with my driver. These shots would give Scott and Jack the basis for an initial diagnosis, and they would provide a baseline against which I would later be able to measure my progress. Our tapes were to follow us from class to class. By the end of school, my tape would contain a synopsis of most of what I had learned, including personalized instructions from Jack and Scott.

When I stepped in front of the camera to hit my first shot, I felt as nervous as if I were teeing off on national television. Various white lines had been spray-painted on the grass. I positioned myself uncertainly among them, then topped the first ball, watching it trickle lamely over the front edge of the practice tee. Jack rewound the tape and told me to try again. Davis Love's little brother, Mark— who is a promising golfer in his own right, and was an assistant instructor at the Learning Center—teed up a new ball for me. I managed to get the next four shots into the air, but all of them sliced to varying degrees—the very ailment I was hoping to cure.

Virtually every golf shot of any length bends in one direction or the other. The reason is that striking a golf ball with a golf club causes the ball to spin, and the spin turns the ball into a briskly aerodynamic object. Golf balls curve for the same reasons that artfully thrown baseballs do. In fact, they curve for many of the same reasons that airplanes fly. As the spinning ball moves through the air, it creates a pocket of lower pressure on one side or the other, and is sucked into it. Curving golf balls can be viewed, therefore, as part of the price we pay for remaining alive. (There is no hook or slice on the airless moon.)

Genuinely straight shots of any length are a great rarity in golf.

My close personal friend Tom Watson—who graduated from the same high school I did, but six years earlier—once told me, "A straight shot is an accident."* Given the tilted, sideways nature of the golf swing, virtually every shot is bound to curve to some extent, and the direction of the curve is not random. A right-hand bend—which is called a slice when it's extreme and a fade when it's not—is caused by certain kinds of swings; a left-hand bend—which is called a hook when it's extreme and a draw when it's not—is caused by certain others. There are other differences as well. Fades tend to fly higher and land softer than draws, which tend to fly lower and run farther. Good golfers try to take advantage of these characteristics by "shaping" their shots to fit the conditions at hand. A high fade is more likely to stick to a hard, elevated green; a low draw is more likely to run a long way down a parched fairway.

Virtually all golfers have a natural or acquired tendency to favor one type of shot over the other. Watson, for example, usually plays the ball from right to left—that is, he draws it. Fred Couples, in contrast, usually plays from left to right. Sometimes, golfers switch. Jack Nicklaus was mainly a left-to-right player in his youth; nowadays, he plays mostly right to left, primarily because a draw gives him back some of the distance that age has taken away. Ben Hogan was on the verge of giving up golf before he finally found a way to eliminate the hook that had plagued his early career, and developed a steady fade.

The pros are about evenly divided between those who draw and those who fade. Crummy golfers, though, almost always fade. Actually, *fade* is a polite word for what crummy golfers do. The more

---

*Watson was not only the captain of the school golf team but also the quarterback and leading rusher on the football team, which under his direction won the conference championship, and an outstanding shooting guard on the basketball team, of which he was a cocaptain. He used to put his clubs away every August, when football practice started, and not take them out again until February, when the basketball season ended. When he left high school for Stanford, in 1967, he had no intention of making a career of golf, and expected to return to Kansas City after graduation to work in the insurance business. I met Watson only once, in 1982, when I was writing a profile of him for *Esquire*. I had to keep rewriting the ending of my story as the magazine went to press, because every time we thought we had put the issue to bed, Watson would win another tournament.

accurate word is *slice*. Like me on the tee that day, crummy golfers almost always swing in ways that produce right-hand banana balls. This fact is one of the great and abiding agonies of bad golfers everywhere. It's the reason why *Golf* magazine has a regular department called Slicer's Corner. (In fact, it's probably the main reason why *Golf* and *Golf Digest* exist.) It's the reason why golf-supply companies sell ice-cream-scoop-shaped tees that supposedly set up a spin-proof barrier between the clubhead and the ball. It's the reason why crummy golfers spend millions of dollars every year on wrist braces, canted drivers, low-spin balls, and other gimmicks intended to reduce or eliminate that embarrassing eastward bend.

The slice, in brief, was the main reason why I had gone to golf school. One of Jack's goals during school, he told me later, would be to turn my slice into a draw—in my view, the equivalent of turning straw into gold.

After the taping, Jack and Scott conducted a joint session on grip, setup, and other fundamentals. We sat on folding chairs in a semicircle and listened to stirring descriptions of good golf swings. Jack said that one of the sources of difficulty in golf is that the ball is positioned "well below what we consider *us*"—that is, it's a long way from our heads, and we have to hit it with a stick. Quoting someone else, he said that it's possible to play good golf with a bad swing "as long as you have an even number of errors"—the idea being that every deviation from proper technique requires an equal and opposite compensation if the ball is to leave the ground. Most golfers—even most pros—have lots of compensations in their swings. Because one's grip is a little bit funny, one has to take the club back in a slightly peculiar way, and because one's backswing is therefore somewhat odd, one has to shift one's weight in a fashion that drains power from one's swing, and so on. If one is superbly coordinated, one may be able to manage a fair number of compensations while still producing good-looking shots. That's why many pros are able to play very, very well with technically nutty swings. But if one is a feeble, tubby, and practically middle-aged guy—that is to say, if one is me—then one's increasingly drastic compensations are only going to lead one deeper into trouble. The best thing to do, Jack said, is to try to strip away the compensations and build in their place a simple, sturdy swing that conforms with known physical laws and contains as few moving parts as possible.

If we were truly the masters of our bodies, building a simple, sturdy swing would be easy. We would watch a videotape of a good golf swing, and then we would simply do what we had seen. Obviously, though, that is not possible. Most bad golfers' bad swings are enormously sturdy structures that have taken years if not decades to erect. Disassembling these structures is extremely hard. But the durability of one's swing flaws is also encouraging, in a way. After all, slicing the ball out of bounds from every tee is a kind of consistency. My swing was bad, but I was able to repeat it with ease. All I needed to do now was to replace all my bad habits with the good ones that Jack and Scott would teach me. After that, hitting the ball into the fairway should theoretically become as easy and automatic as slicing the ball over the fence was now. Okay!

After our introductory lecture, we broke into two groups, eager to get to work. My group, the high handicappers, went with Scott for a lesson in the short game. The low handicappers stayed with Jack to work on full swings. (With characteristic sensitivity, *Golf Digest* had designated the high handicappers Group A, and the low handicappers Group B.) Scott checked our grips, then set about teaching us to chip. At one point, to demonstrate what he wanted us not to do, he tried to skull a shot—to mishit the ball in a way that would send it rocketing out of control across the large practice green. Scott's swing is so pure that he couldn't hit the ball as poorly as he wanted to. Doug, a neurosurgeon with a handicap of twenty-five, said, "Want me to show you?" (Doug had the most equipment of anyone in our group. He had Reebok golf shoes with little air pumps, and he had red vinyl protective covers for the heads of his irons.)

I had always felt that chipping was the one semirespectable part of my game. Short shots around the green were something I had been comfortable with, and I figured that golf school would merely add some polish to a skill I had already begun to grasp. But Scott had something more dramatic in mind. He wanted us to learn a chipping stroke that was quite a bit different from anything that any of us was currently doing. He wanted us to learn to swing our wedges mainly with our shoulders rather than with our hands and wrists.

In virtually all good golf swings, Scott told us, the body does most of the work. In the backswing, the golfer's upper body coils against a firmly anchored lower body. In the swing itself, the body powerfully unwinds, taking the arms, hands, and golf club with it. This turning, or pivot, is the engine that drives a golf swing. Nearly every reasonably healthy body contains more than enough strength to send a golf ball flying a very long way, but most crummy golfers seldom tap more than a fraction of this strength, usually because they rely excessively on their arms and hands in making their swings. (Jack later made a dramatic demonstration of this same general idea. He took an ordinary towel and slightly dampened one end. That end he held above his right shoulder with his right hand; the other end he held near his right hip with his left hand. He stood facing a bushel-sized wire basket containing several hundred range balls. Then, letting go with his right hand, he swung the towel smoothly with his left, as though he were swinging a golf club one-handed. His body pivoted. The damp end of the towel came down in an arc, as the head of a golf club does when you swing, and struck the basket. The basket tipped over, spreading balls across the tee. Jack hadn't lashed at the basket; he hadn't cracked the towel like a whip; he hadn't seemed to expend much energy at all. He had merely turned his body, swinging the towel as he would have swung a golf club, and the towel had grabbed the basket and flipped it on its side. The rest of us tried it but never came close. You could make a lot of money doing that trick in barrooms.)

Scott told us that the chipping stroke he wanted us to learn was simply a truncated version of a properly executed full swing. He had us set up with our hands slightly ahead of the ball; take the club back mainly by turning our shoulders, rather than by cocking our wrists or lifting our arms; and swing the club primarily by turning our shoulders and hips back toward the target, generating force with our bodies instead of merely with our wrists and arms. If you videotaped a full swing and erased everything except the bottom part of the arc, this is pretty much what you would see. In addition, Scott wanted us not to scoop the ball, as I was used to doing, but to strike it with a sharp, descending blow, so that the clubhead would hit first the ball and then the ground, taking a small divot slightly ahead of where the ball had been sitting. Most crummy players try to hit *up* on the ball, hoping to help it into the air. As a consequence, they often hit the ground first, dissipating the club-head's energy and gouging a big, embarrassing divot in back of the ball—a disaster known as a fat shot. It is one of the many cruel paradoxes of golf that the way to get the ball to go up is usually to strike it while the club is moving down. The ball flattens against the clubface for a few milliseconds, then sprongs away at an angle determined by the loft of the clubface at the moment of contact. Just about the only time a player will intentionally hit up on a ball is when hitting a teed ball with a wood. In that case, the tee keeps the ground out of the way, and the slight upward arc adds altitude and therefore distance to the shot.

One of the great advantages of chipping the *Golf Digest* way, Scott told us, was that the same swing could be used regardless of which club we were chipping with or whether the ball was lying in the fairway, in the rough, or in a divot. In addition, Scott said, our new chipping stroke would serve as a sort of foundation for our full swing. Once we got the chipping stroke right, we would be able to sneak up on a full swing by gradually lengthening our backswing and our follow-through, and by broadening the motion of our bodies and arms. Practicing our chipping stroke would help us master the toughest part of the swing arc, helping us to replace our forlorn, ineffective muscle memories with nice, new good ones.

Learning to chip like this was difficult for everyone, and Scott set up a number of drills to help us learn. In one drill, we practiced the correct swing with a string mop rather than a wedge, to give us the feeling of leading with our hands and dragging the clubhead through the ball. In another drill, we chipped balls that had been placed on a white line painted on the grass, so that we could be sure we were taking our divots in front of the ball instead of behind it. In another drill, we did our chipping with a golf club that had a six-foot shaft, which would bonk us in the left side if we let our left wrist get floppy or if we failed to turn through the shot. Scott and Mark Love also worked individually with each of us. At one point, Scott had to hold my hips to keep me from turning them too much on the backswing. Another time, he made me press my right elbow against my side, hold my right hand straight out from my body, and slap his own hand, which he held waist-high in front of me. "Keep your arm still and move your hand by turning your body only," Scott said. "That's the motion I want you to make when you hit the ball." This idea seemed simple in the abstract but clumsy and stupid when I first tried it. Gradually, though, I began to get the hang of it, and I realized that Scott's chipping method required far less effort than my own scooping technique. It was also easier to repeat consistently, because it had fewer moving parts. By the end of the session, I was still shaky, but I had been converted. Scott's chip was clearly a better way to strike the ball. It was also, I would later discover, one of the keys to taming my slice.

We broke for lunch at around noon, by which time everyone had hit three or four hundred balls. (An attendant refilled the enormous ball baskets whenever they got low.) We ate lunch in the clubhouse, where each of us had been given a locker. The shoes I had left in my locker that morning had been shined in my absence, and they would be shined again in the afternoon to undo any damage I might have done to them during my hundred-foot round trip between the locker room and dining room. The Sea Island Golf Club sits on the site of an old plantation, and the parking lot winds around the ruins of a slave hospital. The country club–slavery juxtaposition seemed embarrassingly apt. The relationship between the pampered golfer and the locker-room attendant is essentially the same as that between the Southern landowner and the slave. I comforted myself by deciding that a golfer doing battle with his slice is engaged not in the exploitation of his fellow man but rather in some sort of transcendental wrestling match with certain elements of his soul.

After lunch, my group moved to the practice tee, where our golf bags had once again materialized. All of our strength, apparently, was to be preserved for golf. While we hit balls, Jack walked among us, altering our setups, suggesting drills, and giving advice. Scattered around the tee were about a dozen instructional aids of the sort you see advertised in the back of golf magazines: swing-plane guides, special clubs, hitting bags, hula hoops, an enormous mirror. Jack took me to the mirror and made several changes in my setup. My right shoulder was too high, he said, and it should not be pressing forward. He told me to bend my knees as I would if I were a quarterback preparing to receive a snap from a center, and to keep some tension in my legs. He instructed me to coil my body against my bent right leg on my backswing, and to encourage this he told me to grip the ground with both feet, and not to let my left heel lift off the ground on my backswing as I was accustomed to doing. I should feel most of my weight on my right heel at the top of my backswing, he said, and I should feel virtually all of my weight on my left heel at the end of my swing. I went back to my hitting station, and Jack put a big yellow bag between my feet and told me to try to grip it with my ankles as I swung.

Everything Jack had told me to do felt extremely peculiar, but I did my best to follow his instructions as I hit teed-up balls with my five-iron. Every once in awhile, I would hit a good shot, but I also hit a lot of bad ones. Feeling discouraged after hitting about a hundred balls, I went over to a covered hitting station and got a Coke from a big wicker basket containing soft drinks and fruit juice. We had been encouraged to take frequent breaks, to keep from burning out. Revived by corn syrup and carbon dioxide, I took a deep breath and went back to work.

A little later, Jack took us into the video room in groups of three. In the middle of the room was an Astroturf mat with a big net in front of it. Four video cameras were trained on the mat from different angles, and there were at least as many video monitors, including one mounted in the floor just ahead of the tee. You could set up over a ball on the tee and, without moving your head from the proper position, look at yourself from four different angles on the monitor in the floor. Through a big glass window in one wall, I could see a control room filled with computer and video equipment. Hanging on the walls were sequences of photographs depicting the swings of Seve Ballesteros, Nick Faldo, Payne Stewart, and others. Jack showed us a tape of Tom Kite hitting balls. Using a big knob on the front of the VCR, he could move the tape one frame at a time in either direction. He made lines on the screen with a felt-tip marker, and he pointed out various elements of Kite's swing. Then he loaded our own tapes from the morning session and analyzed them in the same way.

Watching a videotape of yourself swinging a golf club is like watching a videotape of yourself dancing: You don't look as good as you thought you did when you were doing it. Moving frame by frame through the tape, Jack showed me the principal source of my slice. I was turning my hips too far back on the backswing, and then not getting them around again as I swung. As a result, I was swinging almost entirely from the waist up, and my lagging rear end was causing me to "come over the top"—to swipe at the ball from outside and above. Every now and then, my hands or my arms would accidentally compensate for this strangled motion and I would hit a seemingly terrific shot, but I couldn't do it consistently. In addition, because my hips were turning too much on my backswing, my lower body wasn't providing any resistance, and I wasn't developing much power. That's why Jack had told me to grip the ground with my feet: Keeping my left foot anchored would prevent me from turning my hips too far on the backswing and would give my upper body something to pivot around as I swung through the ball. In addition, Jack said, I needed to learn to get my hips around in the other direction as I swung—to really come through the ball with my body as I hit it. He showed us a photograph of Sam Snead hitting a ball. The picture had been snapped just as the ball was leaving the face of the club, at which point Snead had already turned his hips so far that his belt buckle was pointing more or less directly at his target. At the comparable point in my own swing, I saw, my belt buckle was pointing pretty much directly at the spot where I had teed up the ball.

If you wanted to hit a slice on purpose, you would do pretty much exactly what I had been doing unintentionally. You would set up to the ball in such a way that if you drew a line connecting your knees, the line would point well to the left of your target. This is what is known in golf as an open stance. Slicers tend to adopt increasingly open stances because they feel intuitively that the way to keep the ball from going right is to turn the body ever farther to the left. But in this case intuition is dead wrong: Aiming to the left tends to exacerbate rather than eliminate a slice. This is another of the cruel paradoxes of the game. Opening the stance causes the clubhead to cut across the ball on a path that moves from outside to in, and this is the very motion that imparts a slicing spin. The net result is that the harder the bad golfer tries to make the ball go left, the more determined the ball is to curve in the opposite direction. Like steering a boat with a tiller or turning a car out of a skid, hitting a golf ball properly seems at first to defy logic.

The effect of an open stance is magnified by numerous other counterintuitive swing flaws that bad golfers tend to accumulate. My over-the-top swing was one of these. As my body swayed and turned away from my target on my backswing, my mind incorrectly decided that I was now facing too far to the right, and that I had better hurry up and get my club moving in the other direction. Rather than pivoting smoothly with my entire body, I attempted to throw the club back to the left, toward the ball. This movement left my butt behind and caused the clubhead to cut weakly across the ball from right to left: the birth of a banana.

I once played a round with a golfer named Ron who invariably sliced the ball—unless there was trouble on the left. On hole after hole, his drives would bend cruelly to the right, a defect he had learned to live with through years of patient compensation and adjustment. Ron missed a lot of fairways, but he kept his ball in play. He didn't get into real trouble until we came to a hole whose fairway was flanked along its entire left side by a lake. If Ron had taken his normal, open stance, he would have seemed to be aiming straight at the water. He didn't want to do that, so he "closed" his stance—that is, he turned his body clockwise, so that a line drawn connecting his knees would have pointed up the right side of the fairway, as far as possible from the lake. To protect himself further, he changed his swing path, too. Rather than cutting across the ball from right to left, as he was accustomed to doing, he freed up his arms and tried to knock the ball well out to the right. The result? He hit his first hook of the day, and his ball ended up in the water. He viewed that shot as a random event. If he had understood what he had really done, though, he would have seen that his water ball had given him a key to improving his game. His problem, like mine, was that everything he tried to do to solve his problem in fact made his problem worse.

Back on the practice tee, with slow-motion images of my astonishingly awkward self fresh in my head, I returned to my bottomless ball basket with renewed vigor. At first, gripping the ground with my feet prevented me from swaying, and that made my swing feel small and awkward. Still, as I gradually got used to that feeling, I realized that I was hitting the ball pretty well. My shots were somewhat longer than usual, and every once in awhile, one of them would bend slightly to the left: a draw! When class ended at four-thirty, I jumped in a cart with John, a classmate with a similar handicap, and we went out to see if we could squeeze in nine holes before the sun disappeared entirely. On the first tee, I dug my spikes into the ground, held on with my toes, and smacked a long drive that ended up on a part of the golf course that for me was pretty much alien territory: the left side of the fairway.

That evening, I ate dinner in the Cloister's main dining room with three classmates. My dinner companions were Bill, an orthopedic surgeon whose handicap was eight; Joe, a friend of Bill's and an internist whose handicap was twelve; and Peter, a writer whose handicap was eighteen. All three were very enthusiastic about what they had learned that day, and all three felt that their games had already improved. We spent virtually the entire meal talking about golf, with a few digressions about the food, which was very good, and our hands, which were very sore. "I could do this for the rest of my life," Bill said at one point, and we all agreed. Going to golf school seemed to me at that point to constitute something like perfect existence. The food was good; the personal relationships were superficial and thus undemanding; the physically taxing nature of the instruction made golf seem morally acceptable: We were working, not playing. If I had somehow magically been allowed to remain at golf school until I truly got sick of it, I probably would have ended up staying for quite a while. In fact, I might be there still.

The next morning, virtually the entire class arrived at the practice tee early, the sooner to begin hitting balls. I saw Band-Aids on many fingers, and my own hands throbbed as I hit my first few tentative shots. I had bought a new white golf glove in the pro shop the day before, and it was already worn and scuffed and nearly black. I wished that I had bought a glove for my right hand as well. I dug around in my bag and found a pair of neoprene gloves, which I had bought for playing in cold weather. They were thick and spongy, and they made my aching fingers feel much better, although they were so hot that in a little while I had to take them off. What I really needed was a glove for my entire body, which felt old and abused. But Jack told us that sore muscles were a good sign: Absence of pain would have meant we were still using the same old muscles and therefore still indulging our old bad habits.

As we went back to work that morning, I noticed that Jack had given different drills to different students. Hitting balls directly in front of me was Valerie, a meeting planner from Michigan, whose handicap was twenty-six. She was in her mid-forties. She had come to golf camp primarily because she didn't hit the ball very far. She would take a tremendous backswing with her driver, but then pop the ball just a hundred and fifty yards or so. With the help of the VCR, Jack showed her that in her backswing she didn't so much cock the club as wrap it loosely around her neck: she wasn't storing any energy to release in her swing. "I'll bet somebody once told you not to move your head during your swing," Jack said, and Valerie laughed and said that was true. Using the photographs in the video room, Jack showed her that almost all good golfers move their heads back slightly as they coil their bodies in their backswings. Attempting to freeze the head in its address position forces a golfer to rely too heavily on arms and hands, and not enough on shoulders, hips, and legs. Jack gave Valerie a drill in which she would make three partial feints at the ball before striking it. Within an hour, she was hitting her driver close to two hundred yards. (When Valerie checked her phone messages later, she found just one, from her husband: "Don't move your head.")

Working just behind me was John, my golf partner from the evening before. John was about my age, and he owned a computer company in Atlanta. He was a member of the Sea Island Golf Club, and he had taken lessons from Jack before. John's handicap when school began was twenty-two, but Jack told me that John had the swing of a golfer with a handicap half as high. With John, Jack's efforts were focused on tightening a swing that was already basically sound. "When I first saw John," Jack told me, "he would hit one ball two hundred fifty yards and the next ball fifty yards. Now the mishits are going one ninety."

Up at the far end of the line was George, whose handicap, thirty-six, was the highest in the group. George was working on his grip and his stance, and he was taking slow swings at the same kind of big yellow bag that I was attempting to grip with my ankles. George's wife, Maxine, who had a handicap of seventeen, was in the other group. She had taken up golf at the urging of her first husband, a golf nut. Somewhat to her surprise, she had found that she liked the game. She also found that she was pretty good at it. Soon, she was better than her husband. Tensions arose. Her husband didn't like being beaten by his wife. They divorced. Then Maxine met George, who didn't mind being clobbered, and now both had come to Sea Island to get better.

A little later, I asked Jack why we didn't all do the same drills. "There is a common thread that works through what you're doing," he said, "and that is the good solid fundamentals that all of you are trying to learn. But you all have different problems, so you all need different remedies. Look in your own group. Doug had a shut clubface that started here and went there, so we had to work on that with him. Dick had no motion. I'm dating myself, but he reminded me of the way Mr. Peepers, on television, would hit a ball, and we had to work on that. Valerie was too much up and down with her big, loose swing, and she had no windup, so we needed to tighten her up a little. George was too tight, and needed to be looser. John had the right motion, but we need to refine it and get it to hang together better. David, you were hanging back and just throwing the club with your hands, so we had to get you using different parts of your body, different muscles. But even though we've worked differently with each of you, there is a common goal for everyone: a repeating golf swing based on good, sound, solid fundamentals. And as the course has gone on, you've all begun to look more the same. We're all trying to get to Atlanta. Some of us started out in Columbus, and some of us started out in Macon, and some of us started out in Rome. But we're all trying to get to the same place."

At some point during every class, we would put down our clubs, pull our chairs into a circle, and listen to a lecture. On the second morning, Jack gave us a talk in which he stressed the importance of practice, saying that making or breaking a motor-skill habit required patience, determination, and hundreds of repetitions. "I can't tell you how many hours I have spent making golf swings in front of mirrors," he said. "I can hardly pass a mirror without making a swing. My wife and I almost didn't get married because of it. On one of our first dates, we went to a movie, in Athens, Georgia, and had to wait in line for fifteen minutes. We were standing in front of a men's clothing store, and there was a big, dark window, so I spent the time making about a hundred golf swings and looking at my reflection. That just about did it." Jack said the most important thing was not to become discouraged. "The pros have problems that are just as severe to them as yours are to you," he told us. "That's why people say that golf is a game for a lifetime." In fact, he said, Davis Love III (who was now leading the Kapalua tournament by four or five strokes) had been by the week before to work on some problems he had been having with his swing.

Jack then demonstrated the importance of a steady tempo. An assistant leaned a two-foot-long board against the side of a ball basket and rolled balls down it one at a time. Jack stood facing the end of the board and, apparently without effort, hit one ball after another as it rolled toward his feet. Each shot was a pretty draw. "Don't hit *at* the ball," Jack told us. "Just let it get in the way of your swing." He made other heart-stopping demonstrations as well. To prove to us that we didn't need to throttle a golf club in order to hit the ball, Jack hit a number of six-iron shots while holding the club only with the middle finger of each hand. (Try that sometime.)

Stirring demonstrations aside, I found the second morning profoundly discouraging. My clubs felt funny in my hands, and I didn't seem to be able to make my body do anything. All my muscles, big and small, were sore. In a desperate moment, I decided that my old swing, for all its problems, had been better than my new swing, and that Jack had been wrong to try to get me to change. When Jack went off to do something, I asked Mark Love to take a look, hoping that he would say, "Looks good to me." Instead, he pointed out the same flaws that Jack had pointed out and made the same suggestions. I felt trapped and depressed.

The short-game session, with Scott, went a little better. Scott told us the story of a former student who had scooped all his chip shots, hitting up on the ball instead of down. This same flaw had infected his full swing, and he had the common (and typically fatal) swing malady known as the reverse pivot. In a reverse pivot, a golfer shifts his weight to his front foot on his backswing and to his back foot as he swings through the ball—exactly the opposite of what he is supposed to do. A reverse pivot is often the result of a golfer's determination to help his ball up into the air by coming at it from below. It can also be the result of a golfer's determination to keep his head still. It robs much of the power from a swing, since the golfer's body is always moving in exactly the wrong direction. I have a reverse-pivoting friend who occasionally plays fairly well but invariably hits his clubs thirty or forty yards shorter than I do. Scott told us that the obvious thing to do with his scooping student was to work on eliminating the reverse pivot. The only problem was that the student had become phenomenally good at chipping and didn't want to give up his technique, even though he knew it was bad. Scott acknowledged his proficiency at chipping but pointed out some limitations. "What do you do when you have a tight lie and you can't get the clubhead under the ball?" he asked. The scooper said, "I just tee it up in some rough before I hit it." Scott said that fixing his full swing would probably be impossible if he refused to abandon his short swing as well. The scooper eventually decided that he would prefer to hang on to what he had.

After his introductory remarks, Scott climbed into a nearby bunker and told us that the sand shot was "the easiest shot in the game." He dropped a ball into the sand, turned his sand wedge over (so that the back of the clubhead was facing the ball), and swung. The ball popped onto the green and rolled near the hole. "Unfortunately," he said, "hitting the ball with the back of the club is illegal. But sand shots are still easy." Then he hit a few dozen shots the right way, explaining what we were supposed to do. The assistants had set up practice stations in the bunkers that surrounded the green, and we all waded in and went to work. I hadn't really known how to get out of a bunker before coming to golf school. Under Scott's tutelage, we all got pretty good in a hurry, and my measurable improvement restored some of my dwindling self-esteem.

Our putting lesson also went pretty well. On the first day, Scott had asked, "How many of you are good putters?" Only Valerie had raised her hand. Scott said that we all should have raised our hands, because self-confidence is a crucial part of putting. By the second day, I felt like a pretty good putter. Scott had worked primarily on helping us develop consistent putting routines. He said that all good putters set up for every putt in pretty much exactly the same way. He also helped us with aiming and alignment. When the lesson ended, John and I ran off to grab a cart and cram in nine more holes. Afterward we drank beers and watched the end of the

Kapalua tournament on the TV in the locker room. Davis Love was tied for the lead, and I figured there was no way he could lose, since I was watching him from his home locker room and sitting in a chair in which he himself had no doubt sat. But he ended up losing to Mike Hulbert on the first hole of sudden death. The loss was extremely disappointing. But I got over it after awhile.

On the third morning I dragged myself out of bed and ate breakfast alone. I arrived at the Learning Center not one minute early and wrapped my swollen hands around the grip of my five-wood. Once again, I began popping feeble slices down the range. The mere thought of hitting an iron made my elbows ache. The thought of eight more hours of golf school made my mind throb. I desperately wanted to get better, but I seemed to be thoroughly stuck.

After about ten minutes, Jack came over to me and knelt down behind me. He held a towel between my legs. With what I interpreted as a note of exasperation in his voice, he said, "When you finish your swing, I want this towel to be pinched between your thighs." To do that, I realized after making a couple of unsuccessful tries, I would have to have turned almost completely toward my target by the end of my swing—exactly what Jack and Scott had been trying to get me to do, not only with my long clubs but also with my sand wedge. I tried again and caught the towel. I nearly fell down as I did—the movement seemed almost unbelievably awkward—but my shot was long, and it was a draw. "That's it," Jack said. "Now do it again." He stayed on the ground behind me for quite a while as I learned to catch the towel every time and, in doing so, began to understand what it feels like to swing all the way through the ball. Then Jack moved down the line.

I went back to work with sudden enthusiasm; my hands didn't hurt anymore. After hitting a couple of dozen shots with the five-wood, I moved to my three-wood, and then to my driver. Every so often I would abandon my woods and chip ten or twenty balls with my eight-iron, partly to ingrain the feeling of turning my hips and partly to assure myself that I could put away my woods for a few minutes without losing my draw. Then I went back to my five-wood and worked my way up to my driver again. In a short time, I found that I could pound out long, straight drives more or less at will. Suddenly, I was hitting my driver close to 240 yards, about 40 yards longer than I was used to doing, and I wasn't slicing. I picked out a skinny, imaginary fairway at the far end of the driving range (it was bounded on the left by a big tree and on the right by a target green) and hit ball after ball more or less down the middle of it. Jack was up the line somewhere, working with someone else. I wished desperately that he would look over and see what I was doing. All of a sudden I heard his voice.

"Ladies and gentlemen, may I have your attention," he boomed. "At exactly ten forty-four on the last day of golf school, David Owen got his belt buckle turned to the target."

At lunch that day, I asked Jack how good a golfer he thought I could become if I continued to work hard.

"I don't think there's any limit," he said. "Competing professionally is a distinct possibility. The raw talent is there."

Oh, wait, that's only what I was hoping he would say. What he really said was, "You can be a good player. If you have the opportunity and you keep working on the right things, you could certainly play good golf in the eighties in a year or two without any trouble. Now, those wood shots you were hitting this morning were shots that a person could shoot in the seventies with. If you could do that from the tee on every hole, I could play from those drives and shoot par. But I'm trying to be realistic. I think you can get to the point where you would be unhappy to shoot more than forty-two or forty-three or forty-four for nine holes. You build golf like anything else, with plateaus and stairs. Once you move to a certain level, you may fall back, but you don't fall all the way back to the bottom. So if you can get to where you can comfortably shoot in the mid-eighties, then it doesn't take very long for you to have a good day and shoot in the low eighties, and then maybe you have a great day and shoot in the high seventies. And once you do that, the mid-eighties don't excite you anymore, so you set another target and start working toward that."

I told Jack that some of my friends had warned me that golf school would ruin my game.

"Some people say you should never take lessons, for the same reason," he said. "But correct technique can't hurt you. If I change your grip, you may play worse for a while, but that doesn't make the new grip wrong. You just haven't learned the moves that the new grip causes or creates. Sometimes people are unwilling to change, or they take just a few of the things you teach them and build a sort of hybrid swing. They have a Ford front end, and a Chevy back end, and a Plymouth door, and it doesn't go together. Those people may get worse. But good instruction can't mess you up. Now, there are some people who manage to get pretty good doing things the wrong way. Those people are very hard to teach, and I'm not sure they always should change, because unraveling all their compensations may take more time than they have to spend. Learning to do it the right way might not be worth it to them, even though they might not be able to improve without doing it."

"When I go home," I said, "the golf season will be virtually finished. What can I do to hang on to what I have learned?"

"Hold a golf club every day you can," he said. "Keep one by your desk, and when you get phone calls you wish you didn't have to take, prop that phone on your ear and work on your grip. If you're watching TV, keep a club by your chair, and hold on to it during the program. Stand up every now and then, and take a few swings. Get out in the backyard and just swing a club. Don't swing it haphazardly; try to perfect the moves that you are working on. In your case, try to perfect the pivot and the turning through, and try to keep your hands on the club, and you'll be surprised at how much that will help. By the time the weather breaks, you'll be more technically correct, and then you can hit balls for a few days to begin getting your feel back."

"How about during the season?"

"Everybody needs to find their own routine. Some people need to play more, some people need to practice more. A person who is a good ball striker but doesn't do very well on the course may need to play more. John is a good example of a guy who probably needs to play a lot. He doesn't necessarily need to play eighteen holes, but he needs to play a lot of nines. Other people need to practice more, to work harder on their fundamentals. A fairly typical golfer might be able to play once during the week and once on the weekend. To such a person, I would say to go ahead and play those two days most of the time, but I would probably tell him to try to get a practice session in, too. I wouldn't want him just to play and never practice. He at least has to swing a club in the evening, and if he's not playing well he has to forego one of those rounds."

On the golf course that evening, I found to my surprise that I was still able to hit my drives more or less the way I had been during my euphoric session on the practice tee that morning. Even better, when I found my swing slipping away, I discovered that I knew how to get it back. Feet grip the ground, weight to the right heel, then to the left heel, belt to the target, boom, boom, boom. I didn't score very well, in part because I was still working out the bugs in my new chip. But the big shots were inebriating. On the ninth hole, a par-five, I hit the longest, straightest drive I had ever hit in my life, then stroked an easy five-wood to the edge of the green. Putting for eagle! Me!

Well, I didn't get my eagle. For that matter, I didn't get my birdie. For *that* matter, I didn't get my par. But it was almost too dark to see, and the green had some kind of grainy fertilizer on it, and I was too excited to line up my putts, and so forth. Still, I was ecstatic. For the first time in my mostly inglorious golfing career, I believed that I had a fighting chance.

3

G O W F F

WORKING ON MY GRIP WHILE TALKING ON THE TELEPHONE seemed sort of interesting for a while, but after a couple of weeks of winter I began to feel crazy and desperate. When I could stand the off-season no longer, I drove down to Brooklyn to see my brother, John. He is seven years younger than I am, and his handicap is three, and he was the captain of his golf team in college. He is, in other words, the physical manifestation of my most important current fantasies for myself. He sort of hates me now, because I get to play a lot more golf than he does. Still, my adoption of a golf-based lifestyle has given us a solid common interest, and we now see each other more than we would if I had become obsessed with, say, tennis. On this particular day, we met at his apartment in Brooklyn and then walked over to the Eastern Athletic Club, on Clark Street. The club has two computerized golf simulators set up in an old squash court. John and I signed up to use them.

The golf simulators are made by a California company called InGolf. Each one has a big, vinylized-canvas screen—about thirteen feet wide and ten feet tall—onto which are projected full-color views of famous real holes, including the seventeenth at Sawgrass and the eighteenth at Pebble Beach. The pictures are computer-generated, but they're surprisingly realistic. The flags on the greens flap in the randomly generated breeze, and the trees cast shadows. You tee up a ball eight feet from the screen and hit it into the picture, producing a disconcertingly loud *thwack*. Sensors behind the screen measure the speed of the ball and the location of the impact, and other sensors—set in the floor, just ahead of the tee—measure the ball's horizontal and vertical spin. The computer pulls all this information together, and an image of a soaring ball appears in the picture at the point of impact. If the ball hits a tree, it bounces off. If it lands in the water, it makes a splash. John says the machine is very accurate and that the shots he hits on the simulator go the same distance that his real shots do and curve when they are supposed to.

One of the best things about the InGolf machine is that it calculates yardage. Every time you hit the ball, the computer tells you how far it went and how much farther it has to go. The picture on the screen is usually oriented so that the flag is straight ahead, but by pressing keys on the console you can shift the view to the right or the left. This is useful when, for example, you have to knock your ball sideways to get it back on the fairway after slicing it into a grove of trees. (When I put one of my shots behind a tree and asked John what I should do to avoid hitting the trunk on my next shot, he said, "Aim for it.") You can also switch to an overhead view and determine the distance to various obstacles, call up a graphical representation of the flight path of the shot you just hit, or pick any hole and treat it as a driving range. We warmed up by hitting eight-irons at the island green at Sawgrass.

Bruce Miller, who works at the athletic club and is the president of Eastern Indoor Golf, an affiliated company that owns and operates the club's simulators, stopped by to watch us play. Bruce said that he had looked at other machines before buying these. "The main advantage of the InGolf machines is their ability to measure spin," he said. "As a result, they give you exactly the right amount of hook or slice. The guy who invented the system made money earlier in his career by manufacturing computerized wheel-balancing and wheel-alignment equipment that operated on some of the same principles. He's spent his entire life measuring rotation." Other machines measure only direction and force of impact, treating a draw as though it were a push and a fade as though it were a pull. Bruce said that he played on the InGolf simulators almost daily, and that they had made a big difference in his game.

The winter before, my brother had played in an indoor golf league that Bruce had set up. The club has leagues for players with different abilities, and introductory lessons for beginners. John said that it was mildly embarrassing to stand around drinking beer and eating Doritos while beautiful women in butt-floss leotards trotted back and forth between the racquetball courts and the Nautilus machines. But embarrassment is a part of real golf, too. My brother thought the club should install a treadmill next to the golf simulators so that you could pick up a golf bag and pretend to walk to your ball while you waited for your turn to hit. That way, at least, you'd break a sweat. Or maybe there should be a golf cart, so that you could cruise aimlessly around the health club, drinking beer and getting in the way. Later, as I drove back to Connecticut, I hummed happily and practiced my grip on the steering wheel.

Soon enough, though, I began to feel gloomy again—so gloomy, in fact, that I began to believe that it would be necessary for me to fly to Orlando, Florida, to attend the annual Professional Golfers' Association of America Merchandise Show. The show, held in the Orange County Convention/Civic Center, is the most gigantic collection of golf stuff in the world. There are acres and acres and acres of booths and displays. Club pros and equipment dealers from all over the country go there to load up on clubs, balls, clothes, and other paraphernalia, and manufacturers use the show as a forum for introducing cool new equipment. Not coincidentally, the show is held in one of the country's prime wintertime golfing regions. I packed up my new Big Berthas (which I had ordered by mail on the day of the winter's first snow) and took off.

Golf clubs with great big heads, like the ones on my Big Berthas, were very much in evidence at the Merchandise Show. Virtually all of the big-headed clubs also had big names: Launcher, Whale, Wide Body, Fat Eddie, Big Z, Big Ben, Big Head, Mr. Big, Top Dawg, and the Judge. I also saw a driver called the Hammer, which didn't have a big head but did have an internal "hammerpiece," patent pending. There were almost as many putters as there were drivers. I saw a putter with a Teflon-coated head, and another with a head made of marble, and another with a head made of a length of plastic tubing. I spent some time putting pretty well with a funny-looking practice putter that looked like a big black plastic double-runner ice skate; it was supposed to cure the yips, a devastating psychological disorder that causes certain golfers to stab futilely at short putts, thereby ending their golfing careers. When good putters lose their nerve, they have the yips.

One thing I thought about quite a bit at the show was hat hair. Hat hair occurs when you play golf with a hat on for several hours and then take it off. It is the result of perspiration and hat-related pressure, and it consists of roughly equal parts of flatness, dampness, messiness, and sticking-outness. What made me think of hat hair was Greg Norman, who was signing autographs for a large group of admirers. The top part of Norman's hair was sticking tightly to his head, while the bottom part was sticking out. That was odd, because as far as I could tell he had not recently been playing golf or wearing a hat. After thinking for quite a while, I realized that Norman must have had his hair cut to resemble hat hair, making his hairstyle look the same whether he has been playing golf or not—a very practical decision for someone in his line of work.

My three favorite booths were the Kasco booth, the Fantom Golf booth, and the Wilson booth. At all of these booths, people were giving away free golf balls. Of the three, my favorite was the Wilson booth, because there the golf balls were being given away by very attractive young women who had golf bags slung over their shoulders. The golf bags were filled with Ultra golf balls. As I walked in, one of the very attractive young women handed me two brand-new balls. When I walked out, another handed me two more. I wandered around some of the other booths for a little while, then took off my sweater and went back. Pretty soon, my pockets were bulging with so many free golf balls that the only thing left for me to do was play golf.

One of the most surprising things about Walt Disney World, in my opinion, is that its almost unbelievably vast facilities include several very good golf courses. Shortly before my visit, two brand-new Disney courses had been added, bringing the total to five and a half. One of the new courses, called Osprey Ridge, was designed by Tom Fazio. The other, called Eagle Pines, was designed by Pete Dye. Fazio and Dye have my vote as the two best golf-course architects now working. I played Osprey Ridge twice and Eagle Pines once.

The first time at Osprey Ridge, I played with three young radiologists from the Orlando area. One of the radiologists had a beeper in his pocket, and he stopped several times during the round to talk to patients on a cellular phone that he kept beside him on the seat in his golf cart. He would say, "Just a minute. I have to check your file." Then he would put the phone on hold and hit his ball. As a fellow golfer, I viewed this as acceptable behavior. The second time I played Osprey Ridge, the starter grouped me with three men who had come to Orlando to attend some sort of pharmaceutical convention. One of these men was from Puerto Rico. As his putts were rolling toward the hole, he didn't say, "Go in!" the way many native English speakers do; instead, he said, "Enter!" Another of the pharmaceutical guys also spoke to his ball quite a bit, referring to it as "Darling." (Most people speak to their golf balls only in anger; based on my experience as a parent of young children, I would guess that it would be more effective to praise balls when they behave.)

Eagle Pines is a slightly peculiar-looking course, featuring acres and acres of massive bunkerlike waste areas that are filled not with sand but with pine needles imported from Georgia. Dye had them brought in by the train-car load. The idea, as I understand it, was to create nonfairway areas in which high-handicap vacationers would have little trouble finding and hitting their balls, thus speeding up the pace of play. And, in fact, it was very easy to hit from the needles. Still, the waste areas looked a bit forlorn to me. The course had been open for only a month, but I would say that it was already time to order a few more train-car loads.

The starter at Eagle Pines teamed me with three visiting golf professionals—an unbelievably intimidating prospect, especially when it turned out that they wanted me to tee off first. Arms shaking, I sliced my drive into the pine needles on the right. I muttered something about needing to warm up (I had just spent half an hour on the driving range) and stepped aside. Then all three of the pros sliced their balls into the pine needles, too. It turned out that they were assistant pros at a par-three golf course and driving range in Kentucky. From that point forward, we got along fine. Like me, they had snuck out of the Merchandise Show. Also like me, they were in no particular hurry to go back.

I did eventually go back, though, and not just to score free balls. I had an actual mission. Shortly before I left for Orlando, it had occurred to me that what I *really* needed more than anything in the world was to make a golf pilgrimage to Scotland, the birthplace of the game, as soon as the weather turned nice again. How could I expect to become a genuine golfer without spending time in the game's nation of origin? That's essentially what I had decided. The Merchandise Show seemed like a good place to look for someone to help me plan my trip.

I had quite a few prospects to choose from. Putting together foreign tours for American golfers is a thriving mini-industry. I poked around many booths and picked up a large pile of brochures, which I avidly studied each night in my hotel room. After much careful deliberation, I settled on a company called Celtic Golf Tours, Ltd. Celtic sells packaged Scottish and Irish golfing trips; it also sets up custom trips for groups and individuals. Celtic's president is a nice man named Jerry Quinlan, whom I met at the Merchandise Show. After I got back to Connecticut, I spent the darkest weeks of the winter reading books about golf in Scotland and figuring out which courses I wanted to play. Then I called Quinlan. He helped me refine my course selections, then made all my airplane, rental-car, hotel, and golf reservations. All I had to do was send him money. When fair weather finally rolled around, I went back to work on my game. After whittling my handicap down to eighteen, I kissed my wife and children good-bye, and headed across the sea.

For the American traveler, lugging a golf bag through a Scottish airport is—or ought to be—embarrassing, like carrying an elephant gun down the streets of Nairobi. So many Americans make pilgrimages to the ancestral home of golf that it is possible for a visitor to wonder, at the height of the Scottish golf season, whether there is anyone left on the courses at home. It is unsettling to walk into the clubhouse at a British Open golf course and find that every seat is being sat in by an American and that the display of beverages behind the bar includes bottles of Jack Daniel's and Miller Lite.

On the other hand, it may turn out (as it did for me) that all those Americans in the clubhouse are actually only Canadians, and that nearly all of them are drinking domestic ale, and that the golf course itself is virtually empty. It may even turn out (as it also did for me) that the great Scottish golf courses truly are great, and that an over-population of loud-mouthed, know-it-all non-Scots cannot diminish the pleasure that yet another loud-mouthed, know-it-all non-Scot will take in playing them.

Scotland has a powerful appeal for golfers everywhere, largely because golf, much more than most sports, still bears the deep genetic imprint of its origins. Even in its faintly horrifying American form, golf is manifestly the product of Scottish topography. Modern golf courses have fairways because the first holes were laid out in narrow troughs among the dunes along the Scottish seaside, where the ugly weather, sandy soil, hungry sheep, and abundant rabbits stunted the growth of the grass. They have bunkers because Scottish sheep, huddling for protection from the lethal wind, wore away the veneer of turf and exposed the sand beneath. They have eighteen holes because the Old Course at St. Andrews, through a series of accidents that culminated in 1764, ended up with that number. To play the classic Scottish courses is to glimpse the logic that shaped the game we play today. Plus, the beers are bigger and you get to drive on the left side of the road.

My weeklong trip began in Glasgow, to which I flew nonstop from New York. In a rented car I drove first to the west coast, then to the hills of Central Scotland, then to the east coast, then to the far north, and finally back to Glasgow. Although I put less than seven hundred miles on my car, my route covered a substantial portion of the country and took me to eight wonderful golf courses. There is nothing intimidating about a Scottish mileage chart. In less time than it takes some Americans to commute to work, you can drive practically from one end of the country to the other. This fact is underappreciated by the British, who, like most island dwellers, have a compressed sense of geographic scale. When I casually mentioned to a waitress in a pub near Perth that I was going to drive that afternoon to Dornoch—a distance of less than two hundred miles—she looked at me as incredulously as if I had told her I was planning to paddle a canoe to the moon.

My first destination was Turnberry, a little more than an hour to the southwest of Glasgow. Once I broke free of that grimy city's gravitational pull, the drive was beautiful. I saw rolling hills, sheep-dotted pastures, medieval ruins, wind-twisted trees, a sign pointing to the birthplace of Robert Burns, and stone walls so long they must have taken centuries to build. I also drove past two other fabled golf courses: Troon, which, like Turnberry, is a regular stop for the British Open, and Prestwick, where, beginning in 1860, the first dozen Opens were played. To make a comparable brush with golfing greatness in the United States, you'd have to drive for days. (And when you got where you were going, in all likelihood you wouldn't be able to play, since Pebble Beach and Pinehurst No. 2 are the only U.S. Open courses that aren't private clubs. In contrast, all of the British Open courses except Muirfield are open to the public, and Muirfield permits six thousand visitors to play each year.)

Arriving in Turnberry itself, I saw clumps of red-roofed cottages and, on the hill to the left, a hotel grand enough to be the palace of the king of the world. Turnberry's two excellent golf courses—the Ailsa, where the Open is played, and the slightly less distinguished Arran—are to the right, between the road and the Firth of Clyde.

They are laid out on a rolling, treeless stretch of dunes that looks like a wrinkled green-and-brown blanket shaken out toward the water. You can see a spare white lighthouse and the remains of the fourteenth-century castle of Robert the Bruce, both of which stand near the Ailsa's tenth tee. (Staring at the castle from an outcropping above the beach is a rocky profile that is allegedly that of Robert, a nongolfer.) If the weather is reasonably clear, you can look beyond the courses and across the Firth of Clyde to a stark granite thumb called Ailsa Craig, which at one time provided the world's supply of curling stones. The locals sometimes refer to Ailsa Craig as Paddy's Milestone, because it points the way to Ireland, and they sometimes say—at least to tourists—that if you can see Ailsa Craig, it's going to rain, and if you can't see Ailsa Craig, it's already raining. Looking to the northwest in better weather, you can see the Isle of Arran and the Mull of Kintyre.

The golf courses at Turnberry are not ancient. Their forebears were laid out in the early twentieth century by Willie Fernie, the professional at Troon, on a piece of land that the Glasgow & South Western Railway had bought with the intention of building a resort to which people would want to travel on trains. (In advertisements plugging Turnberry, the G & S W billed itself as "the Golfers' Line.") The hotel was built at the same time. During the First World War, the Royal Air Corps turned the golf courses into a training facility. Fairways became runways, and young British pilots honed their nerves by taking off and landing in the same fierce and unpredictable winds that make the golf at Turnberry legendarily challenging. Local fishermen still occasionally come across the remains of an old biplane in the choppy waters just off the shore. The course was rebuilt after the Armistice, then commandeered again, at the outbreak of the Second World War, when it was converted into a full-blown airbase. The golf courses disappeared virtually without a trace. After the war, they were again rebuilt, this time by Mackenzie Ross, whose painstaking reconstruction and renovation is universally viewed as an inspired improvement on the original layout. Most of the dunes you see at Turnberry today are not part of any natural terrain but rather are elements of Ross's masterful imitation.

(One of the old runways still exists and is used as a parking lot during the Open.) The entire complex is now owned by a Japanese megacorporation, and the infusion of yen has been a boon. The hotel and the golf courses are superbly operated and maintained.

It was about eleven when I arrived in Turnberry. After a moment's interior debate, I turned right, into the clubhouse parking lot, rather than left, into the hotel's long driveway. I had an early-afternoon tee-time, and I figured I ought to confirm it. An assistant pro found my name in his big reservation book. "We aren't very busy," he said. "You may tee off now, if you like." I had been thinking I should check in to the hotel and nap for an hour or so, since I hadn't slept on the plane the night before. But how could I go to sleep now, when I had an opportunity to do the one thing that I had come to Scotland to do? To fortify myself, I ordered a sandwich and a bowl of soup in the empty restaurant. During the following half-hour, no one set out from the first tee, which was visible through the window near my table.

After lunch, I dug my golf shoes out of the trunk of my car and lugged my clubs over to a low white building where a half-dozen sleepy-looking men were sprawled on the ground like bored lions in a zoo. These were the caddies. I was assigned a cheerful young man named Donald. He was tall and had a scraggly ponytail and pronounced the name of our game as "gowff." At the first tee, Donald asked me my handicap—at the time, eighteen—and told me to aim my tee shot "between the end of the hedgerow and the first white cottage." Trembling with the gravity of what I was about to do, I pulled my drive slightly into the left rough, and we were off.

Turnberry was the scene of what has often been described as the most brilliant confrontation in the history of golf. This was the heart-stopping two-day battle, known ever since as the Duel in the Sun, between Jack Nicklaus and Tom Watson at the British Open in 1977. Nicklaus and Watson hovered near the lead during the first two days, and were paired together for the third. Beginning one stroke behind the leader (Roger Maltbie) they both shot sixty-fives. This put them in a tie for the lead, with a three-stroke cushion over Ben Crenshaw, their nearest challenger. For the final round, they were paired again. Nicklaus surged ahead, Watson caught up, Nicklaus nosed ahead again. After the twelfth hole, Nicklaus led by two and appeared to some people to have the tournament in his pocket, but Watson worked his way back. On fifteen, Watson sank a sixty-footer for birdie. When they teed off on sixteen, they were even, and the rest of the field was far out of contention.

In an account of the tournament published in *The New Yorker,* Herbert Warren Wind wrote, "I don't believe I have ever before seen two golfers hole so many long putts—and on fast, breaking, glossy greens. They were also doing such extraordinary things from tee to green that it was hard to believe what you were seeing." Watson birdied seventeen, and Nicklaus parred it, leaving him a stroke behind with one hole to play. On eighteen, Watson hit a one-iron down the middle of the fairway, and Nicklaus pushed a driver into deep rough on the right. Watson hit a perfect seven-iron to less than two feet from the pin. From an apparently impossible lie next to a gorse bush, Nicklaus appeared to be done for. But he made a miraculous shot to the edge of the green, and had a thirty-plus-foot putt for birdie. (Scottish spectators immediately rushed to the spot from which Nicklaus had hit and threw coins into the apparently magical gash he had made in the weeds.) Watson said later that he was certain Nicklaus would make that putt, and he did. Watson now needed to sink his own putt to win—a short one except for the circumstances. He drained it. His four-day total of 268 (68-70-65-65) improved the Open record by an astonishing eight strokes. Third place went to Hubert Green, who finished a full ten strokes behind Nicklaus. Green had begun the third day in a tie for second with Watson, Nicklaus, and Lee Trevino (who finished fourth). Green said later, "I won the British Open. Watson and Nicklaus were playing a different game."

The game I was playing at Turnberry was even more different. With a familiar combination of crummy shots and bad putts, I managed to double-bogey the first hole. I was mildly upset with myself, but not distraught. Donald, though, looked genuinely let down. The thought that his mood might be affected one way or the other by how I played was an inspiration to me, and with renewed concentration I managed to par three of the next four holes. In truth, that wasn't really much of an accomplishment. There was very little wind—the principal hazard at Turnberry—and, as it is often said, the Ailsa Course doesn't really begin until at least the fourth hole, which is the first that runs along the water. I didn't have a major disaster until the seventh, a 465-yard par-four that the pros play (from sixty yards farther back) as a par-five. I pushed my drive into the foot-tall, wire-like rough on the right and spent several strokes merely getting it back to a spot where I could see it clearly. There were a lot of other strokes, too, so many I can't remember them. A man sitting with his dog on a dune to the left watched my long struggle without apparent emotion. Donald tried to advise me—"Grip it tight and swing slow to hit out of the rough," he told me—but at some point he abandoned hope and turned the other way. (Scottish rough is so different from American rough that it ought to have a different name; after the 1966 British Open, at Muirfield, the rough on the course was harvested and sold as fodder.)

Turnberry's most famous hole is the ninth. The championship tee is perched on an outcropping of rock that is battered by the surf and from which the fairway is essentially invisible. The carry to the fairway is more than two hundred yards. You aim at a stone cairn on the horizon and try to keep your mind out of your swing. The hole is nearly as scary from the regular tees—the hogback fairway tends to send even reasonably good shots bounding into trouble—although the carry to the short grass is considerably shorter. I redeemed myself in Donald's eyes somewhat by hitting a very long drive right down the middle. I then figured that for fun I would try a shot from the big tees, just like Nicklaus and Watson. Donald stopped me. "You aren't allowed to do that," he said. "You can't play from the championship tees unless you have permission." Donald said that recently when Payne Stewart, then the reigning U.S. Open champion, had played the course, even he had had to wheedle in order to be permitted to play from the tips. If I had been caught playing from the championship tees, Donald would have been disciplined, perhaps even fired. (Hitting a golf ball while caddying is also a capital offense.)

My unhurried round on the empty course took just two and a half hours. When I was finished, I drained another bowl of soup in the bar, and Donald and I headed out again. There were a few groups on the course this time. Gratifyingly, I seemed to hit my best shots while playing through them—exactly the opposite of what I usually do. Donald noticed this and became a bit more aggressive about moving up on golfers ahead of us. I began to fantasize that the people we were playing through thought that I was a professional from the European tour playing a quick warm-up round with my caddy, and this absurd hallucination actually helped me focus on what I was doing. Under the attentive gaze of some slow-moving Canadians, I nearly birdied eight, the hole that had caused me so much humiliating trouble during my first round. I ended up shooting an eighty-five, a score I was thrilled with.

The type of terrain occupied by the Ailsa Course is called linksland. In America, "links" is used as a synonym for "golf course"; in precise usage, it probably should not be. (Before looking into the matter, I had assumed that a course was called a links because the succession of holes somewhat resembled a string of sausages.) A true links is not a golf course but a piece of sandy, undulating, seaside terrain that was fully underwater until the end of the last Ice Age. When the thousand-foot-thick sheet of ice that had weighed upon the British landmass began to recede some six or seven thousand years ago, the island itself rose in relation to the ocean around it, exposing what had formerly been coastal seabed. Sandy ridges that had been shaped for centuries by ocean waves were further sculpted by the wind. Various hardy grasses and scrubby bushes spread across the sand. The new land was too coarse and starved for farming, but sheep could graze there, and they made their own contributions to the topography. The result was a barren, windswept zone that looked nothing like anything that an American golfer would recognize as a promising place to play golf. Still, ur-golfers took their first strokes there eight or nine centuries ago, and they and their successors helped to further shape the ground. The troughs between dunes became fairways. Small ridges were shaped into tees and greens. Increasingly ambitious attempts were made to control the growth of the grass. The land shaped the game, and the game shaped the land. In time, the name of the terrain became inextricably associated with—or linked to, I guess—the game that grew up on it.

True linksland is rare, even in Scotland, because the environmental conditions that gave birth to it were quite unusual. You pretty much need a windswept, smallish island that's close enough to the North Pole to have been squished under a serious layer of ice, and you need vast quantities of sand, and you need a shallow coastal shelf, and you need virtually continual rain, and so on. Scotland's greatest courses—including the handful where the British Open has been played—are concentrated in just a few small stretches of the coastline. There are true links courses in England and Ireland as well, and even a few beyond the British Isles. But they are far from common. If you want to gaze back to the game's beginnings, you pretty much have to go to the source.

When Donald and I had finished our second round, I briefly considered playing a third. (In June, the sun doesn't set on Scotland until after ten; Edinburgh is farther north than the Aleutian Islands.) But after a long moment of indecision, I decided it would be smarter to eat a real meal and get some sleep. I went back to the hotel and checked in.

My room was beautifully furnished. From its ample window I could look down a broad lawn to the golf courses, which were now empty except for a woman walking her dog, and two identical-twin boys wearing rain pants and chipping onto the eighteenth green. At cocktail time, a bagpiper strolled back and forth on the terrace below my window—a hokey touch to which I found I was susceptible. If I had had any energy left, no doubt I would have visited the hotel's reputedly stupendous sports center, just over the hill, and lifted weights for several hours. Instead, I took a long, hot bath, then drove to a pub up the road and had a dinner of salty fried things. A Scottish truck driver was eating there as well, and in a friendly way I asked him the best route to Gleneagles. His answer might as well have been in a foreign language. His accent was so thick that not even the other Scots in the pub could penetrate it. The words he used seemed to have no consonants at all; when he spoke he sounded like someone choking to death. I listened politely, then thanked him. When I returned to my room a little later, I found a starched white cloth slightly larger than a handkerchief on the floor beside my turned-down bed to protect my freshly deslippered feet from any unsavory contact with the carpet. I fell asleep in less time than it takes to three-putt from ten feet.

I got up at four forty-five the next morning, and ate breakfast at my window at five, watching sea mists churn above the Ailsa Course. It was raining lightly, and Ailsa Craig was invisible. After breakfast, I headed northeast to Gleneagles, a drive of a little over two hours. Gleneagles, which was completed in the twenties, is Scotland's second most famous golf resort, and it, too, was built by a railroad company. It easily equals Turnberry in beauty. The long, winding driveway is flanked by trees, a pond, various golf holes, and enormous rhododendrons—which at the time of my visit were explosively in bloom. The massive, stately hotel sits on a rise and overlooks not only the golf courses but also the surrounding farms, valleys, forests, and mountains.

Following my own example from Turnberry the morning before, I ignored the hotel registration desk and drove straight to the clubhouse. There are three courses at Gleneagles. The championship course—called the King's Course—falls well short of Turnberry in the estimation of professionals, but it is still a wonderful course, and it is enough of a test to be the home of the Scottish Open. It was designed by James Braid, a lanky, glum-looking Scot who won five British Opens between 1901 and 1910, and also helped direct the first resurrection of Turnberry. The other two courses are the Queen's, which is reminiscent of but shorter and easier than the King's, and the Monarch's, which is brand new. The Monarch's Course was designed by Jack Nicklaus with the express purpose of attracting wealthy American golfers. As a result, it is one of the few courses in Scotland where motorized carts are not anathema. (On the Ailsa Course, not even pullcarts are allowed.)

None of the courses at Gleneagles is a links course. The resort is far from the sea, perched high in the central hills, and all three of its layouts have trees and ponds, just like most American courses. But King's and Queen's are very definitely Scottish courses. (Monarch's, the construction of which consumed two older courses, very definitely is not.) The glacially sculpted terrain on which they are laid out mimics on a larger scale the seaside topography of a place like Turnberry, with eskers, kames, and kettles in place of dunes. The courses play like links courses, but with their own considerable charms as well.

Like Turnberry, Gleneagles appeared to be virtually empty when I arrived, at around eight A.M. The weather was cold and foggy, and a light rain was falling. The printed weather forecast at the front desk at Turnberry that morning had said the day would be "thundershowery," but it didn't seem too terrible at the moment. I warmed up by hitting a few balls at the new driving range designed by Nicklaus, then set out with a caddy named Bobby Hayburn. I recognized Bobby from one of my favorite videotapes, an introduction to the great Scottish golf courses that is narrated by Sean Connery. Connery, it turns out, is a hopeless golf addict, a fact that lends considerable stature to the game, in my opinion, since Connery is one of the top-ten cool guys of the modern era. If James Bond isn't ashamed to play golf, why should I be?

Bobby was small and wiry and middle-aged, and he had black-framed glasses and perhaps four complete teeth. Judging by the sound of his voice, I would guess that he had been smoking continuously since moments after his birth. He wore a dark coat and boots with spikes on the soles. It took him two or three shots to get a feel for my game, but after that he clubbed me with surgical precision. He would study my lie and the wind and the position of the pin, and then say, "We'll play a firm five," or "We'll hit the nine." Bobby's dead certainty about each choice injected a salubrious and entirely unfamiliar measure of confidence into my golf swing. I found that I could hit the ball as far as Bobby said I could, even if

I doubted initially that he had given me enough club. He also helped me enormously with my putting, something Donald had also done for me at Turnberry the day before. Such granitic conviction about the line of a given putt gave me confidence, and my confidence improved my accuracy. With a caddy in charge, I didn't second-guess myself. (Previously, my usual strategy over a putt of any length had been to think, "A little left? Or right? Or right, then left? Oh, well. I'll aim right. Or left." Then, "Oops.") Even when I missed the line, my stroke was much cleaner, my contact with the ball more uniformly solid. The lesson: Putt with confidence, even when you aren't certain you've read the break correctly. When I putt now, I try to pick a line and try to make myself believe in it, no matter what. Putting the wrong line with confidence usually works out better than putting the right one without.

Bobby and I finished our round long before lunch. I had a quick bite to eat, and we went out again. The rain had stopped, and the course was intermittently bathed in an eerie yellow light. I watched a procession of rain clouds sweep down a valley in the mountains to the east. Gleneagles compatibly occupies one of the loveliest spots on earth, and the views both from and of the golf course are stunning. In addition, the glacial ridges among which the course is laid out isolate most holes from each other, creating a powerful sense of solitude. Bobby told me that there are professionals who play in the Scottish Open simply because they love to look around. There was certainly plenty to look at. Bobby pointed out an enormous heron, a curlew guarding a clutch of speckled eggs, a duck sitting on a nest, a dozen or so stoats, and a tiny roe deer foraging with two Chihuahua-sized fawns.

Midway through the second round, we caught up to and joined two local members named John and Gordon. Play on the courses is intended mainly for guests of the hotel, but Gleneagles is also a club. Membership, at the equivalent of roughly a thousand dollars a year, is more expensive than that at most other Scottish golf courses, but it's still a steal by American standards. John is a retired headmaster, and Gordon is a retired insurance executive. They get to play as often as they like, and they can use the extremely attractive clubhouse and locker room, both of which are new. Gordon told me that he had moved to the area for the sole purpose of playing golf at Gleneagles for the rest of his life, and he had persuaded his friend to take up the game so that he would have someone nice to play with. John said the two of them had played at least five times a week the previous winter, and that they had sometimes been the only players on the course. (In most parts of Scotland, and especially along the coasts, golf is possible all year long—something that's not true in the Aleutian Islands.)

If there's anything I love, it's playing golf with old guys. They shake their heads appreciatively when you hit the ball even two hundred yards, and they tell you about the days when they could hit the ball a long way, too. There is no pressure, and there are lots of opportunities to look better than you are, especially if your tee ball doesn't start slicing until it is beyond their visual range. On one hole, I hit an uncharacteristically terrific drive and followed it with a towering approach shot that miraculously stuck right next to the pin. Gordon asked whether I had just hit a seven-iron or an eight-iron, and Bobby said, with solemn pride, "We hit a wedge." The fourteenth hole on the King's Course is a very short par-four, only about 250 yards from the regular men's tees. The hole is named Denty Den, which means something like "dainty dell." You hit across a little valley to a long, narrow green that is higher than the tee. During my first round, I had driven the green with my three-wood, bouncing the ball off a mound to the right and leaving it about twelve feet under the pin. (Naturally, I had then missed my eagle putt, and then my birdie putt as well.) When we reached Denty Den with John and Gordon, I had the honor, but there was a group on the green. "You're up, David," Gordon said. Bobby intervened. "We'll wait," he said. "We can reach the green."

For most of the morning, I had used my three-wood off most of the tees. I was hitting it pretty well, and I felt a little afraid of my driver. (As a matter of fact, careful scientific studies have shown that most people with middling and high handicaps hit their three-woods farther than they hit their drivers.) Bobby thought I ought to be using my driver, and on one hole he handed it to me without saying anything. Thinking it was my three-wood, I swung fearlessly and hit the ball a long way. "I don't know why we've been leaving that one in the bag," Bobby said, showing me the number on the soleplate. After that, I hit the driver fairly often. My best tee shot of the day came on the eighteenth. The pros play it as a 525-yard par-five; the members play it as a 453-yard par-four. There's a big ridge that runs across the fairway a couple of hundred yards from the green. The pros often play to a flat landing area short of the ridge; the members, with a good drive, can clear the ridge and get an added fifty yards or so of downhill roll. "We'll hit the big one here," Bobby said. I creased the ball, and it flew over the dead center of the ridge. The downslope and hard fairway on the far side gave my ball a turboboost, and I ended up an easy eight-iron from the pin. The eighteenth green is gigantic—a target too big to miss. I took a relaxed swing and dug my eight-iron deep into the ground. The ball squirted feebly. "Goddamnit," Bobby muttered. My ball actually dribbled to the front edge of the green, but Bobby said nothing as he took back my eight-iron—its head now caked with dirt—and handed me my putter. Nor did he cheer up noticeably when I two-putted for my par. I felt that I had failed him.

The relationship between golfer and caddy is unique in sports. A professional's caddy is very much a participant in the game. The best caddies keep their players in the proper frame of mind, injecting needed doses of praise, reassurance, disappointment, advice, and information. A good caddy is part teammate, part cheerleader, part coach. I once spent some time talking with Bruce Edwards, who caddied for Tom Watson during Watson's decade of brilliance, then caddied for Greg Norman, and now caddies for Watson again. In some ways, Edwards knows Watson's game better than even Watson does. At Watson's peak, Edwards made more money than all but a small handful of touring pros, and he deserved it. He not only handled the technical side of his job—compiling yardages, maintaining equipment, and so forth—but also became an expert on Watson himself. Their relationship is as intimate in some ways as a marriage.

Of course, the relationship between a caddy like Bobby and a casual amateur golfer like me is more like the relationship between a prostitute and a john. When Bobby praised one of my tee shots or clucked appreciatively when I sank a putt, I knew that for the most part he was merely building a case for a bigger tip. Still, the human mind is happy to be deceived. When Bobby told me I was hitting my three-wood unusually well, I cheerfully believed him, even though the rational part of my brain suspected that he probably didn't mean it. Sure, I was just a mediocre American hacker who had wandered in off the street and would disappear at the end of the day. But after two rounds together, we had begun to develop a powerful bond based on Bobby's growing respect for my golf game—just like Edwards and Watson. That's what I was telling myself, anyway. And even if I was kidding myself, I really did play better under Bobby's management. Playing with a good caddy is an experience that every golfer ought to have, even at the expense of a trip to Scotland.

It was about two-thirty when we finished our round with John and Gordon. As we left the eighteenth green, I asked Bobby if he felt up to carrying my bag for eighteen more holes. "Aye," he said. We agreed to meet again in an hour, and I went to the clubhouse to rest and get something to eat. When we met again, Bobby suggested that we play Queen's. The afternoon was beautiful, and the course was empty, and we sailed along. It was scarcely dinnertime when we finished. Should we try for seventy-two holes? My heart was willing, but my legs were not. I decided to say good-bye to Bobby and check in to the hotel instead.

The accommodations at Gleneagles I found to be less wonderful than those at Turnberry. The hotel is stunning from the outside, but somewhat ragged inside. My room was a little threadbare, and the bed was dinky. Still, I can't think of any substantial complaints. After an hour or so in the tub, I ate dinner down the hill at the pleasant dormie house, and from the big window by my table I could watch golfers finishing on both King's and Queen's. (There were still golfers on the course at ten, when I finished my meal.) By the time dessert rolled around, my legs had begun to show the early effects of rigor mortis, and I had a little trouble walking back up the

driveway to the hotel. Bobby, for all I know, was out carrying
another bag.

The question of whether the Scots really did invent golf has been
the subject of much tedious scholarship. Did a certain ball game
played on ice by the fourteenth-century Dutch bear a slightly closer
resemblance to golf than to shuffleboard? Are we indebted to the
French or to the Flemish for the concept of the unplayable lie?
When the Dutch shouted *"Voor!"* (assuming they did), did they
mean the same thing that we do when we shout "Fore!" (assuming
we do)? Typical of the scholarly literature is this passage from Robert Browning's *A History of Golf,* a forbidding tome that was first
published in 1955 and is held to be a classic of the genre: "When the
chronicler speaks of the Scots taking advantage of the truce [during
the Battle of Baugé, in 1421] to play ball, it may be assumed that
several different ball games are intended, but one does not go away
out into the fields to play tennis, and pitches for football or shinty
could no doubt be found close to the Scottish lines. It is, I think, a
fair assumption that it was some form of cross-country game that
took this particular group so far from the camp. Moreover, 'men of
note' would not be so likely to be found joining in the *mêlée* of
football or shinty; and in any case the form of the wording suggests
few players rather than many." And so on, ad nauseam.

   Whatever golf's exact pedigree, for symbolic purposes at least the
game's origins are definitely not French or Flemish or Dutch but
purely Scottish. Similarly, we can say with certainty that no matter
where the game originally arose, its birthplace is the city of St.
Andrews, on the east coast of Scotland, between the Firth of Forth
and the Firth of Tay. For St. Andrews is the home of the Old Course,
which, though it may not be the oldest golfing ground in the world,
is undoubtedly the first. Disputing the priority of St. Andrews and
the Old Course is like claiming that Betsy Ross didn't sew the first
American flag. It may be true, but so what?

   I headed for St. Andrews very early in the morning after my
fifty-four-hole odyssey with Bobby Hayburn at Gleneagles. My
route took me eastward, through the same steep valley down which

I had watched those spectral storm clouds glide the day before. The narrow road wound past ancient farms and a couple of cozy-looking inns. There was no other traffic, and I happily sped along, periodically wedging my head sideways between the steering wheel and the windshield to take in more of the precipitous view. Then, suddenly, I realized with horror that for fifteen minutes I had been driving on the American side of the road. I jerked my car to the left and slowed down.

The Old Course is famously disappointing to first-time visitors. Arriving in St. Andrews for the 1946 British Open, Sam Snead glimpsed it from the window of his train and thought it was a farm. "It looks like that might have been an old golf course that's gone to seed," he remarked to a traveling companion. But the course quickly converts those who play it thoughtfully (including Snead, who won the 1946 Open), and its influence is evident in every golf course on earth. It is far and away the holiest piece of golfing turf in the world.

I was eagerly looking forward to being disappointed by the Old Course myself, but I had trouble finding it. I had to stop at a tourist information office on the city's charming main street to ask for directions and a map. Then, after a good deal of driving around, I spotted the mausoleumlike headquarters of the Royal & Ancient Golf Club of St. Andrews, which stands behind the first tee. The R & A is the most distinguished (though only the second oldest) golfing organization in the world. It shares with the United States Golf Association the responsibility for setting the rules for the game.

Like virtually all of the great British golf courses, the Old Course is open to the public. It belongs not to the R & A but to the city of St. Andrews. (The R & A itself is very private, and it has exclusive use of the course for four weeks every year, but it is just one of a number of golf clubs that consider the Old Course their home.) To secure a reserved tee time, an American traveler must usually write many months in advance, book a tour with a company that owns a block of tee times, or check with the starter a day ahead and ask to be included in the daily lottery, or "ballot," for a handful of surplus tee times the following day. But one can also simply show up at the first tee and wait to be tacked onto an existing twosome or three-some. I arrived at the starter's booth at eight-thirty, presented my handicap card—a requirement at the Old Course—and joined seven other American men who were milling around in the drizzle in their rainsuits, waiting for a chance to play.

Unlike Sam Snead, I was not at all disappointed by my first look at the place. The view from the first tee is one of the most enchant-ingly surrealistic in golf. The first and eighteenth holes share a massive, rectangular fairway, which is traversed by a narrow public road called Grannie Clark's Wynd. The first tee seems like a distant extension of the eighteenth green, which rises oddly into a corner, just below an old fence and a road lined with redbrick buildings. The scene has been essentially the same since the days when golf balls were stuffed with feathers, and it sticks in the mind. When you see faded old sepia photographs of important matches beginning or ending on the Old Course, you see what you see when you stand there today.

After I had waited about an hour and a half, the starter reached my name on his list, and I was grouped with two American low-handicappers and a Canadian. "Play away," the starter said. Step-ping up to the first tee was nerve-wracking in the extreme. The hardest shot in golf is always the first one, and this fact is doubly true at the Old Course, where the weight of history and the dark windows of the R & A press heavily on your shoulders as you begin your backswing. The fearsomeness of the shot is paradoxically heightened by the massiveness of the landing area, which is roughly the size of a small airport; it's too big to miss, so if you miss it . . . Still, I managed to hit a pretty decent drive—pulled a bit, but fairly long and definitely in play. Then, as is traditional, I dunked my second shot into the Swilcan Burn, the narrow creek that runs in front of the enormous green and is seemingly too small to catch a ball. My caddy, Jimmy, fished my ball from the water with one of the medieval-looking retrievers that are placed at intervals along the banks, while I glumly waited with my sand wedge.

The Old Course was crowded, but play was significantly faster than it would have been on any comparably busy American course.

(Among Scots, however, who are accustomed to speedier play, the Old Course is viewed as infuriatingly slow.) Oddly enough, one reason the play moved swiftly by American standards was that all the golfers were walking. On the Old Course, as on almost all Scottish courses, there are no motorized golf carts. Contrary to what most American golfers think, four golfers on foot can play faster than four golfers driving two carts in aimless, infuriating circles. Because they walk, furthermore, Scottish golfers look less like candidates for coronary bypasses, and their golf courses look less like interstate highways. The difference is so striking that a sensitive American can scarcely help feeling ashamed.

Maintaining the briskness of play on the Old Course were numerous dour marshals riding motor scooters. One of the marshals hovered near us for a while, and finally told us to move along or risk being asked to leave the course. Jimmy and the other caddies appeared annoyed and told us to ignore the warning, but I was glad the marshal had stopped us, because my two American playing partners were deliberate in the extreme. In the standard American manner—inspired, no doubt, by excessive consumption of televised golf—they agonized over club selection, repeatedly threw grass into the air to check the direction of a wind that was virtually knocking them over, walked back and forth with their hands on their hips, and took two or three practice swings before every shot. Meanwhile, they virtually ignored the only source of information at hand that might actually have helped them—their caddies. I guess they figured they had to know more about the game than a couple of ragged-looking foreigners. I myself waited only long enough for Jimmy to tell me what to do, and then I did it. I like to play fast, and in fact, I think most golfers would play better if they thought about it less. I figure that if you are going to hit a bad shot—as you probably are—you ought to do it quickly. Why make a shank seem planned?

Playing near us at one point were four Japanese golfers who had also received a visit from the motor scooter. These Japanese, who were carrying their own bags, took their warning quite seriously and began running between shots, their golf clubs rattling on their backs. The Old Course is a popular destination for Japanese golfers. Courses in teensy Japan are so scarce, expensive, crowded, and slow that flying halfway around the world can seem like a rational way to secure a tee time. Jimmy told me that he had recently seen a group of Japanese using wood tees on every shot; it turned out that they had never played on grass before, having previously experienced golf only on the pachinkolike multitiered driving ranges of Tokyo.

I played pretty well on the Old Course, largely because of Jimmy. He can't possibly have been as impressed with my swing, length, accuracy, inventiveness, chipping, sand play, and putting as he made out to be, but I was happy to believe every compliment, even though I knew in my heart of hearts that he was working me over. (This is a tradition among Scottish caddies: "Very well topped, sir," a St. Andrews caddy once commented after his client had flubbed his initial tee shot.) With Jimmy's guidance and emotional support, I outplayed my low-handicap partners and had a wonderful time. I was even able to take off my rainsuit before we got halfway around.

Golfers tend either to love the Old Course or to hate it. Bobby Jones detested it when he first played it, at the age of nineteen, in the 1921 British Open; he picked up his ball rather than putt for a triple bogey on the eleventh green, and stomped out of the tournament. I loved it. Its most compelling feature, I think, is its breathtaking spookiness—for the most part, a product of its age and the accidental nature of its early evolution. The place is full of quirky ghosts. The ground has been pounded by the feet of golfers for close to a millennium. Virtually every great player in history has played there, although not always triumphantly. In addition, the course itself is numinous. There are bunkers and bushes and streams and mounds in places where no rational architect would ever have thought to place them. The bunkers come in all manner of odd sizes and shapes. Some, like the gaping Hell bunker, are cavernous; others contain just room enough for, in a famous phrase, "an angry man and his niblick." Many of the bunkers have memorable names: Boase's, Sutherland, the Principal's Nose, the Coffins, Kruger, Mrs. Kruger, and the dreaded Beardies, among many others. The Deacon Sime bunker, in play on the third and sixteenth holes, was named for a local cleric who asked that his ashes be buried in it, figuring that he ought to spend eternity in the spot where he felt he had spent the bulk of his life. Learning the Old Course's nuances is a task of many years. Visitors who decide to save a little money by foregoing a caddy might as well skip the course altogether.

Most modern golf courses tend to be expressions of their designers' ideas about the way the game ought to be played; the Old Course has ideas of its own. The great English golf architect Alister Mackenzie (whose American designs include Cypress Point and Augusta National) once wrote, "I believe the real reason St. Andrews Old Course is infinitely superior to anything else is owing to the fact that it was constructed when noone knew anything about the subject at all, and since then it has been considered too sacred to be touched." You bend yourself to the Old Course's will, rather than the other way around. Devising a strategy for each hole is a matter of respectful accommodation. This is a notion that modern golfers—especially American ones—often find repellent. On my own small course at home, there is a short par-four that has a scrub-covered mound on the right-hand side of the narrow fairway at just about the distance where a well-struck shot with a driver would land. You have to either play short of this mound or be sufficiently confident in your swing to play over it or to the left. Play too short and you have an uphill lie; play too far to the right or left and you are in the trees. The mound—just a piece of intractable local ledge with weeds growing on it—makes the hole. And yet for many years members have argued that the mound ought to be dynamited or declared ground under repair. The terrain has serendipitously offered them the opportunity to devise an appropriate shot, but all they can think is that they are being denied a chance to hit their driver in exactly the same way they would hit it on a driving range. "The mound penalizes a perfect shot," they grumble. But if your ball is in the mound, how perfect was your shot?

Thirty-seven years after his run-in with the eleventh green, Bobby Jones expressed a far more favorable opinion of the Old

Course. The occasion was a ceremony, in 1958, at which Jones was made a Freeman of the Royal Burgh of St. Andrews—the first American to receive that honor since Benjamin Franklin, who was not a golfer but had other qualities the natives found admirable. "The more I studied the Old Course, the more I loved it," Jones said, "and the more I loved it, the more I studied it, so that I came to feel that it was, for me, the most favorable meeting ground possible for an important contest. I felt that my knowledge of the course enabled me to play it with patience and restraint until she might exact her toll from my adversary, who might treat her with less respect and understanding." Hey, that's the way I feel about it, too!

The most famous hole on the Old Course is the seventeenth, the legendary Road Hole. This right-bending 461-yard par-four combines two of the most intimidating shots in golf: a blind drive over the corner of a building and a long shot to a shallow green that sits between a tiny, lethal bunker and a road. The building that you drive over is no longer really a building. It's a black wooden structure that duplicates the profile of some old coal sheds that used to stand on the same spot. (The coal was for trains.) Jimmy told me to aim my tee shot just over the space between the words OLD and COURSE on the ball-pocked black façade, and to fade it very slightly if possible. Miraculously, I followed his instructions precisely and ended up in the ideal landing zone, on the right side of the fairway. Had my shot leaked ten or twenty yards farther to the right, I would have been out of bounds, in the courtyard of the St. Andrews Old Course Hotel (a sign for which provides the aiming point from the seventeenth tee). There's miles of room to the left, but if you go in that direction the hole becomes endless, the green becomes pencil-thin, and the road—which is considered a part of the course and is flanked by a stone wall and treated as a hazard—looks as big as Lake Michigan. I hit a good second shot that stopped just short of the green, giving me a reasonable hope of getting up and down for par. Naturally, I made bogey. But I could see how the thing was supposed to be done.

Despite our Yankee dawdling, we managed to finish our round in well under four hours. I paid Jimmy his £17 fee, and added £7 tip—a generous wage, I figured. When Jimmy glanced at the money, though, he looked as offended as if I had taken a divot on a green. "David," he said gravely, "the traditional tip at St. Andrews is at least ten pounds." I quickly handed him an additional £10—it was just foreign money anyway—and figured it was a privilege to be squeezed by a pro. Hadn't he said that I hit my three-wood an ungodly distance?

After a ritual exchange of business cards with my playing partners, I stashed my clubs in the trunk of my car and found something (lousy) to eat at a pub a block from the eighteenth fairway. Then I wandered back toward my car, figuring I might be able to squeeze in a round on one of the less revered courses adjacent to the Old Course. (These courses are the New, the Jubilee, and the Eden. The New and the Jubilee are about a hundred years old; the Eden is a bit younger.) On a whim, I stopped by the starter's booth at the Old Course and asked how long his waiting list was. "You may play now, if you like," he said. So I did.

The prevailing ghost of St. Andrews is that of Old Tom Morris, who served as the greenkeeper of the Old Course and the head professional of the Royal & Ancient for much of the second half of the nineteenth century. In photographs, Morris looks like a squat, grumpy Confederate general, with what appears to be a tobacco-juice spit trail down the center of his biblike white beard. He was a legendary clubmaker, course designer, and champion. He was the runner-up in the first Open Championship, in 1860, and he was the outright winner in four of the next seven—the last when he was forty-six years old. (His son, known as Young Tom, won the following four.) Old Tom didn't invent golf, but he might as well have. He made a huge impression on the game, not only at the Old Course, whose modern configuration he helped to shape, but also at the numerous courses he designed.

In Morris's youth, the Old Course was significantly different from the way it is today. When Morris, as a young boy, first began playing, there were just nine greens, each with a single hole. A golfer played to each of the nine holes heading out from the clubhouse, and then to each of the same nine on the way back in. Returning golfers had priority over those heading out. In 1832, when Morris was eleven, the greens were expanded, and a second hole was cut in each—a change necessitated by growing congestion on the course. Even with twice as many holes in the ground, traffic jams were common. Virtually no distinction was made in those days between greens and tees—or, for that matter, between greens and tees and fairways and rough. The entire course was referred to as "the green"; the "putting ground" referred initially to the area within a club's length of the hole. Golfers teed up within a few paces of each hole, originally using a pinch of sand extracted from the hole itself. Putting was a highly inexact art that had more in common with modern chipping. You didn't stroke your ball into the hole; you knocked it in the hole's general direction, over a surface that today would cause grumbling if it were presented as fairway.

At the age of eighteen, Morris was apprenticed to Allan Robertson, a renowned ballmaker and one of the dominant golfers of his time. A ball in those days consisted of a small leather pouch stuffed with a hatful of boiled goose feathers. Cramming in all those feathers—using a variety of wedges, pokers, and prods—was a difficult art. Finished balls were then hammered into roundness. Well-made ones were quite hard and durable, as long as they remained dry. They were also expensive, since a good ballmaker might manage to turn out just three or four in a day. Morris and his golfing partners spent a lot more time looking for stray balls than you or I do.

These early balls, later called featheries, didn't behave the way modern golf balls do. They didn't go as far (although a good golfer could still occasionally whack one two hundred yards), they curved prodigiously, and they were easily affected by the wind. These characteristics helped give rise to a golf swing that was longer, flatter, and looser than any good modern swing. The idea was to take a big, wide, below-the-shoulder turn and sweep the ball off the ground, launching it on a low, hooking trajectory that would minimize the effects of the wind and maximize the amount of roll (as well as reduce the likelihood of damaging the precious ball). Vari-

ants of this swing—which is often called the St. Andrews swing—
dominated golf until the twentieth century, and they still linger in
the Scottish gene pool.

Beginning around mid-century, the feathery was fairly rapidly
displaced by the gutta-percha ball. Gutta-percha is a kind of resil-
ient Malayan tree sap; like balata, which it resembles, it is a crude
cousin of rubber. It was harvested with rapacious enthusiasm by
forest-leveling nineteenth-century British colonials, and it found its
way into a variety of products, including dental prostheses, doll
parts, electrical insulation, and golf balls. Gutta-percha balls traveled farther and lasted longer than feather-filled balls, and they
were easier and cheaper to manufacture. Feathery makers rightly
saw gutta-percha as a threat to their livelihood. Allan Robertson
made Tom Morris promise never to play with one; when he heard
that Morris had betrayed him, Robertson sent his protégé packing.
Morris became the greenkeeper at Prestwick, on the opposite coast
of Scotland. He did not return to St. Andrews until 1865, by which
time the feathery was a thing of the past.

The gutta-percha golf ball underwent a rapid and complicated
evolution, with many interesting dead ends. Ball makers discovered
that balls with surfaces that had been scored, dented, dimpled, or
otherwise scarified had aerodynamic advantages over the earliest,
relatively smooth versions. They also discovered that solid balls
were less satisfactory than balls with something other than gutta
percha in their middles. Over the years, the golf ball industry at-
tracted its share of wacky inventors. There were balls with blobs of
mercury or free-moving steel weights in their centers; there were
balls whose surfaces were scored with curving grooves that were intended to produce a flight like that of a rifle bullet; there were balls
with pits, and balls with bumps, and balls that appeared to have
been covered with wicker. The most important innovation—the
change that signalled the beginning of golf's true modern era—was
that of Bertram Work and Coburn Haskell, two Ohioans who, in the
late 1890s, made the first golf ball with a core made of tightly
wound elastic. Their invention was significantly improved a couple
of years later, when a man named John Gammeter (who, like Ber-

tram Work, was an employee of the B. F. Goodrich Company) invented a machine to wind the cores, which had originally been wound by hand. Haskell golf balls (as they were known) worked so much better than other balls that they became the new standard within a very few years. No golf ball innovation since that time has instituted as big a change over what had been before.

Old Tom Morris lived long enough to play with Haskells. He died in 1908, at the age of eighty-seven, having competed in his last British Open just twelve years before. Tragically, Young Tom Morris died long before his father did. He died in 1875, at the age of twenty-four, after becoming deeply depressed following the death of his wife in childbirth. Golf pilgrims can visit the Morrises' graves, in the cemetery at the crumbling old St. Rule's Cathedral, on Sundays, when the Old Course is closed. (Old Tom used to say that golfers might not need a day of rest, but the course did.)

During my visit to St. Andrews, I stayed not at the Old Course Hotel but at a small and very charming hotel to the west of town called Rufflets. This is where Jack Nicklaus and his entourage stay when the Open is played on the Old Course. My room was small but comfortable, and the meal I ate in the attractive restaurant was easily the best I had in Scotland. As usual, though, I didn't pay much attention to my surroundings, staggering into the hotel only to eat dinner and sleep. The next morning, a little after six, I set out for Carnoustie, just up the coast from St. Andrews, across the Firth of Tay.

"Mugs don't win at Carnoustie" is a Scottish golfing verity. The Open has been held there five times, and five nonmugs have won: Tommy Armour, Henry Cotton, Ben Hogan, Gary Player, and Tom Watson. In recent years, though, the course hasn't had as much attention as it deserves. Few golfing pilgrims bother to make the trip, even though Carnoustie is little more than an hour from St. Andrews. You could play the Old Course in the morning and Carnoustie in the afternoon—but not many golfers do.

When I arrived at the course, at a quarter to eight in the morning, I found an empty parking lot and a small, grim concrete building that looked like the long-neglected terminal of a struggling rural airport. The town itself had a drab, beaten look, and the sky that morning was very low and very gray. I peered through a locked glass door and saw a line of pullcarts parked in a stairwell. No one was sitting at the starter's window. I was about to drive away, figuring the course must be closed, when another car pulled in. Its driver was a young member named John, and he invited me to join him and two of his friends, who pulled in shortly afterward. (Membership at Carnoustie costs the equivalent of about 350 dollars a year—about the same as at other Scottish courses. As John's guest, I later paid the equivalent of about fifteen dollars for my round.) John told me that he had once belonged to one of the clubs in St. Andrews, but that he had dropped out because there were too many Americans. I was the only American in sight at Carnoustie. We put on our shoes in the parking lot, chose teams (my partner was Ray, a middle-aged man in the snack-food business), and teed off.

My total golf immersion of the previous few days suddenly paid off in a big way. I parred the first three holes, then parred four of the next six, narrowly missing par putts on the other two. It was the best nine holes I had ever played. By the turn, my partner and I had nearly closed out the match on my ball alone. I kept apologizing for how well I was doing, explaining that I was playing way over my head. Then I would crease another drive, or nail another approach, or send another putt dead into the center of the cup. I was afraid that I might suddenly begin to play poorly out of sheer embarrassment. After four holes, I insisted that my handicap be reduced for the purpose of our match. I said that if I was going to play the round of my life, I didn't want to worry that my playing partners were looking at me with narrowed eyes. After a good bit of friendly joking, we cut my allotment of strokes in half, and I returned to my zone.

At the turn, we stopped for refreshments at a tiny green shed beyond the ninth green. A woman who looked like Mrs. Tiggy-Winkle served us tea in chipped china cups. Behind her was a huge Pyrex pot in which she was hard-boiling several dozen eggs. Also squeezed into the shed was a prehistoric refrigerator, some cans of fruit juice, a haphazard arrangement of unappealing candy bars, a dozen or so dreadful-looking sandwiches, and a can of condensed milk for the tea and coffee. My playing partners and I sat knee-to-knee in wobbly chairs in front of the counter and sipped our tea.

The magic spell that had carried me triumphantly over the front nine abandoned me on the tenth tee, and I blundered into various familiar difficulties. Typical was my experience on the sixteenth, the cornerstone of Carnoustie's killer finish. The hole is a 250-yard par-three with an elevated green that from the tee looks like a tiny island bobbing in a storm-wracked sea. During a practice round before the Open in 1975, Jack Nicklaus failed to reach the sixteenth green twice with a three-wood and once with a driver, and asked that the hole be remeasured. I pulled my tee shot into the dunes and tall grass on the left and had to hack my way back into play a yard or two at a time. It's not a friendly hole.

After the round, I was treated to lunch by my hosts, who told me they were determined to undermine Scotland's reputation as a nation of tightwads. We ate across the street, at the clubhouse—a modern but slightly more cheerful building than the concrete bunker near the first tee. The menu was standard for Scotland: fried fish, fried chicken nuggets, lasagna, french fries. My companions had been planning to go back to work in the afternoon, but I talked them into playing another eighteen. I had hoped to play the Championship course again, but they suggested that we play Carnoustie's second course, called Burnside. (There's also a third, called Buddon.) I paid my £3 green fee to the starter and selected a pullcart from the ladies' restroom.

The wind—Carnoustie's principal weapon—had begun to blow in earnest by the time we teed off, and I didn't shoot many pars. For that matter, I didn't shoot many bogeys. Jim told me that once while playing the Championship course in the winter, he had seen a ball whiz past his head, and he had looked up to berate the inconsiderate golfer who had hit it—only to discover that the ball had been his own. The wind had blown it off the elevated green toward which he had been walking.

Scottish golfers tend to look down their noses at American golf-ers, American golf courses, and American golf in general. More than once I was asked by a Scottish playing partner whether I didn't think that the game as played in America was merely "target golf" and thus unworthy of comparison to the game as played in its gale-ridden native land. I was asked whether I didn't think that the bump-and-run shot (a Scottish golfer's favored short approach shot) was morally superior to the high pitch (ditto for an American). I was asked whether I didn't think that American golf courses were absurdly overmanicured. I was asked whether I didn't agree that American golfers were criminally lazy.

Some of these very pointed questions I felt were unfair. American golf is indeed a target game, but so is Scottish golf. When you play any hole on any golf course in the world, you begin at one point and progress toward a very small target—the hole. Indeed, every shot (assuming it's played with care) has its own target, whether the shot is a three-hundred-yard drive or a two-inch putt. The Scots do tend to play closer to the ground than American golfers do—they are more likely to run a ball onto a green than to lob it up into the jetstream—but that's just a reflection of the difference in prevailing conditions. Scottish courses (especially links courses) tend to be windier than American courses, their fairways tend to be harder and scrappier, and their greens are designed to accommodate balls skidding toward them at very low trajectories. So what? There are a lot of American golfers who don't know as much as they should about controlling a ball in the wind, but there are also a lot of Scottish golfers who don't make anywhere near enough use of their wedges and have never had to fade a five-iron around a maple tree. I've played with Scots who couldn't have pitched a ball over a bunker to save their lives, just as I've played with Americans whose shot-making ends once they've determined their yardage. The fact is that any golfer could become a better golfer by learning the other guy's tricks.

The American obsession with immaculate playing surfaces is harder to defend. Our courses don't need to be as green, smooth, and weedless as they often are. Most of the great Scottish courses didn't even have watering systems until fairly recently. At Carnoustie, the minimal watering was being done by a small number of moving sprinklers attached to great big hoses; twice I had to move a hose in order to play a shot. Of course, in most years the Scots can count on a prodigious amount of rain. But their example still proves that a great course doesn't need to look like a billiard table. Besides, it's easier to hit long drives on a dry course, and crappy lies are a historically important part of golf.

As for the lassitude of the typical American golfer, I can't think of anything nice to say. Those lush American fairways wouldn't seem quite so embarrassing if they weren't covered with tubby middle-aged guys driving kiddie cars. The game is meant to be played on foot.

After my second round at Carnoustie, I headed north, to Dornoch. The Royal Dornoch Golf Club is on nearly every list of the world's greatest courses, although it is far enough out of the way to be omitted from most tourists' itineraries. If it were situated two hundred miles to the south, it would have a place on the Open rota. It's one of the best golf courses on earth, but it doesn't get a whole lot of traffic. I played three rounds there. For the second and third, I teed off by myself because there was no one around to play with.

Golf was first played at Dornoch in 1616. Old Tom Morris designed nine of its holes in the late 1880s, and many other hands have shaped it. Dornoch is a links course. Unlike Turnberry or St. Andrews, though, it sits on a cliff and in some parts is as hilly as Gleneagles. It is sometimes compared to Pebble Beach, which is also perched above the water and also has sweeping views. The comparison isn't completely apt, but it correctly indicates Dornoch's stature.

After Cypress Point, Dornoch may be the most beautiful course I have played. It is certainly one of the ones that I am most eager to return to. Two holes especially stick in my mind. One is the eighth, a par-four that from the members' tees measures a little under four hundred yards. The hole begins on a high plateau; about two hundred yards out, the fairway drops precipitously to a moonscape of moguls and bunkers. You aim your drive over the precipice—actually the edge of an old quarry—then walk up hopefully and peer over the rim to see where you've ended up. From the edge, the view of the western end of the course, and of Dornoch Firth beyond it, is stunning. My other favorite hole is the twelfth, a par-five called Sutherland, after the greenkeeper and club secretary who, among other things, oversaw the lengthening of the course, in 1904, to accommodate the Haskell ball. The twelfth also has an inviting tee shot. You stand on a small rise and drive into a dune-flanked valley that bends gently away from you to the left. It's not an especially hard hole, but it's a beautiful one, and the one that comes first to my mind when I now think wistfully of Dornoch.

The town of Dornoch should be important to American golfers because it was the birthplace of Donald Ross, one of the most influential and prolific designers of American courses. Ross was the architect of Pinehurst, Oak Hill, Oakland Hills, Scioto, Inverness, and some five hundred other courses, many of them among the most distinguished in the country. Ross's ideas about what a golf course should be have influenced every designer who followed him, and they were formed indelibly at Dornoch. It was there that he first saw the flowing, natural holes for which he is now renowned.

I stayed at the Royal Golf Hotel, which is situated on a hill above the course, little more than a short pitch from the first tee. I played a round before lunch, a round before dinner, and a round before bed. Midway through my final round, I joined a young electrician from Inverness who had one of the prettiest golf swings I have ever seen. He told me that he loved Royal Dornoch, and that he didn't really mind paying its membership fee, which, he said, had recently been raised to the equivalent of about three hundred dollars a year. The hotel's manager and I had a putting contest on the floor of the bar that night, and I left my bag tag among several hundred others hanging from the ceiling.

The following day, on my way back to Glasgow, I played a round at Tain, a Morris layout on the other side of Dornoch Firth, from which, on a clear day, the cliffs of Dornoch are visible. Jerry Quin-

Ian, the man who put together my tour, had arranged for me to play with Tain's general manager and one of the members. I got lost in the town and didn't arrive at the club until the stroke of eight, when we were supposed to tee off. The manager, whose name was Norman, and the member, whose name was Ian, were already on the tee. Ian looked peeved and impatient. I jumped from my car, pulled on my shoes, breathlessly hit a drive without so much as a waggle beforehand, and took off after them.

Norman and Ian, it turned out, were playing in a club competition. Even so, they played at a pace that would have staggered the average American golfer, and I had to concentrate just to keep up. I had to watch them closely to make sure I put down my bag on the side of the green that was nearest the next tee, and I always had to be aware of whose turn it was to do what. If there was any doubt about the putting order, one of them would quickly establish it. "First David, then myself, then Ian," Norman said on one hole as he pulled the pin. Each golfer was expected to line up his putt or select his next club while the other players were putting or hitting. Even so, we played more slowly than the two players behind us, who occasionally had to wait for us before playing their shots.

Tain is a links course, but it looks more like a farm. We shared it with a few stray sheep and chickens, and at one point I had to retrieve my ball from an out-of-bounds pigpen. The course was the only one I had played in Scotland that didn't strike me as particularly distinguished. Still, my round there was one of the happiest of my trip. After I had diligently jogged along with them for a couple of holes, Norman and Ian apparently forgave me for being late, and we chatted between shots after that. Norman told me where to aim off every tee—the bunker on the left, the last tree to the right. To my surprise, I managed to hit the ball on the proper line surprisingly often. On later reflection, it occurred to me that my unaccustomed accuracy was probably the result of nothing more astonishing than simply aiming at *something*. Previously, like most golfers, I had aimed my tee shots at nothing smaller than the entire fairway—in effect, aiming at nothing. By not aiming at something small and precise, I had failed to take advantage of my brain's powerful ability to guide my muscles without my conscious direction. I first noticed this ability while stealing candy from my children's Halloween bags. I found that I could peer into one of the bags, identifying a particular piece of candy that I wanted to steal, and then, without looking into the bag (because I was warily watching my children across the room), reach in and invariably pick up the very piece of candy that I wanted. How was this possible? Because our brain knows what to do, if we give it a chance to do it.

After our round, Norman and Ian bought me a beer in the clubhouse bar. The two players who had been behind us on the course were also there. Ian good-naturedly complained to them that they had talked too loudly during their match, and that their voices had bothered him. "If you had been playing at the proper pace," one of the players said, "you would have been too far ahead to hear me." Ian laughed hard at that, both because it was a terrific comeback and because it was true. The little exchange exactly captured the graciousness and good manners that characterized every round I played with Scottish playing partners. If we Americans put our minds to it, we could play that way, too.

4

THE EMPEROR
OF GOLF

KARSTEN SOLHEIM'S BEARD HAS BEEN CALLED THE EIGHTH wonder of Arizona. It is white, it is the size and shape of half a lemon, and it sticks to the end of his chin like a puff of shaving cream. Solheim grew it in the early seventies, after injuring his chin in a traffic accident in India, where he had been traveling on business. His business is making golf clubs. The clubs are so popular that Solheim has an international following, and his beard makes him instantly recognizable. The king of Morocco once hailed him from an adjacent fairway on the Old Course. Japanese tourists sometimes stop him on the street and ask him to pose for snapshots. At the Masters a few years ago, officials had to tell him to confine his autograph signing to an area near the clubhouse so that his fans would not interfere with the players.

Solheim's company is called Karsten Manufacturing, and his golf clubs are sold under the trade name Ping. During the first eight years that he was in business, his factory was his garage. His first product, which he introduced in limited numbers in 1959, was a putter. It was unlike anything else available at the time. It was weighted in a way that made it more stable, and hence more accurate, than other putters. But it was not an immediate success. Solheim and his wife hawked it for years in pro shops and on practice greens at professional tournaments without attracting much serious attention. Many golfers viewed Solheim as a kook. Then, in 1967, Julius Boros, a well-known professional who had been suffering a putting slump, switched to a Ping putter and won the Phoenix Open. The company began to grow at a nearly geometric rate. Today Ping putters dominate the market, and they are used by more than half of all players on the men's, women's, and seniors' professional tours. In a closet at the company's headquarters in Phoenix are racks containing more than twelve hundred gold-plated Ping putters, each one representing a victory in a professional tournament. Solheim's first irons, which he introduced in 1961 and began manufacturing in earnest in 1969, carried his design ideas further. As the irons caught on among golfers, they precipitated a revolution in the golf-equipment business. Ping irons looked ugly, and they cost a lot, and they had to be fitted by a pro, but they hit the ball straighter and with more control than other clubs did, and they became extremely popular. Today, they are the most widely used clubs in America, despite the fact that they are among the most expensive. It has been said that if you were to check the golf bags of any foursome in the country, you would be almost certain to find at least one Ping club. In addition, virtually all manufacturers now make clubs that borrow, sometimes shamelessly, Solheim's numerous innovations, and many companies market their clubs in ways that Solheim pioneered. The success of Karsten Manufacturing, which is privately owned, has made Solheim a very wealthy man. *Forbes* has estimated his personal fortune at close to half a billion dollars.

Solheim's innovations have sometimes been accompanied by controversy. In the late sixties, he had to redesign his irons after the United States Golf Association decided that one of his improvements—a slight, stability-enhancing bend in the shafts of the clubs—did not conform with the rules of golf. In the late eighties, he tangled with the USGA again—this time over the size and spacing of the grooves on the faces of his irons. In 1989, the PGA

Tour—an organization, unrelated to the USGA, that governs the principle men's professional golf tournaments in America—voted to ban his irons (and similar ones made by other manufacturers) from use in tour events, claiming that the shape of the grooves on their faces gave some players an unfair advantage in certain situations. Karsten Manufacturing sued the PGA Tour and won an injunction preventing the tour's ban from taking effect. Then the tour countersued, claiming that Karsten had knowingly broken the rules. Several years of acrimony, and the expenditure of many millions of dollars in legal fees, ensued.

Many people who follow golf closely came to view the lawsuit, in which Karsten claimed damages of at least a hundred million dollars, less as a legal battle than as a titanic personal struggle between two stubborn, powerful men: Solheim and Deane Beman, who was then the commissioner of the PGA Tour and the main force behind the ban. After all, the part of the golf club that was under dispute was so small that you could have filled it with a few human hairs, and the effect of the grooves on the game was far from clear, even to many of those who had studied the matter closely. Other observers saw the fight over grooves as a sort of symbolic battle over golf's, well, soul. For many years, the USGA had been the rule-making body for both amateur and professional golf. The tour's ruling threatened to change that and, in doing so, make it harder for amateur golfers to convince themselves that they played the same game the pros played—a happy fantasy that has long been one of golf's attractions. Still others saw the lawsuit as a contest between the forces of progress and the forces of reaction. Solheim, in this view, represented technology's unstinting dedication to enhancing the quality of modern life, while the PGA Tour represented stodgy old ignorant arbitrary convention (did I mention that I use Ping golf clubs myself?). But it's really a lot more complicated than that.

When I rediscovered golf, at the age of thirty-six, the golf clubs I used were some ancient Tommy Armour PGA irons that my brother had acquired secondhand and played with for a long time but no longer wanted. Those Tommy Armours looked pretty much exactly like the kind of golf clubs that people used to think of simply as golf clubs. They had smooth, sleek, chrome-plated heads, and they looked as though they might have been made by a guy whose real job was making door handles for Cadillacs. The only problem with them was that they were very hard for a relatively uncoordinated golfer like me to use. Hitting a ball on almost any part of the clubface except the exact sweet spot would send a painful, bone-rattling jolt up the shaft and into my arms. When I was just starting out, I hit many shots that produced such jolts, and the fear of hitting more of them made me tense my arm muscles defensively before taking a swing—exactly the wrong thing to do.

Eventually it occurred to me that I ought to invest in some nice new golf clubs that might be easier to use. I knew from reading various golf-related publications that my new clubs ought to be so-called "game-improvement irons"—the generic term for golf clubs made by Karsten Solheim and his numerous imitators. Such clubs are easier for bad golfers to play with, and they have advantages for good golfers, too. Since I had already rationalized the purchase of roughly five hundred dollars' worth of new woods, rationalizing the purchase of roughly eight hundred dollars' worth of new irons was easy.

Just as I was working out the final details of my idea, in early 1992, Solheim introduced his first new irons in a decade. They were called Ping Zings. I first heard about them at the PGA Merchandise Show, held in Orlando in January of 1992. Zings were easily the hit of the show, despite the fact that Karsten salesmen had no samples, no photographs, and no drawings to show potential customers. There were no signs announcing the new clubs, and no brochures describing them. The first sets would not be ready for months, the salesmen said, and even then, they would be available only in limited quantities. Still, buyers crowded into the Ping booth and placed thousands of orders. (When the first photographs of Zings did become available, shortly before the clubs reached the market, several golf publications ran them on their covers.) I was immediately caught up in the mob mentality and tried to order a set myself.

A salesman explained to me that I could not, because I wasn't a golf pro. As soon as I got home from Florida, though, I placed an order with the professional at my club. "What are the Zings like?" he asked. I said I didn't know.

My new clubs arrived in March, and for several months I had the only set at my club. (Now, quite a few of my regular playing partners have them.) Like the numerous Ping models that had preceded them, they were ugly by conventional standards. Placed face down, a Zing clubhead looks like an ear, or like a miniature fifties-era ashtray, with swoops and dips along the edges—the result of removing weight from the center of the clubhead and placing it in various strategic positions around the perimeter. In addition, it has a dull gray finish (produced by tumbling it with hundreds of other clubheads in a large drum for several hours) that is intended to be less distracting to a golfer than the shiny chrome finish on forged blade irons like my old Tommy Armours. Nonetheless, I thought my new clubs looked really great. I also loved the way they felt when I hit balls. My shots were longer and straighter, and my elbows and finger joints didn't hurt as much as when I was finished. I still hit plenty of terrible shots, but my bad shots tended to be only pretty bad, and my pretty bad shots tended to be pretty good.

Very rapidly, I became a convert to the Solheim religion. In the fall, I arranged to pay a visit to the great man himself, at his headquarters in Phoenix. I wanted to hear the story of his life, see how his golf clubs were made, and kiss the hem of his garment. Naturally, I took my golf clubs with me.

With more beard, a mustache, and a string tie, Solheim would look something like Colonel Sanders. He is a bit less than six feet tall and is a little on the heavy side. He has wavy white hair. For over eighty years, gravity has been tugging at the lobes of his ears and the tip of his nose. For the last few years, he has been blind in his right eye. He wears half-rim aviator glasses. He drives a white BMW that one of his sons bought for him a few years ago, but he is otherwise unostentatious. He and his wife, Louise, live in a nice but by no means palatial house near the first tee of Phoenix's Moon Valley

Country Club, which he owns. (He also owns a country club in England.) Some people who know him say that his memory isn't what it used to be, but he says his memory was never very good, a deficiency he traces to a childhood accident in which a carpenter dropped a two-by-six on his head. Age has forced him to trim his business schedule in recent years, but he still goes to work before seven in the morning, still ascends to his office by climbing a long staircase two steps at a time, and still designs many of his company's new golf clubs. Except for his habit of making sandwiches out of two pieces of white bread and a dozen or so brick-shaped chunks of butter, he has no vices. He is obstinate, funny, kind, and deeply religious. He and his wife are active in a local Baptist church and in a number of religious organizations; they attend early-morning prayer services, and they always say grace before meals. His employees like him. They address him as Karsten, and they greet him with pleasure when he takes one of his frequent walks through the buildings where his golf clubs are manufactured, opening unlabeled locked doors with keys from a massive ring that he carries in his pocket. The receptionist in the company's main building has several photographs hanging above her desk; one is of herself, one is of herself and her husband on their wedding day, and one is of Solheim.

Despite his easy relationship with his employees, Solheim is used to doing things his own way. When he eats in the grill at Moon Valley, he typically knows what he wants before he arrives, orders it as he is being seated, and is sometimes served while his guests are still reading their menus. He bought Moon Valley, in 1984, because it was in danger of going bankrupt. He has since spent several million dollars expanding the club's facilities and redesigning its golf course, which is now the home of the Standard Register Ping tournament, a stop on the women's professional tour. (Solheim is a staunch supporter of women's golf, and he and his wife are the founding sponsors of the Solheim Cup, a biennial international competition that is the women's equivalent of the Ryder Cup.) Like the company, Moon Valley operates the way Solheim wants it to operate. The new putting greens, the lockers in the men's locker room, the shower controls in the women's locker room, and the dish-washing equipment in the kitchen, among other details, were designed by him. A maintenance worker using a tractor to move a pile of dirt from one part of the golf course to another at seven-thirty in the morning is not surprised to see Solheim suddenly waving his cellular telephone at him, directing him to move the dirt somewhere else. The man who shines the golf shoes of Moon Valley's members uses a special kind of polish that Solheim imports from Norway. A suggestion box hangs from the branch of a tree outside the clubhouse. It is fifteen feet above the ground.

Solheim was born in 1911 in Bergen, Norway. When he was two, his family emigrated to Seattle, where his father, a shoemaker, hoped to find the prosperity that had eluded him at home. A short time later, Karsten's mother died, at the age of twenty-one, while giving birth to his brother, Ray, and a short time after that his father went to Alaska to look for gold. Karsten and Ray were left behind, in the care of separate foster families. During the next three years, Karsten lived first with a German family, then with a Swedish family. When he was six, his father returned to Seattle, remarried, and reclaimed his sons.

When I asked Solheim about those years—we were riding in a white limousine between his headquarters and the foundry where his clubs are cast—he answered vaguely, then changed the subject. His wife, Louise, who is the executive vice president of Karsten Manufacturing, told me later that in nearly sixty years of marriage she had only rarely heard him discuss his childhood. "When I think about it, I feel very sad," she said. "He must have felt really lost. His mother was gone, and his father had left him with a family that didn't speak Norwegian, which was the only language he understood. When his father remarried and took him back, Karsten hardly knew what language to speak. They didn't start him in school until he was seven, because he couldn't speak English, although I think he would have learned better, and faster, if they had put him in school immediately. But he never talks about those days, and he never complains, and he doesn't seem to have any bad memories."

In school, Solheim distinguished himself as a woodworker. He had learned to handle tools while helping his father in the family's shoe shop, and he quickly left the other students far behind. When the principal asked the school's two woodworking teachers about building a bookcase for his office, both recommended Karsten for the job. The Solheim living room today contains several pieces dating from that era. There is an elaborately carved footstool, a piano bench, a small book stand that he designed himself, and a cabinet with an intricately joined hexagonal compartment on each side. Solheim is still proud of these pieces, and he showed them to me when I visited his home. "I can hardly believe I did that," he said, looking at the cabinet and lifting a lid to show me how the parts fitted together. "Nowadays, kids will make a breadboard shaped like a pig, and they call that woodworking."

After school and on weekends, Karsten worked in his father's shoe shop. He was unusually small for his age until his growth spurt in late adolescence, and to talk to customers over the counter, he had to stand on a wooden box. After high school, he spent a year studying engineering at the University of Washington, paying his tuition with money he had earned with an early-morning paper route. He couldn't afford to stay. The country was in the depths of the Great Depression, and his father needed him in the shoe shop.

A few years later, at church, he met Louise Crozier. She had been born in Spokane, but her mother had died when she was a month old and her father had sent her to be raised by an aunt and uncle in Texas. She was precocious, learning to read before she was four. When she was ten, her father, who taught science and business in a school district outside Seattle, decided he wanted her back. Louise didn't want to go but accepted the change stoically. "I remember that when I got on the train, a tear was rolling down my nose, but I held my head up high so that no one would see it." She and her father boarded with another family for a year, then moved to the country, where he supplemented his teacher's salary by raising chickens.

Shortly after Karsten and Louise met, they heard a sermon by a visiting evangelist who was a grandson of the founder of the Salvation Army. The evangelist said that the ideal age for a woman to marry was eighteen, and the ideal age for a man was twenty-five. After the sermon, Karsten asked Louise how old she was. She said she was seventeen. She asked Karsten how old he was. He said he was twenty-four. Neither said anything else then, but ten days later, Karsten proposed, and six months after that—in June of 1936, just after Louise's eighteenth birthday—they were married. They spent their honeymoon in northern Washington. As they were driving home, Karsten's Model T stopped dead. "I got down under the car, and took the pan off, and realized that the connecting-rod bearing was gone," he told me over lunch at Moon Valley one day. "Well, there was a farmhouse right there, and I asked the farmer if he had any bacon rind. He got me a piece, and I trimmed it a little, and I put that bacon rind where the bearing should have been, and I tightened up the cap, and we drove the forty miles home without any more trouble. Of course, when we got there, the bacon was crisp."

Solheim continued to work as a shoemaker for several years. There were two other shoe shops within a block of his. One day, he noticed in the window of one of them a sign advertising new heels for women's shoes at fifteen cents a pair, a price that was lower than his. He put an identical sign in his own window. His next customer asked, "Why did you cut your price? Aren't your heels as good as they used to be?" An hour later, another customer asked the same thing. Solheim took down his sign, raised his price to thirty cents, and put a piece of prime leather on his counter. When a customer asked why he charged more than the man down the street, he said, "The cost of our labor is the same, so the difference must be in the quality of the material," and he let the customer feel the piece of leather on the counter. Within a year, both of his competitors were out of business, and Solheim had learned a marketing lesson that he would never forget.

In 1940, an injury to his arm forced Solheim to abandon the shoe business. He got a job selling aluminum cookware and rapidly became the company's star salesman. Shortly after the Japanese attack on Pearl Harbor, he took a university extension course in engineering, and was hired as a draftsman by Convair, in San Diego. This was the first of eighteen moves during the first twenty years of their marriage. Convair had a contract to build ships for the Navy. Solheim suggested changes in the company's production methods that enabled a single shift to accomplish what had formerly required three. He was promoted rapidly, and later took a job at Ryan Aeronautical, where he helped to design and build the first jet airplane.

After the war, Solheim went back to selling cookware. This career move seemed odd to me, and I asked Louise about it. She said, "I think the answer is simply that Karsten likes to work, and that he has enjoyed every job he has ever had. He liked his engineering jobs, but he also liked selling cookware, and he was very, very good at it, and when the war ended, he figured there would be less engineering work. You never see Karsten sitting around wondering what to do next. The test pilot at Ryan told me once that no matter what everyone else might be doing, Karsten was always busy. I think the only thing he ever dreaded was being stuck in an office by himself. He likes to have people around him, and he says that that's how he gets his best ideas."

When the Korean War began, in 1951, Solheim went back to Ryan, then back to Convair, where he helped to design the Atlas Missile Ground Guidance System. Three years later, General Electric recruited him, and he moved his family to Ithaca, New York. He took advanced electronics courses at Cornell, worked on the first transistors, and played an important role in the project to build the first portable television set. At around the same time, he invented a new kind of television antenna that was meant to go inside the house, right on top of the TV. The antenna he designed had two adjustable arms that reminded some people of the ears of a rabbit. GE wasn't interested, so he gave the idea to some friends at an electronics company in Chicago. "The reason GE wasn't interested was that their marketing people had estimated that they would be able to sell only forty thousand of them," Solheim recalls. "But we did a dry run, and I kept hearing workers on the assembly line saying, 'I'm going to get one of those,' 'I'm going to get one of those.' So I knew that they would be a success, and right at that moment, I decided that marketing people shouldn't talk to the people who are selling the merchandise; they should talk to the people who are buying it. That's been my philosophy ever since. Marketing is easy if you have a product that people want." When the Chicago company sold its millionth set of rabbit ears, it sent Solheim a gold-plated set.

Solheim has often had ideas for new products or for improved versions of existing ones. For example, he once attached an electric-resistance coil to the bottom of a frying pan, creating what might have been, had he pursued the idea, the world's first electric skillet. Another time, he attached small wings to the windshield wipers of his car, so that the lift created by the wings as the car drove forward would press the moving wipers' blades more firmly against the glass. When his son Allan—the Solheims have three sons, all of whom are now vice presidents of Karsten Manufacturing, and all of whom frequently appear, with their father, in the company's television commercials—signed up for the Soap Box Derby, Solheim told him to set his car's wheels as far back as possible, so that the car would remain on the steep starting ramp for a longer time, and thus have a faster start. He also told Allan to build the car as light as possible, and then bring it up to the maximum permissible weight by adding pieces of lead to the very rear of the car. Putting the weights in the rear would keep the heavy part of the car on the starting ramp longer, giving the car an extra push. Allan won race after race, and he might have won the national championship, except that he decided to try an improvement of his own. Having noticed that skaters propel themselves by pushing outward against the edges of their skates, Allan reasoned that he could increase the speed of his car on the main part of the raceway by turning the steering wheel back and forth, and simultaneously shifting his weight from side to side. At a race in Ohio, he came off the starting ramp ahead of his opponent, as usual, but when he began to rock back and forth, he rapidly fell behind.

While working for GE in Ithaca, Solheim received a fateful invitation. Some friends from work were going to play golf, and they wondered if he would like to join them. He had never played before, but he went along, and although he played very poorly, he was fascinated by the game. He was forty-three years old. He played frequently after that and improved steadily. Like most golfers, he found the game alternately inebriating and painfully frustrating. The part of the game that frustrated him most was putting. No matter how carefully he tried to control his stroke, he had trouble making the ball follow the same line two times in a row. Eventually, he decided that the fault lay not in his technique but in his golf club.

Solheim decided that the putters commonly in use at that time were poorly designed. Most of them had heads that were uniform in thickness, so that the weight was evenly distributed from one end of the head to the other. Solheim reasoned that this design was inherently unstable. "Hitting a golf ball with one of those putters is like hitting a tennis ball with a Ping-Pong paddle," he says. "The weight isn't in the right places, and it twists in your hands." In his garage, he took a small rectangular aluminum bar and attached a lead weight to either end. He then attached a shaft near the center of the aluminum bar. With this crude club, he went to the practice green and found that his putting accuracy was dramatically improved. Adding extra weight to the blade's heel and toe had enlarged its sweet spot, increasing his margin for error. With his new putter, he didn't have to hit a ball in exactly the right place in order to make it go straight. He could hit a ball near the heel or toe of the club's face without causing it to deflect severely. He added his new putter to his golf bag.

Not long afterward, GE transferred Solheim to the company's new computer department, in Palo Alto, and he began to play golf occasionally with a local pro. One day, the pro praised Solheim's putting. Solheim said, "Oh, you should have seen me before I built this putter." The pro putted a few balls with it and told Solheim, "You ought to market that." A similar thought must have been lurking in the back of Solheim's mind, because he went straight from the golf course to his office and made a rough drawing. He recalls, "I took a piece of paper, and I said to myself, 'Well, I'll put a block of metal at the toe and another at the heel.' Now, I couldn't put strings between the two blocks, like a tennis racket, because golf balls are too hard for strings. So I put a metal plate between them. That was the face of the putter. To make it so that a left-handed golfer could use it, too, I put another plate on the back. Then I needed something to attach a shaft to, so I added a small bar of metal across the bottom." Solheim took the drawing to a welder at Kaiser Electronics, one of GE's suppliers. Later that afternoon, the welder returned with a finished putterhead. Solheim took it home that evening, drilled a hole in the bar on the bottom, and stuck a shaft in the hole. He dropped a golf ball on the ground, and stroked it. The ball rolled straight. Because of the way the pieces of metal were joined, the new putterhead acted like a tuning fork. It made a sharp, clear, ringing sound—a ping—when it struck a ball. "I remember Karsten running into the kitchen with this thing," Louise told me. "I was making dinner, and he said, 'I've got a name for my putter!' And I said, 'That's nice, honey.' If it made him happy, it made me happy. Of course, I never dreamed what would come of it."

Allan Solheim, who is now in his fifties, was a high school student when his father began making putters. "We lived in Redwood City, California, at the time, and then, in 1961, GE transferred my father to Phoenix," he told me one day as we were sitting in his office. "When my parents looked for a house in Phoenix, they looked for one with a big garage. We used to hang the putters from a line in there, while the glue dried in the grips. Eventually, the putters took over the house, too, and there were boxes everywhere. We used to heat up the heads on the burners of the electric range. You had to heat them up in order to get the shaft in, and also to make the metal oxidize, so that your finger wouldn't leave a print when you touched it."

In the early days, Solheim would visit pro shops and putting greens, trying to explain what made his putter different. To demonstrate the principle of heel-and-toe weighting, he built a putter whose head had four holes bored in the top of it. There was one hole at each end, and two in the middle. To the back of the putterhead he attached a wishbone-shaped yoke that held a pen. He would put lead weights in the two middle holes and putt a ball across a long sheet of paper that he had spread on the ground. The pen in the yoke would make a crooked line on the paper as the putter head struck and was deflected by the ball. Then he would move the weights to the heel and toe, and putt again. This time, the line would be straight.

"It was very, very slow," Solheim told me. "And I didn't give those putters away. In San Francisco, once, I spent a long time on a putting green with a very well-known pro. He said he was interested in my putter, and that he wanted one. But he didn't want to pay. I told him, 'If you don't want to pay, I'm not going to give it to you.' Because I knew that if I saw something I really wanted, I'd be happy to pay for it. The fact that he wasn't willing to pay for it meant that he certainly wasn't planning to use it."

At first, the touring pros viewed Solheim as an eccentric. His putter looked and sounded funny, and his shoes had holes in them, and he looked like a nutty inventor. When pros consented to try his putter, it was often because they felt sorry for him. But putting is a notoriously whimsical skill, and golfers in a slump will often try anything to get their feel back. The company's big break came in 1967, when Julius Boros won the Phoenix Open with a nonmusical Ping model called the Cushin. Orders began to pour in. Gene Littler, George Archer, Gary Player, and Jack Nicklaus, among other well-known professionals, began to use Ping putters, and to win tournaments with them.

"We got so far behind in our orders that it wasn't funny," Louise recalls. "The phone would ring in the middle of the night, and it would be somebody from Japan, wanting putters. I remember Jack Nicklaus suddenly wanted the rights to distribute our putter in England, and Gary Player wanted South Africa. I went to New York to meet with their agent, and he asked me how many putters I thought we could put out in a week. At that time, Karsten was still working at GE, and I don't think we had ever put out more than two hundred in a week. But I took a deep breath, and I said, 'A thousand.' "

While the Solheims were building their putter business, Karsten was also thinking about irons, and wondering if his ideas about weighting could be applied to them as well. To find out, he took his own golf clubs into his garage and tooled a cavity in the back of the head of each one, to move the weight away from the center. He built up the perimeters with small welds, then covered the cavities with a piece of metal shim stock so that no one would see what he had done. He took the clubs to a driving range and hit a bucket of balls. The modified clubs felt better in his hands, and they produced a significantly higher percentage of straight shots than the old clubs had. He took the clubs to several local pros but was turned away. Finally, one pro agreed to try them. The pro hit a few balls, then said, "When you make these clubs, send me two sets."

Solheim's early manufacturing methods were crude. He tooled the cavities in his clubheads by hand, with a used mill that he had bought for eleven hundred dollars. (That eleven hundred dollars is the only money he has ever borrowed for his business.) To test the aerodynamic properties of some of his early clubheads, he would hold a prototype out the passenger window of his car while his son Allan drove at high speeds along empty roads on the outskirts of town. "My job was to get the car up to a hundred miles an hour and hold it steady right at a hundred," Allan told me. While the car sped along, Solheim would hold each prototype against a simple spring scale, looking for the configuration that produced the least drag.

Perimeter weighting wasn't the only performance-enhancing feature of Solheim's first golf clubs. While tinkering in his garage, Solheim had discovered that he could greatly increase the stability of a golf club by placing a four- or five-degree bend in its shaft, just above the bottom of the grip. The bend was barely noticeable, but it helped prevent the clubhead from twisting at impact, and it produced straighter shots. Solheim demonstrated the principle to me over lunch one day by bending a paper clip into the shape of a golf club and having me press its head against my water glass. Ever since that demonstration, I have been tempted to take a hammer to the shafts of my golf clubs.

"The bent shaft would have revolutionized golf," he told me. "It would have made it much easier for the average player to hit the ball straight. But the USGA ruled that it was a violation of the rules of golf, and we got rid of it. In some ways that ruling was a good thing, because it made me think about other ways of improving golf clubs. Around that time, I had started checking the quality of what other manufacturers were producing, and I had found that it was very, very low. For example, the six-iron in one set might have the same loft as the seven-iron, which meant that the set really had two seven-irons and no six. Or the lie of the clubs might be different, or the shape of the sole might be wrong. There was virtually no quality control in those days. So I made a gauge in my garage that would let me calibrate clubs, and then I would take that gauge and a vice and a hammer and a wrench, and I would go over to the golf course and show people how their clubs were off, and I would tell them that I could fix them. A lot of them didn't want me to touch their clubs, but some did. And while I was hammering away, there would be a fellow standing on the first tee with his driver in his hand, waiting to tee off, and he didn't dare hit his ball until I had finished."

Solheim decided that one way to improve the quality of golf clubs would be to cast the heads in molds rather than to forge them, as was done almost universally at that time. In forging, a piece of metal is first heated, then pressed into shape, then tooled by hand to its final dimensions. The process has many variables. Differences in the temperature of the metal at the time of forging can create differences in the performance of a club. So can differences in the skill of the person doing the finishing. Solheim had been casting his putterheads with great success, and he decided to do the same thing with the heads for his irons. (Ping clubs are now cast at a foundry in Phoenix called Dolphin, Inc., which is a subsidiary of Karsten Manufacturing. Dolphin makes a lot of things besides golf clubs, including photoreceptor drums for IBM photocopiers, parts of cruise missiles, and fittings used on most of the world's jet airplanes.) He also decided to create a fitting system that would enable him to match individual golfers with clubs that complemented their bodies and their swings. At that time, virtually all golf clubs were sold in just a few variations on a single standard size. Tall golfers, short golfers, fat golfers, thin golfers, golfers who hooked the ball, golfers who sliced the ball, and golfers who did everything in between—all of them used essentially the same clubs. Solheim's fitting system enabled him to sell clubs that were tailored to the peculiarities of each customer. Solheim decided to sell his clubs only through golf professionals, who could be taught to fit the clubs properly, and to build every set to order.

As his club business grew, Solheim developed a reputation among tour professionals as a club doctor. Players would drop by his factory or even his house, sometimes late at night, and asked him to check their clubs. In 1976, Jerry Pate asked Solheim to check his irons, which had been made by another manufacturer. Solheim determined that Pate's five-iron didn't fit with the rest of his set. "The sole of the club wasn't the right shape," he remembers. "It didn't have the right grind on it. That's one of the problems with forging. It's hard to make two clubs that are exactly the same. Anyway, I told him that I could grind it to the right shape, and I did." A few weeks later, at the Atlanta Athletic Club, Pate used the same five-iron to hit a crucial shot in his victory in the U.S. Open. On the final hole, with a one-stroke lead, he hit his tee shot into the rough, leaving him just over 190 yards from the pin. His ball was in tall grass, and there was a pond in front of the green. He selected his reground five-iron. His ball flew straight at the pin, carrying the pond and stopping two feet from the cup. He sank the putt for a birdie, clinching his victory. Today, there is a plaque on the course at the spot where he hit that shot.

The headquarters of Karsten Manufacturing are spread among more than twenty buildings on two large blocks in northern Phoenix. The complex is easy to miss, because the buildings don't have signs. (An Australian golf-club manufacturer once told Solheim that signs merely make life easier for thieves.) The smallest building in the two-block complex is a 2200-square-foot cinder-block box that served as the company's first nongarage headquarters. Solheim took me to see it one day in a chauffeured golf cart. "I felt like a king when we bought that building," he said as we parked outside. "That was in 1967. I had five desks in front, and I divided the other three sections into shipping, grinding, and assembly, and I thought I had it made." He laughed. Today, the building is the company's repair shop, where golfers bring old Ping clubs to be reshafted, regripped, or modified. Solheim abhors waste. His original work-bench, which he built in his Redwood City garage in the fifties, is still in use in the repair building. (Solheim's feelings about waste extend to his company's advertisements. He sometimes complains to the marketing department that Ping ads are insufficiently clut-tered. "Karsten doesn't approve of white space," a marketing em-ployee told me. "He'll say, 'There's a little bit of room left in the corner. Why don't you put a picture of one of our balls in there?' ")

Solheim took me inside another building to show me the com-pany's computer-aided design department. When Solheim began work on the Zings, several years ago, he would grind his prototypes by hand, then take them to the computer department, where pro-grammers would recreate their dimensions electronically. Modify-ing the design in the computer was easier than doing it by hand. The computers directed the milling of the original molds. All the prototypes were tested on a computerized mechanical golfer called the Ping Man, which Solheim designed. The tests were recorded on high-speed video equipment capable of shooting up to twelve thousand frames a second.

"We've learned a lot from that camera," Solheim told me when we visited the video department. He showed me still pictures and parts of tapes from several tests. "One thing we learned is that a golf ball is in contact with the face of a golf club for only about one twenty-five-hundredth of a second. The back of the ball com-presses when the clubhead hits it, and then the ball is gone. Noth-ing that the golfer or the club does after that can affect the flight of the ball." We looked at a tape of a wooden club striking a ball near the club's toe. The club twisted back and forth violently after con-tact. "Look at that," Solheim said. "That club is twisting thirty de-grees in each direction. You couldn't twist the shaft with your hands like that, but the ball made it whip back and forth. What we learned is that you need to have enough weight in the right parts of the clubhead to compress and release the ball before the shaft can start to twist. If you can keep everything stable for that fraction of a second, the ball will go straight. That's why we move the weight around in our clubheads."

Golf clubs made by other manufacturers, especially clubs that were designed before Solheim's ideas about perimeter weighting became widely accepted, sometimes look as though they were built for the purpose of producing mishits. On old-fashioned forged irons, the weight is often spread relatively uniformly through the clubhead or even concentrated near the middle. Such configurations move the head's center of gravity toward the shaft, greatly reduce the size of the sweet spot, and make the club especially prone to twisting. Before Solheim, aesthetic considerations were often paramount in golf-club design. "I don't want to mention any names," he told me, "but if you really want to understand the importance of distributing the weight in a golf club, why don't you take a tennis racket and put some weight right in the center of it. Put something solid, about three or four inches in diameter, right in the center of the racket. Try to play tennis with that, and you'll have some idea of how those other clubs work."

Virtually all modern golf clubs, except putters, have grooves on their faces. The grooves are like treads on a tire. Their purpose is to displace foreign material—such as water, dirt, or bits of grass—that comes between the clubhead and the ball. When foreign material gets in the way, the ball spins less and is thus harder for a good player to control. The grooves' size, shape, and spacing are all governed by rules published by the USGA. For example, the rules say that grooves can be no more than thirty-five thousandths of an inch wide and no more than twenty thousandths of an inch deep, and that the space between any two grooves must be no less than three times the width of one groove. For many years, the grooves on all golf clubs, including Pings, were V-shaped in cross section, in accordance with the USGA's specifications. In 1984, the USGA revised its rules. Because of the nature of the casting process, the

V-grooves on cast clubs—which by then were being made by a number of manufacturers—tended to have slightly rounded bottoms. In recognition of this fact, the USGA announced that two new types of grooves would also be permissible. Both of the new types were roughly U-shaped in cross section. Solheim realized immediately that a U-shaped groove—also known as a square groove or a box groove—would not only be easier to cast than a V-shaped groove; it would also work better. A U-groove would have a greater volume than a V-groove of the same width and depth, and as a result it would displace more water, dirt, and grass. Solheim redesigned his clubs.

Solheim's first U-grooves didn't work very well. Their edges were so sharp that they nicked the covers of golf balls. To keep that from happening, he modified his design by slightly rounding the grooves' edges. In 1986, the USGA decided that this rounding had made Ping grooves too wide by approximately the width of a human hair. Solheim objected to the USGA's measurement method and said he wouldn't change his clubs. The USGA responded by voting to ban Pings in USGA-sanctioned play (including the U.S. Open), and Solheim sued. There was a great deal of expensive arguing back and forth. The two sides settled out of court in 1990, with Solheim agreeing to change the width of his grooves from that point forward, and the USGA agreeing to permit golfers to continue using older Pings without being held to be in violation of the rules.

This is arcane stuff, and it seems even more arcane when you actually study the disputed grooves. In Solheim's office one day, I used a jeweler's loupe to examine Ping clubheads from various eras, and I honestly could not see the difference between a pre-1990 U-groove and a post-1990 U-groove, even though the loupe had a groove-width measurement scale superimposed on its lens. For that matter, I wasn't entirely certain that I could see the difference between a U-groove and a V-groove. It is impossible to overemphasize how teensy the disputed area was. Teensy or not, though, it caused a lot of trouble. And Solheim's disagreement with the USGA was like a pillow fight in comparison with his subsequent battle with the PGA Tour.

At around the time the USGA was objecting to Solheim's method of measuring grooves, the PGA Tour was taking exception to the grooves themselves. In the late eighties, the tour's leadership complained to the USGA that U-grooves gave tour-caliber players an unfair advantage when hitting relatively short shots from light rough. On such shots, the tour said, a player using U-grooves was able to put more backspin on a ball, and thus stop it more quickly on a green, than a player using V-grooves. The tour said that U-grooves made short shots from light rough easier than they ought to be, thereby reducing the advantage of hitting a ball in the fairway to begin with. The tour wanted the USGA to eliminate U-grooves altogether.

The main force behind the tour's complaints was its commissioner at the time, Deane Beman. Beman, who is in his fifties, had been a distinguished golfer in his day. He won the British Amateur Championship in 1959, and he won the United States Amateur in 1960 and 1963. He joined the professional tour in 1967 and won four tournaments before a hand injury forced him to retire, in 1974. He became the tour's commissioner the same year. Beman had been a businessman before turning pro, and he set about shoring up the tour's finances, which were shaky. During two decades in office, he transformed the PGA Tour from a nickel-and-dime athletic organization into an immensely wealthy nonprofit corporation. He increased tournament purses by a factor of more than ten, instituted a pension program for players, and increased the tour's assets from less than a million dollars to roughly 200 million. Over the years, quite a few tour players accused Beman of pursuing policies that they felt ran counter to their own best interests—for example, by leading the tour into the design and construction of golf courses, a business in which it competes directly with current and former players—but even his detractors acknowledged that he had brought about huge gains in the fiscal health of professional golf.

In addition to being a businessman, Beman is a traditionalist. He believes that improvements in equipment in the last couple of decades have changed professional golf for the worse. At his urging, the USGA conducted tests on U-grooves. The tests concluded that under certain circumstances players using U-grooves were indeed able to stop their balls faster than players using V-grooves. But they also indicated that despite this apparent advantage, the players using U-grooves were not able to stop their balls any closer to the hole than the players using V-grooves. In other words, according to the USGA, there was a difference in the behavior of the ball, but no resulting advantage in scoring. This sort of variation is common in golf. Some golf clubs are designed to hit the ball high, and some are designed to hit it low. Some balls are designed to spin very rapidly, making them more likely to stop quickly. Some balls are designed to spin somewhat less, making them more likely to travel farther and curve less. All these differences are tolerated under the rules, and golfers attempt with varying degrees of success to use them to their advantage. Indeed, the idea that a change of equipment can lead to a change of fortune on the course has been a part of golf since its very beginnings.

Unhappy with the results of the USGA's groove tests, the PGA Tour conducted its own and came to a different conclusion. In 1989, the tour's tournament policy board voted to ban U-grooves in competition, beginning in 1990. Karsten Manufacturing went to court to block the ban, claiming among other things that the board's vote had been illegal. The vote had indeed been unusual, and in fact, it had violated the tour's bylaws. Although the board had ten members, only three had voted to ban the clubs; the other seven had abstained, citing conflicts of interest. These conflicts were very real. All seven abstaining members were professionals who had contracts or business arrangements with equipment companies that competed with companies that made clubs with U-grooves. The tour later amended its bylaws in an effort to make the earlier vote retroactively legal. But the court granted Karsten an injunction against the tour, and the injunction was upheld on appeal.

Golf Digest covered the grooves controversy extensively. At the height of the yelling, I called Jerry Tarde, who is the magazine's editor, to ask him about the case. Like many people not directly connected with one side or the other, Tarde viewed the entire matter with a certain amount of disbelief. He said, "It's almost as though P. G. Wodehouse had created the plot. There are golfers like Jay Sigel and Tom Watson who feel passionate about how much these grooves have affected the game, and yet it all seems to be an argument over nothing. And the irony of it is that everybody is arguing the wrong side. You have the manufacturer claiming that its clubs make less of a difference than the skill of the players, and you have the tour claiming that skill of the players makes less of a difference than their clubs. It's crazy."

Big lawsuits tend to take on a life of their own, however, and the Ping lawsuit certainly did that. Still, there were real issues at stake for both sides. The PGA Tour's argument was that it ought to have the right to decide what equipment its players can use in its tournaments. There are plenty of precedents in other sports. Major league baseball players aren't allowed to use aluminum bats, for example, even though high school and college players are. Tennis players can't use double-strung rackets. The tour felt that it ought to be able to exercise the same degree of control. John Morris, a spokesman for the tour, told me, "The point we have tried to make consistently is that we should have the right to determine our own rules of competition—not the rules of golf, but the rules that cover our own tournaments." For Karsten Manufacturing, the issues were equally important. Karsten was the leading manufacturer of golf clubs when the ban was announced, controlling nearly 30 percent of the market. Its share dropped significantly after the ban. A number of well-known golfers who had used Pings before the ban switched to other clubs shortly afterward, in some cases because they were tired of being razzed by other players. Karsten's lawyers argued that the tour's ban was arbitrary and that its position was weakened by conflicts of interest. They pointed out that the tour itself had pursued the idea of selling golf clubs and other equipment under the PGA Tour name, a move that would bring the tour into direct competition not only with Karsten but also with some of its own players. The tour even trademarked the name Tour V-Groove, apparently with the intention of licensing manufacturers to make tour-approved clubs.

The conflict-of-interest argument is powerful. So many tour players receive so much endorsement money from so many manufacturers that it is impossible to trust them entirely when they talk
about golf clubs. Karsten's company is unusual among major equipment manufacturers in that it doesn't pay players for merely using
its clubs in competition, although it does annually distribute a substantial performance-based bonus pool among players who carry a
Ping putter and at least ten other Ping clubs. In less than twenty
years, Karsten had gone from being a nonentity to being the industry's leader, and its success had cut into the business of other companies. Could the paid representatives of those companies be
trusted to judge Karsten impartially? The advantage of leaving
equipment decisions to the USGA—as the PGA Tour had done
before U-grooves came along—is that the USGA comes closer to
being a disinterested party than the PGA Tour does.

Of course, I had my own conflict of interest. I believed that my
Zings had improved my golf game, and I wouldn't have wanted to
give them up upon qualifying for the senior tour. I'm sure that my
satisfaction with my golf clubs prejudiced me in Karsten's favor.
And if I can't be trusted, what about the players who are paid half
a million, or a million, or even two million dollars a year to use
clubs made by one of Karsten's competitors? Such people might
have too much at stake to make objective judgments about equipment.

Even many people who supported the tour's position in principle
wondered why the tour chose grooves to make a fuss about. Metal
woods, oversized woods, graphite shafts, long putters, high-spin
balls, and any number of other recent equipment innovations have
arguably had a far bigger impact on golf than U-grooves have. The
sand wedge, which was invented by Gene Sarazen in 1932, has had
an enormous effect. (Good golfers will sometimes shout at their
balls, "Go in the bunker!," a shout that was never shouted before
Sarazen came along.) Beman himself made a significant change in
the game back during his pro career, when he began pacing off golf
courses and carrying a yardage book in his pocket during tournaments. No one had thought of doing that before, and it was frowned

upon as being nontraditional by, for example, Ben Hogan, who unerringly calculated his own distances by eye. Hogan notwithstanding, golf survived the arrival of yardage books. It also survived the change from hickory-shafted clubs to steel-shafted clubs. It survived the change from the wooden ball to the feather-stuffed ball, and from the feather-stuffed ball to the gutta-percha ball, and from the gutta-percha ball to the rubber-cored ball, and so on.

It will also survive U-grooves. In June of 1993, just before the lawsuit was scheduled to come to trial, the two sides settled. The settlement was described by the tour as a compromise, but it looked more like a total victory for Karsten. The tour agreed to lift its ban on U-grooves and promised not to reimpose it. It said that all equipment decisions in the future would be made by a committee of impartial outsiders. And the tour's insurer agreed to pay Karsten's legal costs, which were titanic. (Karsten rewarded the touring professionals who had stuck with him through the lawsuit by paying them bonuses of several hundred thousand dollars apiece.)

One of the saddest things about the grooves controversy is that it preoccupied the game's most innovative equipment maker for a period of several years. Solheim's ideas about club design are so widely accepted today that it's easy to forget how revolutionary they were when he first introduced them. Solheim, very simply, invented the modern golf club. (With a bit of a stretch, he might also be said to have anticipated the modern tennis racket, since the original Ping putter embodied the same physical principles as the oversized tennis racket, which didn't come along till later.) Conceiving of perimeter weighting was a less stupendous achievement than, say, inventing the oral polio vaccine, but it has made a huge difference to golfers at all levels, as have Solheim's ideas about manufacturing standards, club fitting, shaft flex, and so on. Had Deane Beman taken a slightly less paranoid view of square grooves (or had he been a somewhat less gifted golfer), he might have seen Solheim as a powerful ally and a force for salutary change.

It is interesting to wonder what else Solheim might have come up with if the grooves controversy hadn't consumed so much of his time. In recent years, Karsten Manufacturing's renown has been eclipsed somewhat by that of Callaway Golf, the makers of Big Bertha metal woods and irons. I am a devoted Callaway customer—I own virtually complete sets of Big Bertha woods in both steel and graphite, and I think my Big Bertha Heaven Wood is the best and most versatile golf club I have ever owned—but it's worth remembering that the Big Bertha idea is really just an extension of Solheim's original heel-and-toe innovation. A Big Bertha driver is a perimeter-weighted metal wood. It works for the same reasons that Solheim's first putters and irons did. Big Bertha irons (like the irons of most current manufacturers) are the direct descendants of that first set of cavity-backed irons that Solheim tooled in his garage thirty years before. Furthermore, quite a few of the celebrated marketing innovations of Callaway Golf—including the premium pricing and artificial scarcity of Big Bertha irons—were borrowed directly from Solheim.

By the time this book goes to press, my Zings will be three years old. They will be, in my view, fully depreciated, and I will face the happy chore of deciding whether or not to replace them with something newer and more expensive. Zings have recently been followed by Zing 2s, for reasons I'm not certain I understand. (I have heard many explanations: that Zing heads are too heavy and therefore occasionally snap their graphite shafts; that touring pros think Zings hit the ball too low; that touring pros think Zings hit the ball too high; that touring pros think Zings make the ball too likely to draw; that touring pros think Zings make the ball too likely to fade; various other things.) I've been thinking of ordering a set of Zing 2 wedges as a way of giving the new clubs a sort of test drive. I've also been thinking of abandoning Karsten and switching to Big Bertha irons, because I love Johnny Miller and because Callaway's new television commercials are so compelling. I've even been thinking of trying those weird-looking Cleveland Classic irons that Corey Pavin uses. The idea of buying a new set of clubs when my old clubs are still perfectly serviceable may seem distastefully extravagant to some people. But if I just kept using my same old golf clubs year after year, how could I be absolutely certain that a new set wouldn't change my life?

5

IN THE HUNT

JOHN DALY WAS THE FIRST TO GO. THE MEN WHO PICKED him were so excited that one of them ran to the lobby to call a friend. I looked over the crowd. Roughly four hundred men were hunched intently over the small, numbered tables that filled the ballroom, and roughly four hundred women—their wives—were yawning and looking around. During the next few minutes, Paul Azinger, Ben Crenshaw, Hale Irwin, Phil Mickelson, Mark O'Meara, and Payne Stewart were snatched up. All had been on my list of possibilities. Then, suddenly, my table's number was called, and my two teammates and I had twenty seconds in which to decide. In a final frenzy of deliberation, we settled on Lance Ten Broeck. Ten Broeck had never amounted to much in thirteen years on tour—his best finish ever had been a second at the Chattanooga Classic in 1991—but choosing him would give us Corey Pavin on the second day and Bobby Clampett on the third. Pavin had been the tour's leading money-winner the year before, and Clampett is a well-known nice guy and one of the more thoughtful golf analysts on television. (A decade before, when he was just starting out on tour, he had been picked by many as a possible "next Nicklaus," but like many before and after him, he had not lived up to those impossibly high expectations.) As our captain hurried to the microphone to announce our selection, I leaned back in my seat and waited for our names to go up on the big board.

It was Tuesday night at Walt Disney World, and I was sitting in the ballroom of the Grand Floridian Hotel with the other amateur participants in the 1992 Walt Disney World–Oldsmobile Golf Classic, a regular event on the PGA Tour. We were picking our professional partners for the tournament's pro-am competition, which would begin on Thursday. Virtually all professional tournaments include pro-ams, in which ordinary hackers like you and me pay a great deal of money for the privilege of slicing drives out of bounds and missing short putts under the bored gaze of touring professionals. The Disney pro-am is different in that it lasts three days and takes place during the real tournament. Most pro-ams are held during a single practice round on the day before the pro competition begins. Another difference is that the Disney tournament is held at Walt Disney World, a fact that makes it somewhat easier for would-be participants to persuade their wives that paying the entry fee (which was five thousand dollars the year I played, and is considerably higher today) would be a smart move for the entire family.

I had come for the usual reasons. I wanted to rub shoulders with my golfing idols, to watch real golfers playing real golf close at hand, and to indulge various ludicrous fantasies. I hadn't played much competitive golf myself, apart from a handful of scrambles and the two-day member-guest at my club a couple of months before, and I wanted to try to gain some sense of what it's like to compete under tour conditions. I was fully aware that playing in the Disney pro-am isn't the same thing as, for example, playing in the U.S. Open, but I figured that it was slightly more like the Open than the fifty-cent nassaus I had played at my own club. I would be in a position to observe real pros playing for real money, and by using my ample powers of self-delusion I would be able to convince myself that I was just like them. In brief, I wanted to play in the

Disney pro-am more than I had wanted to do virtually anything in my entire life.

The amateur field at the Disney Classic consisted of 396 golfers divided into 132 three-man teams. The teams had been put together in a blind draw based on handicaps. Each team would be joined by a different pro during each of the first three days of the tournament. (On Sunday, the top pros would play on alone for the $180,000 first prize.) The other amateurs on my team were Phil Lengyel, who is a Disney executive, and Randy Hundley, who played catcher for the Chicago Cubs back in the seventies. Randy now owns a baseball fantasy camp in Palatine, Illinois. He has curly reddish hair, a plastic hip, and a tree-trunklike neck that turns only if his head and shoulders turn with it. Randy isn't a candidate for the Hall of Fame, but he played hard, at the cost of virtually every gram of cartilage in his body. He still has quite a few working parts, however. When you shake hands with him, you have to flex the muscles in your fingers in advance to protect your metacarpals. His handicap, ten, was the lowest on our team. That meant that he was our captain, a position to which he was ideally suited, since he had spent a couple of years managing one of the Cubs' farm teams, and Phil and I were minor-league all the way. My handicap was a fragile fourteen, and Phil's was a shaky eighteen. Phil, who was in his mid-forties, was a last-minute replacement for a local businessman. "I hope you're a player," he had said to me jovially earlier in the evening, "because I'm just along for the ride." I was just along for the ride, too, I figured. My real goal for the week was to try not to make too many embarrassing mistakes.

When many people think of Disney World, they think mainly of overweight tourists wearing funny clothes and taking pictures of other overweight tourists taking pictures of the Pirates of the Caribbean. But the world's most surreal amusement park is not just an amusement park. In recent years, for example, it has also become North America's most popular honeymoon destination. In fact, it is a popular place to get married in the first place, and Pluto, Donald,

Goofy, and other Disney characters can be hired to mingle with wedding guests. Most surprising of all (as I had learned already, during my January trip to the PGA Merchandise Show), Disney World has quietly become one of the country's best golf resorts. The complex's forty-three square miles—only a fifth of which have been developed—include five excellent courses. During January, I had played the two newest courses, Pete Dye's Eagle Pines and Tom Fazio's Osprey Ridge. The Disney Classic in 1992 was played on the three older courses—the Palm, the Magnolia, and Lake Buena Vista, all of which were designed by Joe Lee and have been around since the early seventies.

I had had my first taste of the tournament courses earlier that day, when I had played practice rounds on Palm and Magnolia with my fellow competitor Arthur Levitt, Jr. (Levitt, a former president of the American Stock Exchange, was later to be chosen by Bill Clinton to run the Securities and Exchange Commission.) Levitt's handicap was higher than mine, but we were compatible golfmates, and we sped our way around both courses without encountering much traffic, except for an occasional pro. When we were getting ready to play our tee shots on the sixteenth at the Palm, Lanny Wadkins zoomed up in a cart with his caddy and asked if he could hit a ball, too. The sixteenth is a 170-yard par-three that plays across a lake from a slightly elevated tee. The green is big and undulating, and it is guarded in front by great big rocks. Wadkins dropped a ball on the tee, slapped at it with an eight-iron, and watched impassively as it soared high over the water and stuck two or three feet from the cup. "Misread the grain," he said. He dropped another ball, and slapped it to about twenty feet. "Thanks, fellas," he said before speeding off. Levitt and I waited until he was well out of sight before hitting our own shots.

I had a very good time playing my practice rounds with Levitt, even though I wasn't exactly sure what I was supposed to be practicing. I knew that Disney's Bermuda greens had a very pronounced grain, and I knew that the grain had a powerful effect on putts, but I could never seem to see which way the grass was growing, and I wouldn't really have known what to do about it if I had. The green that gave me the most trouble was Magnolia's eighteenth, which is fairly large and rises steeply from front to back. The pin was in the front, and I put my approach shot way in the back, at least sixty feet away. I figured that my downhill putt would be dead straight and that it would run like crazy, so I barely nudged it. My ball rolled perhaps twenty feet, and veered wildly to the left. Surprised, I dropped a second ball and tried the putt again, this time aiming well to the right and giving it a real whack. My ball rolled perhaps ten feet farther, and still veered to the left. It took me three more tries merely to get the ball below the hole, and two putts from there to get down—an altogether frustrating experience, and one that dampened any meager confidence I might otherwise have felt.

During both of those practice rounds and another the next day, I remained in a state of simmering anxiety. Mainly, I was brooding about my shot off the first tee on Thursday. The first shot is the only shot in a round of golf that really counts, psychologically. If the first shot is good, every succeeding catastrophe can be viewed as an aberration. Conversely, if the first shot is lousy, every good shot seems like a fluke. The Disney Classic isn't televised, and it doesn't attract big galleries, but I knew that at least a few people would be watching on the first tee, and I didn't want to screw up in front of them. I also wanted to make a good impression on my playing partners and our pro. Later that day, I spent an hour or so at the driving range trying to bang my swing into shape and working on various versions of a first-tee strategy. I was carrying a two-, three-, four-, and five-wood. (I hadn't brought a driver, figuring that that club was too dangerous even to have in my bag.) Should I swing hard with the two-wood and trust to luck? Should I take an easy pass with the five-wood and be relatively certain of hitting the fairway? Should I compromise with the three or four? I changed my mind with virtually every practice ball I hit.

During a final practice round the next day, I struck up a conversation with a playing partner's caddy, who turned out to be the golf coach at a nearby college. Every year, he said, he brought his golf team to Disney so that they could gawk at the pros and pick up a little spending money by caddying for amateurs. I hadn't thought about hiring a caddy; most of the amateurs were using golf carts. But I took the coach's business card. I had loved playing with caddies in Scotland. Would I love playing with one in Florida? Or would having a cocky college golfer snickering at me behind my back make me more nervous than I already was? I figured I would probably end up taking a cart.

On Thursday, we were scheduled to tee off on the tenth hole of the Lake Buena Vista course, which I hadn't played but had heard was supposed to be shorter and easier than the other two. I took a courtesy car over to the course at about nine-thirty. The car (which was one of two hundred that had been provided by local Oldsmobile dealers) was driven by a retired Orlando resident, who told me that he didn't play golf and had never seen a tournament but enjoyed driving people around. ("It's something to do," he said. "I ought to play golf, but for some reason I don't.") He was short and round and bald, and he gripped the top arc of the steering wheel tightly with both hands, as though he were chinning himself. He dropped me off near the pro shop, and I made my way timidly through the crowd with my golf bag on my shoulder, feeling nervous and out of place. Much to my relief, I ran into the college golf coach I had met the day before. "I guess I might like a caddy after all," I said, happy just to have run into someone I recognized. The coach told me that he had only one caddy left, a student from Sweden named Anders. He pointed to a kid sitting by himself at a table near the concession stand. Anders was small and slightly built and looked about fourteen. Other golfers had passed him over, the coach said, because they figured he wasn't hefty enough to lug around their great big games. "Perfect," I said. Anders didn't look like the type of hotshot who would laugh behind my back. The coach introduced us. I handed Anders my bag, and we went to the driving range.

The tenth hole at Lake Buena Vista is a par-five that plays about 520 yards long for the pros and about 30 yards shorter for the amateurs. I had obsessively studied a diagram of it in my room the night before. "Easy starter for the back nine," my yardage book had said. I wanted to believe that, but I took a good long look at the

fairway on my way to the range, and it looked plenty narrow
enough to miss. At a quarter to twelve, Anders and I made our way
to the tee, where I made a final, feverish study. My heart was
pounding. I hadn't hit any of my clubs very well on the range, and
I feared for my first tee shot. Phil Lengyel was already there, accompanied by a caddy who turned out to be a friend of his from Disney.
Lance Ten Broeck, our pro, arrived a minute or two later. He chatted cordially with us and various officials while we waited for the
last few minutes to tick away. Randy was nowhere to be seen. I had
spotted him earlier, on the putting green, but he had since disappeared, and I was suddenly worried that he might be confused
about when and where we were supposed to tee off. What would
happen, I wondered, if he didn't show up? Would we have to play
without him? Would our team be disqualified?

At eleven fifty-nine, as Lance was taking a few warm-up swings
with his driver, a golf cart emerged from somewhere behind us and
stopped by the first tee. A middle-aged man who looked like a
retired boxer was at the wheel. He was wearing a baseball cap and
a blue-and-orange Cubs T-shirt. Sitting beside him was Randy,
looking regal. Randy climbed slowly from the cart, smiling and
nodding to the handful of people standing around the tee. "I'm an
old broken-down baseball player," he said to Lance as they shook
hands. The look in Randy's eye said, "I've been a professional
athlete longer than you have, son." Randy had a bright red batting
glove on his left hand; his right hand was striped with adhesive
tape. The bottom of his bag was held together with duct tape; at one
point the shaft of one of his irons poked through, and he had to
nudge it back up inside. To Phil and me he said, "Let's just go out
there and have some fun," but I could tell that he didn't really mean
it. Randy wanted to win.

Lance was up first. Comfortingly, from my point of view, he hit
a great big hook that ended up in serious trouble on the far left. No
one laughed. No one snickered. Lance looked largely unperturbed.
If I screw up, I thought to myself, at least I'll be in good company.
Then it was Randy's turn. He swaggered onto the tee like a home-
run hitter coming to the plate with the bases loaded in the bottom

of the ninth. Using the biggest golf club I have ever seen, he took a huge swing and launched his ball very nearly out of sight, right down the middle of the fairway, perhaps eighty yards farther than Lance's. My jaw dropped, and my mouth was still hanging open when my own name and hometown were announced a moment later. I have no memory of swinging my club (the two-wood, which Anders had handed me). Somehow, though, my ball ended up in decent shape on the left side of the fairway, and I felt an enormous weight lift from my shoulders. Then Phil sliced into trouble on the right, and we were off.

Many touring professionals hate pro-ams. They don't like being distracted from the nearly impossible task of earning a decent living on tour, and they don't like exposing themselves to the contagious and potentially terminal swing flaws of their amateur partners. The pro-am is such an integral part of the Disney Classic, though, that pros who don't like amateurs usually stay away. The pros who do play tend to view the tournament as a chance to unwind a little toward the end of their long season, and maybe to take their kids to Typhoon Lagoon. Lance was more than friendly as we headed up the fairway, actually making conversation as we walked along. Then he turned off into the weeds to look for his ball.

Like all the pros in the Disney Classic, Lance was competing for a share of the tournament's million-dollar pro purse, but for today he was also a member of our pro-am team. The team's score on every hole would be the best score (including handicaps, for the amateurs) made by any of the four team members. Our first hole was Lake Buena Vista's number-four-handicap hole. That meant that Randy, Phil, and I—all of whose handicaps were higher than four—would each get to subtract one stroke from whatever score we actually shot. Lance wouldn't get to subtract anything from his score, of course. But pros don't usually need handicap strokes. That's why they're pros. In a pro-am, the pro's main function is to provide a scoring ceiling for the team by steadily shooting par after par, leaving the amateurs to try to capitalize on their handicaps. My goal on that first hole was to make a nice, undramatic par, which would count on the score card as a birdie four.

When Anders and I got to my ball, I saw that I had a good lie on the edge of the fairway. I might have been able to get close to the green with a really well hit three-wood, but I chose my relatively undangerous six-iron instead. I hit it well, roughly up the middle of the fairway, leaving me a little under a hundred yards from the front of the green. When we got to the ball, Anders checked the pin position in his yardage book, and I chose a wedge. I hit the ball slightly fat, but it still made the front of the green—a huge relief. I was the first to putt. My nerves, which I had contained reasonably well until that point, suddenly went haywire, and I pushed my ball wildly to the right, leaving it fifteen feet below and to the right of the hole. I was crushed. I could still get my par, but I would need a great second putt to do it. I realized that I had let my team down, and I felt terrible about it. I had had my first mild taste of tournament pressure, and I had screwed up.

My despair was unnecessary, as it turned out. While I had been concentrating on my own problems, Randy had followed his gargantuan drive with a beautifully struck three-wood to the left side of the green, about twenty feet from the hole. He could three-putt and still make par, which, minus his stroke, would give us a net birdie. He studied the slope of the green for a while, then bent over his ball and—while continuing to look at the hole—stroked it in for a net double eagle. After just one hole, we were three under par. My screw-up hadn't mattered at all. While Randy, Phil, and I exchanged high fives, Lance tottered to a bogey six. The tournament volunteer carrying our team's miniature scoreboard put a gloomy black one after Lance's name, and a fiery red three after ours.

At that exact moment, my nervousness evaporated. Randy merely birdied the next hole (the par-three eleventh, a short hole on which only Phil got a stroke), but thanks to Phil we picked up net birdies on the next two. On the fourteenth, a 370-yard par-four, I hit a good drive with my three-wood and followed it with an eight-iron to the fringe at the left front edge of the green. Lance read my putt for me. "It breaks to the right," he said, "but the grain in the fringe will push it to the left. Putt it straight." I did, and my ball tumbled into the cup for a net eagle. On the next hole, an even shorter par-four, I hit a good drive and a good approach, and, with Lance's help again, two-putted for a net birdie. We had played six holes, and we were nine under par. Like all successful pro-am teams, we had somehow managed never to be all good or all bad at the same time. Randy had been hot, then Phil had been hot, then I had been hot. When we came to the electronic scoreboard behind another green, I was astonished to see that our names were near the top of the pro-am leaderboard. "Don't you think about that leader-board," Randy said sternly when he saw me gawking. "Let's just keep having fun."

Lance, meanwhile, had begun to have a little fun himself. After his shaky start, he played pretty well. I think he enjoyed playing with us, and especially with Randy. We were all business, and we played very quickly, finishing our first nine in a little over an hour and a half—a remarkable time for a pro-am. Lance, who was thirty-six at the time of the tournament, is just about exactly a year younger than I am. He was dazzlingly promising as a young player, but he has always struggled on tour (it took him nine years to push his career earnings over $200,000). He has a reputation for being something of a party animal—his nickname among tour players, a caddy told me, is Last Call Lance—and there was speculation that youthful dissipation might have blunted his game. With Randy lead-ing the charge, however, Lance played very well, recovering the stroke he had lost on the first hole and finishing the day with a very respectable sixty-nine, which was three under par. (The first-day leader was Lee Janzen, who shot a sixty-four.)

Lance's performance paled in comparison with ours, though. We ran into a dreary patch midway through our second nine, settling for a few disappointing net pars, but our wheels never came all the way off. My favorite hole was our last one, the ninth. I hit a straight but short drive to the middle of the fairway, then hit my five-wood to the back of the green, leaving me a tricky thirty-foot putt. I misjudged the speed, and left my ball six feet short. Everyone else was out of the hole. Lance and his caddy studied my putt from both directions, finally deciding that it would break about a cup to the right if I hit it just hard enough to get it there. The moment I hit the ball, I was worried that I hadn't stroked it hard enough. Just as it seemed to run out of gas, though, it took one final roll and fell into the cup. There were quite a few spectators gathered around the green, and they actually clapped and cheered when my ball fell into the hole. My net birdie left us nineteen under par for the day; we had shot a net fifty-three.

I desperately wanted to find out how we stood in comparison with the rest of the field, but Randy led Phil and me directly to the driving range. Randy had decided that the time had come to do something about Phil's slice, which had gotten him into trouble fairly frequently during our round. "Let's take a look at that grip," Randy said. Phil had a decent-looking Vardon grip, in which the little finger of the right hand overlaps the index finger of the left. This is the standard modern golf grip, but Randy didn't like it. "Let's move those hands apart a little," Randy said, "the way you'd hold a baseball bat." In fact, Randy wanted Phil to swing his golf club like a baseball bat, too. Not coincidentally, this was the way Randy swung his. Phil tried his new swing, and hit a few decent shots, but Randy wasn't satisfied. "Where are your hands when you finish hitting a home run?" he asked. Phil had to admit that he didn't know, since he had never hit a home run. (Come to think of it, Randy didn't hit all that many either.) Randy made a few more adjustments, and after ten minutes or so Phil actually began to draw the ball—something he said he had never been able to do before. Grip changes usually take agonizing weeks to get used to, but Phil seemed fairly comfortable with his new one right away. Every shot was better than the last, and he was increasingly ecstatic.

I was hitting some pretty good shots myself. Our heady round had given me an enormous dose of confidence, freeing up my swing. We all beat balls for about half an hour. Then Randy went back to the hotel to have dinner with his wife. I hung around for a few more minutes, then made my way back to the leaderboard to see where we stood. Astonishingly, out of 132 teams, we were tied for second place, just one stroke out of the lead. I went back to my room and called my wife, my mother, my father, my brother, and virtually everyone I had ever played golf with.

. . .

Like many of the other participants, both amateur and professional, I was staying at what was then called the Disney Inn. (It has since been leased to the military as a rest and recreation center, and is now called Shades of Green.) The complex is perhaps the least prepossessing of the hotels at Disney, but it is ideally situated for golf. My room was roughly equidistant between the first tee of the Palm and the first tee of the Magnolia, and there was a practice green just a hundred yards outside my door. Randy's room was down the hall, a location that he had made even more convenient by parking a small fleet of golf carts on the little terrace outside his sliding glass doors. His room was as crowded as his terrace. His wife, his son, his daughter-in-law, and his granddaughter were staying in it as well.

The next morning, I got up early and bought copies of all the local papers, in which the Disney Classic received major coverage. I quickly skipped over the main articles until I found the pro-am results. There were our names, right near the top of the list, just after the scores of the pros. My only regret was that the score after my name—fifty-three—was too ridiculously low to be a real golf score. Still, I loved seeing my name in the paper. When I went to breakfast a little later, I saw Phil smiling and drinking coffee and gazing happily at the same page.

Our pro on the second day was Corey Pavin, who the year before had won two tournaments, been the tour's leading money winner, and been named the Player of the Year. He had also won already in 1992, at the Honda Classic back in March, giving him a career total to date of ten tour victories. Corey is not a particularly long or powerful hitter, but he is a legendary shot-maker and putter. He's a real golfer's golfer, the kind that other pros shake their heads and marvel at. Of the three pros in our rotation, he was the one I was most eager to play with.

I didn't feel nervous at all on the first tee of the Magnolia— perhaps not a good sign, as things turned out. I hit a big high leaker to the right, and my ball ended up in heavy grass on the bank of a creek, just a few feet above the water. I felt terrible and embarrassed, but then I took my nine-iron and popped my ball over some trees and a big bunker. It ended up in the fairway, about a hundred yards from the hole. "Good shot," Corey said, and I felt immensely better. I ended up with a double-bogey, but Randy got a par and a stroke, and we had another red number.

Corey didn't do nearly as well as we did. He set the tone for his round by missing an eighteen-inch putt for par—an astonishing lapse for a golfer who is often spoken of as one of the two or three best putters in the world. Actually, I got a small thrill when his ball didn't go in. One of the most inebriating experiences in golf is watching a terrific pro make a terrible shot. It's something you don't get to see very often on television, because the pros you see on television are almost always the ones who are in the lead, and a pro who is in the lead is one who, by definition, is not making terrible shots. At the Disney Classic, though, I had quite a few opportunities to watch pros make shots that were very nearly as bad as shots I might have made myself. By the time Corey missed his putt, my attitude toward our professional partners had become pretty much the same as the attitude of most professionals toward their amateur partners: Just stay out of our way. Corey wasn't having much of a tournament, but, by God, we were in the hunt (as the pros say when they are within hailing distance of the lead). I don't think Corey improved our score on a single hole; if he made any birdies, they were on holes where we had already nailed down a birdie of our own. But we didn't mind having him around.

To his enormous credit, Corey didn't become sullen or angry when his round began to go astray. He remained friendly and talkative, and he asked as many questions about us as we did about him. He and his caddy helped us constantly with yardages and putts, and in that way they made a big difference in our round. I will also be eternally indebted to him for improving my sand game. On the second hole, a short par-four for the amateurs, I put my approach shot in a bunker just short of the green, then put my sand shot fairly close to the pin. "I like that sand stroke," Corey said. I had never been a very good bunker player before that, but I have been a pretty good one ever since. When my ball goes into a bunker now, I say to myself, "Corey Pavin says I know how to do this," and most of the time I hit a good shot. My sand game changed forever in that bunker on the second hole.

I got a chance to test my newly Pavin-approved sand stroke a short time later, on the sixth hole, a 175-yard par-three with an elevated green that is protected by three big bunkers, one of which is shaped like the head of Mickey Mouse. I hit a four-iron over the pin into the narrow bunker behind the green. Randy, who didn't have a stroke, missed the green well to the left, and Phil, who did have a stroke, missed it far to the right. Both would be lucky to get fours, and Corey was in lousy shape as well. "It's all up to you, Dave," Randy said as we walked morosely from the tee. The green ran downhill from the bunker I was in, and the pin was only about twenty feet away. I had to pop the ball softly out of the sand and let it trickle down to the cup. I thought of Corey and popped the ball softly out of the sand. It trickled down to the cup and stopped about two feet to the right, and I made the putt for a net birdie.

The rest of my day was a little rocky, but Phil played very well with his brand-new baseball swing, and Randy had his usual flashes of brilliance. He changed our hitting order whenever we missed a net birdie. "You're a good leader," he would say before Phil or I teed off. (On one hole when I was our leader, Randy didn't say it right away, and I was worried that he was going to forget. I took a long time teeing up my ball and waggling my club, waiting for him to remember. I was just about to remind him when he said it on his own. I smiled and hit a good shot.) If Phil or I sliced one into the trees, he would say, "Good swing at it, pard." His little pep talks really did make me feel better about my bad shots, and inspired me to try to make good ones. We followed the previous day's pattern of playing well one at a time, though once again we struggled a bit in the middle of the back nine. (I decided that night that we were simply running out of fuel, and I packed a grocery bag of apples, peanut-butter crackers, and water for the following day.) Randy moved a little more slowly as the round wore on, and he washed down his taped fingers with rubbing alcohol, but he never lost the glint in his eye.

Through it all, Anders was an extremely able and affable caddy. He worked hard. He met me at the driving range each morning and stood behind me with a wet towel to clean each club as I was finished with it—just like one of the pros' caddies. Before each round, he transferred all the information from the pin-placement charts into his yardage book so that he could figure our exact yardages quickly on every hole. And he was a lot of fun to be with. His coach told me later that Anders had been a very good golfer at home in Sweden, but that he was having trouble adjusting to American courses: He didn't get as much roll on his drives in Florida as he had on the semifrozen fairways of his homeland, and he was overswinging in an effort to make up the difference. Still, he knew the game. Having a good golfer as a caddy can be a huge advantage. Anders was a good adviser not only on putts and club selection but also on course management. He would remind me when it made sense for me to try a high-risk shot, and when it didn't, and he always knew who had a stroke and where everybody stood. Very gently but effectively, he kept me thinking about my game.

At the eighteenth, a very long par four, I summoned all of my remaining strength and hit a long drive up the right side. When I got to my ball, a kid standing behind the ropes with an autograph book asked, "Are you the pro?" I laughed good-naturedly and said I wasn't, but the question filled me with intoxicating ambition. I surveyed my approach shot, envisioning my ball flight, as the pros do on television. Then I took an all-pro swing, and—with the beaming face of that kid vividly in my mind—buried the head of my five-wood deep in the dirt about six inches behind my ball. My ball moved twenty or thirty yards, about half as far as my vast, fragmented divot. Humiliated, I slunk up the fairway with my hat pulled low on my forehead, made two more futile attempts to reach the green, and finally picked up my ball.

Randy, meanwhile, had reached the back of the green in regulation. He now faced pretty much exactly the same downhill putt that had exasperated me during my practice round with Arthur Levitt, Jr., three days before. I hesitated to say anything, then suddenly felt I had to. Just as Randy was about to stroke his ball, I stopped him and said, "When I had this putt on Tuesday, it took me four tries to get my ball past the hole, and it broke about six feet to the left." Randy looked me in the eye for a long time, then took another look at his putt. When he set up over his ball again, he was aimed several feet farther to the right. He gave the ball a mighty whack, and I breathed a sigh of relief as it did more or less what I had said it would, ending up about three feet just below the hole. He made that putt, and slapped my hand. We were seventeen under par for the day, and thirty-six under for the tournament. For the time being—there were still quite a few groups out on the courses—we were leading the tournament. In fact, we were ahead by eight strokes.

We met at the driving range later that afternoon. Also at the range was J. P. Hayes, a twenty-seven-year-old kid from Texas who had gotten into the tournament at the last minute as an alternate and now, after shooting sixty-five and sixty-six, was tied for the lead with Payne Stewart. He was hitting beautiful iron shots and acknowledging the congratulations of other pros. I felt pretty good myself.

After our practice session, I mentioned to Randy that I was going to take a quick look at the scoreboard on my way to dinner. "You stay away from there," he said. "That scoreboard doesn't concern us." But when Randy went off to talk to someone else, I snuck through the pro shop and around the caddy area, and took a look anyway. Our lead had been whittled from eight strokes to three, but virtually all the groups were finished now, and we were still on top. As I stood gaping at my electronically illuminated name, I happened to notice someone sitting in a cart ahead of me, also gaping at the board. It was Randy.

I could also tell from the scoreboard that the group in second place was just about to finish its round on the ninth green. I went and joined the gallery in the bleachers, and waited for them to appear. They turned out to be entirely ordinary-looking middle-aged guys, playing with Peter Jacobsen. Jacobsen and one of the amateurs reached the green in two. I held my breath while they putted. One of the amateurs putted and missed. Jacobsen putted and missed, settling for par. Another amateur putted, and the ball went in for a net birdie, cutting our lead to two. But we were still ahead, and we had improved our position by three strokes in relation to the rest of the field. I slipped away from the gallery and stood in front of the big scoreboard by the putting green for a very long time. Finally, I watched the scorekeeper use a big yellow marker to fill in the box that contained our two-day total of minus thirty-six. Ours was the only score that was highlighted in that way. We were leading the tournament, and there was no one else who could catch us that day.

I spent the evening putting on the carpet in my room, chipping balls onto my bed, and looking at all my free stuff. Free stuff is one of the best things about playing in a good pro-am. Every participant in the Disney Classic received a pile of loot that included two expensive Gore-Tex rain suits (one for the player and one for his wife), a couple of hats, a dozen personalized golf balls, a sort of blanket with a big Goofy on it, various accessories emblazoned with the tournament's logo, a basket of fruit and cookies, some one-year passes to the Disney golf courses and the Magic Kingdom, several other things I can't think of at the moment, and a very nice leather bag with a logo on it for carrying everything home in. Of course, all this stuff was free only in the sense that I hadn't paid for it at the exact moment it was handed to me. Still, it seemed free, and seeing it strewn around my room made me feel kind of rich.

The next morning, I got up early and ate a long, leisurely breakfast with Phil, while both of us dreamily meditated on our names in the sports section of *The Orlando Sentinel*. We had an afternoon tee time for our final round, and that meant that we had a long, nervous morning to kill. I spent mine putting on the practice green, hitting balls at the driving range, napping, and taking two showers. Randy visited me on the putting green and encouraged me to try putting while looking at the cup, as he did. I tried it, and putted quite well that way, but was reluctant to make such a drastic change in my game on the very brink of our ultimate test. Randy then told me to practice getting down in two from all over the green. I was glad to have an assignment, and the long minutes slowly ticked away.

Walking around the area near the clubhouse with the knowledge that we were leading the tournament was quite exhilarating. A guy in the pro shop and a guy in the bag storage room both recognized me and spoke to me in a way that seemed somehow more animated and respectful than the way in which they spoke to people who were not on top of the leaderboard. "You guys still leading?" a total stranger asked me, and I said I guessed so, trying to sound as though I hadn't given the matter much thought. For a couple of hours that morning, I had a teeny inkling of what it must be like to be John Daly. When I hit a bad shot on the driving range, I thought, "Meaningless. We're leading." The scores in *The Orlando Sentinel* proved that we were hot stuff, so what did it matter if I was shanking practice balls? Next to me in the line, a guy with one of the worst swings I have ever seen (he would weirdly wrap his club almost all the way around his back, and then lash at the ball while lunging forward) said to a friend, "You think eighteen under will do it?" Not to catch us, pal, I thought to myself. On the other side of me was another amateur, morosely hitting bad shots while his wife sat on his golf bag behind him and critiqued his swing. "Take it away in one piece," she said. "Your arms are disconnected. You're lifting. Your shoulder isn't coming through. That was all right, but look where you're aiming." The man had placed a golf club on the ground in front of his ball, to help with his alignment. "That was too fast," his wife went on. "You've got to stay behind the ball. You're not turning." Everywhere, it seemed, there were terrible golfers making a last, desperate effort to elevate their sorry games to the point where they might have a hope of nipping at our heels.

Finally, our tee time crawled around. All morning, I had scrupulously avoided looking at any of the electronic scoreboards. Our principal rivals, I knew, had had an early tee time, and they would be finished by the time we began. Would they fall apart coming down the stretch? Would they let out all the stops? I knew that Randy wouldn't want me to know.

Unfortunately, avoiding the scoreboards was impossible once I got close to the golf course. As I made my way to our first tee—the tenth on the Palm—I couldn't help noticing that the group that had trailed us by two strokes the day before had already gone out and shot twenty-two under par. "Oops," said one of the caddies. The other guys were leading the tournament by a mile, at fifty-six under, and we were going to have to shoot twenty-one under to beat them. That was a very intimidating number. Still, we were the only group left in the tournament with a chance.

Our pro for the day was Bobby Clampett. Bobby was viewed as a potential superstar back in the early eighties, when he started out on tour, but he won only a single tournament, in 1982, and then sort of drifted away. "Bobby's too smart to be a good golfer," one of the caddies had told me. Nowadays, he is best known as a television commentator, for CBS, although he still manages to put together a good tournament once in awhile. He was having a good tournament at Disney. He didn't have a realistic shot at winning, but he was well on his way to earning a decent paycheck for the week. And, like Lance and Corey, he couldn't have been nicer to us.

Once again, Randy waited until the last possible moment to make his entrance. His room was actually visible from the tenth tee. At a minute before our tee time, I saw him open the sliding glass door and climb into one of the carts parked on his terrace. He looked ready to play, and despite his professed apathy about where we stood, he already knew what we had to shoot. He introduced himself to Bobby, and we teed off.

Randy, Phil, and I started well, making net birdies on the first three holes, but then we had to settle for net par on the next two. Then Bobby got us back on track with a real birdie of his own, and we more or less found our groove again. (Bobby had a good round except for three skulled sand shots—maybe the three worst sand shots by a pro that I have ever seen.) I struggled during our first nine, but during the second, I suddenly came into my own and played the best five holes in succession that I had ever played up until that point, making four pars and a birdie and improving our score by four shots. (I made the birdie with a twenty-foot putt after

Anders, while handing me my putter, had looked me in the eye and said, "Make it"—proving, I suppose, that I play better when people tell me what to do.) We had a small traveling gallery at that point—the first time we had been followed by people who had no personal connection with anyone in our foursome. Still, we didn't bring the course to its knees the way we needed to. With several holes to go, we realized that, barring a miracle, we were playing for second place. Bobby generously said, "Let's go out and get you some eagles," but when we came to the final tee we were just fourteen under par for the day, and six strokes off the lead, and we needed a par to stay in second place all by ourselves. We got it, barely, with a net par from me and then a real par from Bobby. It was disappointing not to win. But missing by six strokes was probably easier to take than missing by one or two.

At the award dinner that night, we trouped up onto the stage with the other top nineteen teams to receive enormous trophies with little statuettes of Mickey Mouse on top. The applause was muted, and the dinner conversation consisted primarily of grumbling by nonwinners, who universally assumed that anyone receiving a trophy had played with an inflated handicap. "If he wants it that much, let him have it," I heard someone at the next table mutter about someone else. I heard another man say, about a member of the winning team, "He's the biggest sandbagger in the country. I don't know why they even let him play in this tournament." Someone else told me confidentially that one of the double-digit handicappers on the winning team was really a three, and that he had been on the winning team the year before, and that he had been asked not to come back next year. None of this was true, but the rumors were pervasive. The tournaments' organizers seemed sensitive to the general bitterness; the trophies were handed out very quickly and with a minimum of fuss. On the shuttle bus back to my hotel after the dinner, another passenger glared at my trophy, his eyes narrowed to slits. "I've been playing in this thing ten years," he said, "and I never got one of those." All in all, I was just as glad that we hadn't come in first.

Were we sandbaggers? I don't think so. I would be surprised if any of us shot his handicap on any of the three days. Randy was very long off the tee, and he was quite good with his putter, but he was very shaky from a hundred yards in. He chewed up the par-fives, but he was in his pocket fairly often, too. Phil and I meandered back and forth between the sublime and the ridiculous. The key to our success was that we very rarely all stank at the same time, and we let very few stroke holes go by without capitalizing on them in some way. Our pros were pretty much irrelevant to our scoring; Pavin didn't even make the cut. (The guys who won played with Ed Fiori, who tied for thirty-eighth, and Peter Jacobsen and Ronnie McCann, both of whom missed the cut.)

Anyway, screw all the complainers. I got my picture taken with Mickey Mouse, and they didn't.

The next day, Sunday, was the pros' final round. I had a mild case of post-tournament depression, so I slept late and then spent the middle part of the day playing eighteen holes on the Palm course with two guys I met on the driving range. One of the guys, whose name was Gary, said he would be going to Texas the following week to try to qualify for the Senior PGA Tour. I was very impressed, and more than a little intimidated, until I had watched him play for a while. Gary seemed to make an awful lot of bogeys and double-bogeys for a guy who was planning to earn his living going head to head with Lee Trevino, Raymond Floyd, and Jack Nicklaus. "I'm a great putter," he told me at one point. But his great putting did not seem to include the making of great putts. If Gary does make it on the senior tour, there's hope for all of us. I am indebted to him, however, for showing me how to hit a sand shot from a wet, hard bunker: ball back in stance, clubface square.

I picked up the big tournament on the back nine. Mark O'Meara (who is legendary for playing well in tournaments that have big pro-ams) was leading at that point. The crowd following him and Ted Schulz, who had begun the day tied for the lead with O'Meara at twenty under par, was gigantic and impenetrable, so I decided to follow Payne Stewart and John Huston, who were two groups ahead. I heard a man standing near the ropes on the tenth hole say to his wife, "He's going to try to hit it up there. That part is the green." Almost the moment I started following, Stewart fell apart (beginning with a bogey on the par-five tenth after he had reached a greenside bunker in two) and Huston began to play like a maniac. Huston birdied seven of the last nine holes and ended up burying O'Meara by three strokes. His final score was sixty-two, or ten under par, and his tournament total was twenty-six under, which was within a stroke of the tour record. The key to Huston's success? Perhaps the fact that he putted at least one long lag putt while looking at the hole, in the style of Randy Hundley.

When the tournament was over, Mickey, Minnie, Goofy, Donald, and a small marching band came dancing onto the eighteenth green to give Huston a trophy and a great big check. It was somewhat unsettling to see cartoon characters in enormous shoes cavorting on a putting surface. Huston's wife and young daughter were not present; he had sent them home the day before, because he was playing well and didn't want the distraction of having them around. Huston accepted his money and said the customary nice things about Disney, Oldsmobile, the fans, and so on, but made no mention of his amateur partners or—surprisingly, I thought—the amateur team that had come in second. When the ceremony was over, I followed Huston to the press tent, where, during a lull in the interviewing, I asked him how he had liked playing with amateurs. He said, "We really move along at a good pace here with the amateurs. They pick up when they're supposed to. They don't waste time. I actually think we play faster with foursomes here than we do with threesomes on normal tour events. And that's really sad."

That evening, there was a farewell cocktail party beside the pool at the Disney Inn. There was a plastic foam volcano floating in the pool. I ran into Randy, his wife, and their son, Todd, who is a catcher for the New York Mets. We chatted for a while. Then Randy brought up the possibility of playing a little more golf. We laughed at the thought, then fell silent. Maybe we *could* play some more golf. I looked at my watch. It was five forty-five; at most, there was an hour of daylight left. Randy said, "Let's do it," and suddenly the

three of us were running to put on our shoes and find golf carts and
scrounge up some clubs for Todd, who is left-handed. The bag
room was closed, but Randy sweet-talked an attendant into giving
us a set of clubs and two carts. "We'll bring them back tomorrow,"
he said. I took one of the carts to the tenth tee of the Palm; Randy
and Todd took the other cart back to their room, to get a third cart,
which Randy had parked on their terrace. We met on the tee just as
the sun was scraping the tops of the trees. I hit, then jumped into
my cart to race after my ball just as Randy was teeing up his. Then
he jumped into his cart, and Todd teed up a ball. On most holes, we
didn't bother to putt. We also didn't bother to look for balls that we
didn't find immediately. I used up all my personalized balls, figuring that if I was going to lose balls with my name on them, I would
rather do it in Florida than on my course at home. On one hole, as
I was about to hit my ball out of a fairway bunker, I heard Todd yell
from the tee. His characteristic shot was a long, low, screaming
left-hander's hook—the kind of shot that splits the shortstop and
third baseman and skims into right field. I threw myself down, and
his ball bulleted into the sand just past my head. I dusted myself off,
made my shot, and hurried on.

After a certain point, it was so dark that balls in flight were
essentially invisible. You had to hit your shot, then crouch down
and run back to your cart, like a soldier avoiding sniper fire. The
first guy on any green would wait to retrieve all three balls. When
it was my turn, I would cover my head with my arms or crouch
down near the flag, figuring that was the safest spot. Then we raced
on to the next tee.

Randy suffered our only injury. A line drive of Todd's ricocheted
off a palm tree and smacked him hard in the rotator cuff. The
wound took some steam out of his swing, but he kept playing, and
we finished the back nine in a bit less than an hour. The original
plan had been to play nine holes, but we could still make out our
hands in front of our faces, so after a moment's deliberation we
raced on to the first tee. There was no time to rake bunkers, no time
to look for balls in the rough. "Skip the par-threes!" Randy shouted
as we raced down one fairway. "Go straight across!" Randy and

Todd had a minor cart crash, and Randy worried for a moment that the impact had thrown out his hip replacement. As it got darker, we had to spot each other's balls off the tee. There was a great deal of pressure to hit the ball straight. On one hole, Todd hooked a drive into the rough on the edge of a tree-filled swamp. As he was setting up to his shot, he heard a splash in the water behind him, and he took off like a gunshot, without hitting his ball. Earlier in the day, I had seen a small alligator in a creek on the course; at night, all alligators are large.

Surprisingly, we all played pretty well. There was no time to overthink a shot, no time to get locked up over a tricky putt. I made my best guess, whacked my ball, and moved on. To my astonishment, I generally drove my ball a long way, hit an unusually large number of greens in regulation, and even holed a couple of endless putts. The lesson? If you don't know what you're doing, thinking about it harder probably won't help.

We made it through our par-three-less second nine in a bit under half an hour. There was still some light left when we finished. I could just make out a slightly deeper blackness alongside the fairways: trees. Reluctant to leave, we putted on the ninth green for a while. We momentarily considered trying to squeeze in another hole or two, but good sense eventually won out. Randy said good night and went back to his room. Todd and I hung around for a bit longer, then drove our carts over to the practice green near the Disney Inn and chipped for a while. The green was partially illuminated by some big lights in a nearby parking lot. If we chipped toward the holes nearest the parking lot, we could see if our balls got close. Eventually, Todd said he'd better head back before his wife began to wonder where he was. We shook hands and said good night. I was too embarrassed to keep chipping by myself. So with a slow step and a heavy heart, I headed back to my room to pack.

6

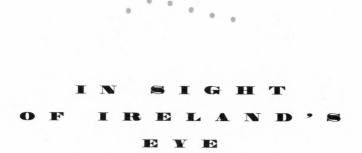

IN SIGHT
OF IRELAND'S
EYE

"COLD AND VERY WINDY," SAID THE FORECAST IN *THE Irish Times,* "strong-to-gale-force west to northwest winds, squally rain and hail showers, but sunny intervals also." I kicked myself for having left my sunglasses at home. But it was my first trip to Ireland, and I hadn't realized I would need them.

I went to Ireland in November, about a month after the Disney Classic, to play half a dozen courses in the Dublin area, on assignment for *Golf Digest.* In truth, the weather was pretty nice. Only once during my dozen rounds of golf did it rain really hard, and on that occasion the wind was blowing so fiercely that the rain fell horizontally, leaving the fairways relatively dry. I grew up in Kansas City, in the middle of Tornado Alley, so I know how to get around while leaning forward at a forty-five degree angle. Besides, the storm blew out to sea toward the end of the morning, and I played a second eighteen holes in sunshine after lunch. In the course of a busy week, I discovered that there are a number of memorable courses within striking distance of Ireland's capital, and that early winter isn't necessarily the worst time to play them. I also discovered that Ireland is a worthy destination for Americans who feel a deep chromosomal yearning to play golf on terrain like that on which the game began. Jerry Quinlan, the man who helped me put together my Scotland trip, had urged me to add Ireland to my earlier itinerary as well. A day or two into my trip, I could see why.

This time my trip was planned not by Quinlan but by the Irish Tourist Board, which assists *Golf Digest* in working out the logistics of its Irish golfing tours. Because I was a potentially impressionable journalist who was in a position to say things in print that might influence the travel plans of other Americans, I was given a letter of introduction from a public relations officer at Aer Lingus, the Irish national airline, and told that if I presented it at the ticket counter I could probably have my coach seat bumped up to first class. This is a type of special treatment that I frown on and invariably decline. Human beings are infinitely suggestible. If I were to accept an expensive upgrade—which to certain people might appear to be a bribe—my opinions as a journalist would become suspect, and my readers would be justified in doubting my impartiality, not only about air travel but about the whole of Ireland. Besides, I would be embarrassed to use my position as a reporter to secure special treatment for myself. A gentleman doesn't ask for freebies.

When I arrived at the ticket counter shortly before my departure, I discovered with surprise that the letter from the Aer Lingus public relations officer had somehow become neatly folded inside my ticket envelope. At that moment, the thought occurred to me that if I failed to seek an upgrade, the public relations officer might be considered not to have done his job. Indeed, he might be fired, and his family publicly humiliated. Seething with inner turmoil, I opened the letter and let it fall, right side up, on the counter before the ticket agent. "Oh," she said, after skimming its contents, "I believe we do have room for you." I stammered an incoherent reply.

When I reached my seat in the first-class compartment of the airplane, a beautiful young Irish stewardess took my jacket and hung it on a wood hanger in a spacious closet. Another beautiful young Irish stewardess handed me a glass of champagne. Yet another handed me so many bundles of complimentary amenities—

headphones, eye shade, slippers, clothes brush, shoehorn, blanket, toothbrush—that I was scarcely able to stow them all beneath my gigantic leather-upholstered seat. The man sitting beside me, who turned out to be an important executive in a chain of Irish luxury hotels, had many interesting things to say. We chatted through dinner—the best meal of the entire week, as it would later turn out—and over cognac afterward. Then I put on my eyeshade, permitted a beautiful young Irish stewardess to tuck my blanket around my shoulders, and slept soundly for two hours—the first time I had ever fallen asleep on an airplane.

(A week later, when it was time for me to return to the United States, I arrived at the Dublin airport several hours early and went straight to the first-class ticket agent. "I'm entitled to an upgrade," I said, thrusting my letter in her face.

"I'm afraid we're full," she said.

"Full? *Full?*" I said. "Did you see who signed this letter?"

"I'm awfully sorry," she said, "but the section is fully booked."

"Do you know who the hell I am? I'm a goddamned journalist, for Christ's sake."

"Awfully sorry."

"You'll be 'awfully sorry' after I talk to your supervisor," I sneered. "Pretty high unemployment rate you've got over here, isn't it?"

"The section is full," she said.

"So, this is the legendary Irish hospitality," I sneered as I gathered my various documents together. "Tell me, do you have children?"

All to no avail. I ended up in the middle seat of a middle row in the middle of the plane, and I didn't sleep a wink all the way back to New York.)

When I arrived in Dublin, on a Sunday, I checked into my hotel, threw my suitcase on my bed, and drove to the Royal Dublin Golf Club, a few miles north, and east of the city's center. Driving to the course, I essentially retraced my route from the airport, a fact that filled me with poignant remorse: by taking the time to drop off my suitcase, I realized, I had cost myself at least nine holes of golf, and possibly a full eighteen. I would still have time to squeeze in a full round before dinner, but the thought of all that redundant driving was a torment.

One reaches Royal Dublin by driving across a narrow causeway. The course was laid out shortly before the turn of the twentieth century on a peninsula of sand that had not existed before the turn of the nineteenth. The peninsula materialized following the construction of the Bull Wall, an enormous breakwater that was built to prevent tide-swept sediment from clogging Dublin's harbor. (Among the Bull Wall's designers was a prominent out-of-work sea captain named William Bligh.) Like Turnberry, Royal Dublin was converted to military use during the First World War; a concrete bunker that was used in rifle practice is still a part of the course, and unexploded shells occasionally nose up out of the turf. After the war, the course was rebuilt and redesigned by Harry S. Colt, whose layout is still mostly intact and whose other credits include Pine Valley.

Royal Dublin is sometimes compared to the Old Course at St. Andrews, primarily because both are links courses, both run all the way out and all the way back, and both are flat and quirky. The comparison surely originated in Ireland. Royal Dublin has little of the primordial spookiness that permeates the Old Course. There are fewer notable holes, and the smokestacks of Dublin make a less stirring backdrop than the spires of St. Andrews. Still, Royal Dublin is a very good place to play golf. It has been the site of the Irish Open, and it is the home course of Christy O'Connor, Sr., who is properly celebrated as the modern father of Irish golf. (O'Connor, Sr., is also the uncle of Christy O'Connor, Jr., who defeated Fred Couples in the pivotal match of the 1989 Ryder Cup, which preserved the cup for Europe.) Best of all, it's just a short drive or a cab ride from the city's center.

There was an interclub match going on when I arrived, so I couldn't tee off right away. Royal Dublin was playing the Kildare Country Club, a brand-new course to the west of Dublin that was also on my itinerary. I stood by the first tee for a while, and was interested to see that the typical Irish club player and the typical

American club player have similarly lousy swings, producing similarly lousy tee shots into trouble. An assistant pro standing near me dismissed the K Club—as it is universally known—as "a millionaires' club." He invited me to hit some balls, then led me not to a driving range but to a small back room equipped with a bit of Astroturf and a tattered net. I declined his invitation, and poked around the pro shop instead. When the final match had teed off, he paired me with a member named Tom Higgins, a single-digit handicapper who told me he was in the meat business. Higgins invariably said, "I never miss these putts," before stroking any putt of less than five feet or so, giving himself a booster dose of confidence that, it turned out, was 100 percent effective. We played for a pound a side. Higgins pointed out local features as we played. He took me over for a closer look at Curley's Yard, an old stone-walled enclosure that is tangentially in play on a couple of holes; a local golfing legend, Michael "Dyke" Moran, was raised in a cottage within. Higgins told me that the course lies within a celebrated bird sanctuary, and that wildlife of many types is plentiful in the area. He also mopped up the course with me, but then refused to collect our wager, saying it would be bad manners to take money from a guest.

Royal Dublin's best-known hole is the eighteenth, a sprawling par-four that used to be a par-five. Christy O'Connor, Sr., won the Carrolls International at Royal Dublin in 1966, when the eighteenth was still a par-five, by eagling it in the course of playing the last three holes in five under par—eagle-birdie-eagle. To reach the green with your second shot, you have to flirt with out-of-bounds on the right by cutting off a massive, ditch-bordered, ninety-degree dogleg. Errant balls disappear, usually forever, into a scrubby unmowed field called the Garden. Darkness had fallen by the time we reached the tee. I was happy to hit the front of the green in three and make a few futile exploratory putts in what I presumed to be the direction of the hole.

On my way back to my hotel, I gave a ride to an elderly man who had approached me in the parking lot. As we set out, I asked him how long he had been a member. "I am a caddy," he said with pride. "I have worked on a hundred and fifty-seven golf courses—

eighty-three in Ireland, seventy-one in England, and three in Scotland. As I lie in bed at night, I recite their names. I used to carry between twelve and fourteen bags a week, in season; I now carry two, because I won't work for less than I am worth. I preferred caddying in England, because the pay is better there, but my wife missed her family in Dublin and wanted to return. I couldn't cook, so I had to come along. I have caddied for ten Ryder Cup players, some before, some after, none during. I caddied for Paddy McGuirk when he won the Carrolls International, in 1973. He insisted on carrying a ridiculous selection of clubs. He carried a one-wood, a two-wood, and a five-wood. He couldn't hit the two-wood, and he didn't need the five-wood, because he also carried a two-iron. He hit his driver from the fairway sixteen times in that tournament. He would grip it down, cut the hell out of it, and pray."

I dropped Dorgan at a busy corner on the north side of the city and then plunged into the driving nightmare that is central Dublin. Like many cities laid out before the invention of the oxcart, Dublin is prone to traffic jams, and the shortest path between two points is likely to be a wildly jagged line. As my principal navigational beacon, I used the numerous signs directing visitors to an exhibit of Jimi Hendrix memorabilia. I had looked up the address of the exhibit on my map and knew that any arrow pointing toward it was also pointing vaguely toward the center of town.

On the recommendation of the Irish Tourist Board, I was staying at a hotel called Jury's, on the southeast side of Dublin. The travel guides classify Jury's as luxury accommodations, but I was reminded of a down-at-heels Holiday Inn. The place is imbued with the sort of grim characterlessness that apparently seems quintessentially American to people who don't think much of Americans. Worse, Jury's is a long way from the fun parts of Dublin, and an even longer way from the best golf courses, most of which are to the north. Nonetheless, it does have a lively bar, called the Dubliner, and I spent some time there that evening. A man in his sixties sat down next to me and struck up a conversation. We talked about Bill Clinton, Irish politics, racial intolerance, Catholicism, colonialism, and a former friend of his who had snubbed him that very evening by coming to the bar with someone else. Suddenly, he looked at me gravely and asked, "Do you want a woman for the night?" With a furtive motion of his eyes he indicated a woman standing to his left, whom he nonetheless did not seem to know and who appeared at any rate to be the wife or girlfriend of a man standing on her other side. Perhaps he thought she looked like a prostitute. "No, thank you," I said. He raised his eyebrows wryly and said, "No?" I said, "Really, no." And we went back to talking about Clinton.

Early the next morning, I headed north again, to Portmarnock, a club that deservedly has a place on nearly every list of the world's great courses. The 1991 Walker Cup was held there, the members of the European tour voted it their favorite course, and Tom Watson once famously wondered why it had never been chosen to host the British Open. Portmarnock is situated on a small, Florida-shaped peninsula that is swept by shifting winds from the Irish Sea. During the club's first half-century—it opened in 1894—it was accessible only by boat or, at low tide, by horse cart. Today you can drive to it, and navigation is simple. The clubhouse (which, like Royal Dublin's, has white walls and a red roof) is visible from far away. You keep your eye on it as you follow the coast and wait for a chance to turn toward it.

   I arrived in gale-force winds and driving rain. There were just a few cars in the parking lot: mine, the pro's, two others. A young man in a rainsuit was putting on the practice green, but he wandered away, and I never saw him again. I paid my fee at the office in the clubhouse and headed back into the weather. The bored caddymaster, wearing storm gear and standing near the door of the pro shop, watched without comment as my first shot rose almost vertically against the wind and then seemed to bend back gracefully toward the tee. Halfway up the fairway, I encountered three workmen huddled in the cab of their truck, smoking cigarettes and drinking coffee. They boredly watched me hit my second shot, and in spite of their attention, I hit a good one. The first few holes at Portmarnock are easy holes, even into the wind. They give you a chance to put your swing in order before the real test begins.

Despite the conditions, I loved the course, which meanders through shallow valleys defined by ragged dunes. The back nine must be one of the great nines in golf. My favorite spot was a bench beside the thirteenth tee. The bench faces not the golf course but the Irish Sea, which comes dramatically into view as you climb the dune to the teebox. While waves crashed on the beach below my feet, I looked out over the dark water at Ireland's Eye, a desolate rock with the remains of a seventh-century convent at one end. The thirteenth is a long par-five. The fourteenth, a par-four, plays back alongside it, with Ireland's Eye now the aiming point from the tee. On the tee of the fifteenth, which runs claustrophobically parallel to the beach, Ireland's Eye is again a dark presence, though now to the right. The fifteenth is a notoriously difficult 185-yard hole that Ben Crenshaw once called the best par-three in the world and Gary Player once called the best par-five. Its crowned, elevated green is guarded by bunkers, tall grass, scrubby dunes, and the howling wind. I aimed a four-iron virtually toward England and watched the gale push my ball back into a bowl-shaped depression on the opposite side of the green. I managed to scrape out a par, and true to Gary Player's description, it felt like an eagle.

Portmarnock wouldn't be a good place to spend a golfing honeymoon. Like Royal Dublin, it has no women members, and female guests and visitors are tolerated only under grumpy-sounding restrictions. The women's tee markers at Portmarnock are placed seemingly at random, often in the footpaths leading from the men's tees to the fairways. The club has a nice locker room for members, a pretty nice locker room for visitors, and a teensy changing room for women, across the hall from the manager's office. There's also a stuffy-looking dining room where jackets and ties are required. I took my lunch business back up the road to a pub called the Golf Links. On a mirror over the cash register was a painting of Portmarnock's fifteenth hole. On other mirrors were painted the layout of the course and portraits of Tom Watson, Jack Nicklaus, Nick Faldo, and Ian Woosnam, among others. I had a tolerable lunch of curried something or other, then headed back to the course, stopping for a moment to look through a chain-link fence at a new golf course and a hotel under construction at the landward end of the Portmarnock peninsula.

The smartest thing I did before leaving for Ireland was to pack two of everything that might get wet. After my morning round, I had spread my wet rainsuit and gloves on the backseat of my car. Now I put on my dry ones. (I had brought two pairs of shoes as well, and the evening before I had dried the ones I had worn at Royal Dublin with the wall-mounted hair dryer in my hotel room.) The rain had stopped and the sun had come out by then, but the wind was still blowing hard, and the rainsuit kept it from cutting through me as I played a second eighteen—this time with three vacationing Germans who did not believe in talking while playing, except to curse, in English, their many dreadful shots. With the improvement in the weather had come a minor increase in the amount of bustle on the course. The three workers I had seen huddling in their truck in the morning were now languidly stacking slabs of sod on one side of a fairway bunker, which they were rebuilding. I now knew the Championship Course well enough to tell the difference between it and Portmarnock's third nine, called the C Course, which is inter-leaved among the original eighteen holes and is reputed to be comparable in quality. I would have loved to play it, too, but there wasn't enough light left by the time I finished with the Germans, so I saved it for another trip.

The night before, I had decided to abandon Jury's and move from Dublin to Howth (rhymes with *both*), a picturesque fishing village and resort on a bulb-shaped promontory overhanging the northern part of Dublin Bay. Howth, which from most directions looks like an island, is clearly visible from both Portmarnock and Royal Dub-lin. It is perfectly situated in relation to most of the best courses in the Dublin area, and it would have made an ideal base of opera-tions for my trip. On the strength of a somewhat ambiguous recom-mendation in a guidebook, I checked into the Howth Lodge Hotel, which was squeezed between the water and a picturesque railroad crossing. The room (like my rental car) smelled like the inside of an ashtray, the telephone service was prehistoric, and the shower was a tentative drip, but I much preferred the place to Jury's. After checking in, I drove around town for a while, and turned into the driveway of the Deerpark Hotel, just up the road from the Howth Lodge. As I read the sign, a wave of gloom swept over me: The Deerpark has its own golf course. Why hadn't I known? My spirits sank further a moment later as I passed the interesting-looking ruins of a castle, just to the side of the driveway. My good mood returned when I got to the end of the drive, however. The Deerpark looked like a motor lodge, and the golf course was inconsequential. I cheerfully drove back down the hill.

In town that evening, I visited a pub called the Pier House, down near the water's edge. The comfortable old bar was filled with workingmen—or, as is nearly as likely to be the case in Ireland nowadays, nonworkingmen. (During the American presidential campaign, Irish editorial writers had to explain to their readers why a single-digit unemployment rate was considered a political issue.) Astonishingly, the television in the pub was tuned to the PGA Grand Slam, an event in which Fred Couples, Nick Faldo, Tom Kite, and Nick Price—the reigning champions of the four major tournaments—were battling for golf's world heavyweight title. You would never find golf on the TV in a comparable American bar. I marveled at the contrast and found myself wishing that golf in America could somehow shed its country-club taint and truly become a sport for everyone, as it clearly was here. Then the bartender asked me whether I would mind if he switched the channel to a football match, since no one except me seemed to be interested in the golf.

Just around the corner from the Pier House is the King Sitric, a seafood restaurant that is reputed to be one of the few good restaurants in all of Ireland. (Irish food really is terrible. The country's culinary history has less to do with pushing forward the frontiers of fine dining than with averting mass starvation. Such national dishes as there are tend to be soft and white, or else made from parts of things that pickier eaters would throw away.) The King Sitric looked formal and empty, so I ate instead at the Abbey Tavern, just around the corner and up the hill. The Abbey has a dark, medieval-looking bar downstairs, a semihorrendous restaurant upstairs, and a cramped annex in which a terrific troupe of Irish folk musicians performs in the evenings. The whole place smells attractively of smoldering peat, the principal heating fuel. While eating over-cooked salmon and mushy vegetables in the dining room, I over-heard an American at another table telling two female companions about his childhood. "We lived in Kansas City until I was seven," he was saying. "Our house was at the corner of West Sixtieth Terrace and a big street whose name I can't remember. It's the street that runs down the big hill into the Plaza." I stepped over to their table and said, "Wornal Road," then returned to my seat.

Even when it isn't raining in Ireland, it is sort of raining. There was no storm during the night, but the next morning the streets were mottled with dark puddles, and the inside of my miniature rental car was as wet as if it had been filled to the dome light with water and slowly allowed to drain. I mopped the windshield with some old socks and headed for St. Margaret's, a new course just north of the Dublin airport.

Irish golf has known two major periods of growth. The first was roughly a hundred years ago, when Royal Dublin, Portmarnock, and quite a few other fine courses were constructed in response to the sudden popularity of the Scottish game. (This period, inciden-tally, corresponds precisely with the establishment of the game in America; the great old American courses are roughly the same age as many of the great old Irish ones.) The second major period of growth is now. Speculators all over the country are bulldozing old farms, partly in the hope of tapping a recent upsurge in domestic demand, and partly in the hope of attracting international travelers. St. Margaret's is one of the best known of the new courses. It had opened less than a year before my visit, and its owners were hoping that it would one day be chosen as a site for important professional tournaments. There was no one in the clubhouse or pro shop when I arrived, so I went for a drive around the area. On a narrow, hedge-lined road around the corner, I saw another new golf course under construction. What had once been an ancient farm now looked like a mud hole.

When I returned to St. Margaret's, not only the pro but also another golfer had arrived. The other golfer's name was George. He was a sales representative for a big British chemical company, which, among other things, sold fertilizers and herbicides to the superintendents of golf courses. He had come to St. Margaret's on a friendly sales call. We teed off together and had the course to ourselves.

The sky was perfectly clear, but the wind was very cold and it was blowing very hard. On a downhill, downwind, 150-yard par-three, where I might have hit an eight-iron in calm weather, I hit a pitching wedge and watched my ball sail into a creek on the far side of the green. St. Margaret's was originally a cow pasture, and it still looks like one. Hundreds of foot-tall trees have been planted, but it will be years before any are big enough to affect course strategy. On several holes, golfers are more or less on their honor to stick to the fairway and not save yardage by cutting through a grove of microscopic saplings.

The course, though brand-new, was in very ragged condition, and George critiqued it as we played. St. Margaret's had been opened too quickly, he said. In just two months, the greens had been ravaged to the point where a number of them had had to be resodded or even rebuilt. We watched some workers fussing around the edges of a ruined green that, after resodding, looked as lumpy as a quilt. Sod for the original greens had been imported from Britain, and it hadn't taken. On many holes, putting was point-less. On others, we played to scrappy temporary greens that de-feated the design of the holes. George pointed out places on several real greens where careless contouring had created ridges and bumps that had been scalped by the mowers. In addition, he said, the course's designers had paid insufficient attention to soil com-pacting during construction, with the result that drainage was dreadful. Indeed, we had to step carefully to avoid the many boggy areas on the course. George said that such problems were common on a number of new courses, because the owners were under financial pressure to begin earning revenue as soon as possible. He told me that I would notice similar deficiencies at the K Club, where I would be headed in a couple of days. Like a number of other Irishmen I spoke with during my trip, he managed to suggest that these problems, along with various others, were somehow American in origin, even though the course had been designed and built by locals. At any rate, we agreed that it would be several years before St. Margaret's merited a return visit.

The next day I drove north, to Baltray, a small, old fishing village on the outskirts of the ancient port city of Drogheda (whose name, when pronounced by a resident, sounds a little like a throat being cleared). Baltray is the home of County Louth Golf Club, a wonderful links course situated near the intersection of the Boyne River and the Irish Sea. The course, which is usually referred to simply as Baltray, is reminiscent of Portmarnock, but eerier. The seaside holes look like what the moon would look like if the moon were covered with grass. The dunes beside the fairways are jagged, stark, and weirdly sculpted, and the greens seem like smoother continuations of the undulating ground around them. The course was overhauled in the thirties by Tom Simpson, who also did work at Ballybunion, Muirfield, and Sunningdale. Simpson liked to build tough, interesting greens that were not overly dependent on bunkering, and the greens at Baltray are considered to be among his finest.

In 1908, when Baltray was sixteen years old, a member named Col. McWeeney wrote the following tribute:

> Doctors may boast of their skill pharmaceutical,
> Measure out drugs in a grave sort of way,
> If you want health to pervade every cuticle,
> Go and play golf on the Links at Baltray.
> Tuberculosis is cured in two doses there,
> All the wild ills of the flesh fade away;
> Double pneumonia, asthma, insomnia,
> Weap for their sins on the Links at Baltray.

There's a good deal more than that (including "Burn all your band-
ages, rise to health's pinnacle/Crutches are golf sticks in play at
Baltray"). The doggerel may be unforgivable, but the colonel's enthusiasm is understandable. Baltray is a terrific course.

In the morning, I played with Kevin Breith, a young man with a
good swing who had been an assistant pro at Baltray the year
before. I asked him what he did now. "Play golf," he said. The wind
was blowing so hard that divots occasionally flipped out of divot
holes, sand blew out of bunkers, and my pullcart tipped over twice.
On the 476-yard, par-five eleventh, which was playing straight
downwind, I hit a three-wood off the tee, then hit an eight-iron ten
yards past the pin. Playing in the opposite direction on another
hole, I hit a strong, hard, drawing six-iron from 110 yards and
watched it fall short of the green. At the fourteenth tee, Kevin and
I put down our clubs and climbed over the dunes into what I
suddenly realized was a fairway. A second course was under construction at Baltray, and some friends of Kevin's were working on
it. We walked over to a tractor. In its cab, three large men were
chatting and smoking cigarettes. "Typical Irish workers," Kevin
said. On the ground near the tractor were a number of bumps, dips,
and other defects that had been highlighted with white spray paint.
Kevin's friends were supposed to be excising these blemishes, but
for the moment, they were taking a break.

After lunch, I played a second round by myself. A storm threatened but never arrived. At one point, half the sky was dead black,
half was flawless blue, and an enormous rainbow stretched from
one horizon to the other. I saw a number of golfers struggling with
umbrellas, which threatened to blow out to sea. I was stuck behind
four local priests who treated balls like souls, never giving one up
for lost, and who never so much as acknowledged my presence
behind them. Several times I considered teeing off over their heads
as they thrashed around in the gorse a hundred yards beyond the
tee, looking for their topped drives, but I decided instead to be
grateful for the opportunity to enjoy my surroundings. I saw the
priests later in their black robes in the club's dining room, where

they were drinking tea and taking turns anxiously auditing their check.

After my round, I drove into Drogheda and looked around. The city, which rises from both banks of the Boyne, was founded by Vikings more than a thousand years ago. Traces remain of the wall that surrounded the city in medieval times. I inspected St. Laurence's Gate, the sole survivor of the city's ten massive original entrances, and marveled at the enormous trucks maneuvering around corners on the narrow, steeply sloping streets. At St. Peter's Catholic church, on West Street, I ducked in briefly to look at Drogheda's most compelling tourist attraction, the preserved head of St. Oliver Plunkett, who was martyred by the British in the late seventeenth century. Then I returned to Baltray.

I spent the night in one of thirteen bedrooms that the club maintains for visitors. My room was small, spare, and not very comfortable, and the bathroom was down the hall, but I loved spending the night in the clubhouse. Poking around later, I realized that the club's secretary had placed me in the smallest and most decrepit of the thirteen rooms, even though I was the only guest. That evening, I visited the bar and ate dinner in the dining room; both are popular local hangouts. I turned in early but heard partying until all hours. At seven-thirty the next morning, as I was packing my suitcase, the cook knocked at my door to tell me my breakfast was ready. We were the only two people on the premises. In the dining room, he had laid out coffee, tea, cornflakes, toast, eggs, tomato, bacon, and two kinds of sausage. As I ate my breakfast, I watched the sun spread over the course. The first golfers were just arriving as I left.

I spent the rest of the morning driving to Straffan, a village to the west of Dublin. Straffan lies in a region of genteel farms and is the home of the Kildare Hotel and Country Club—the K Club—whose members had been competing against those of Royal Dublin on the day I arrived in Ireland. On a map, the distance between Baltray and Straffan is unintimidating; in a car, it is seemingly measured in light years. To drive from the north of Dublin to the west of Dublin, you have little choice but to drive through Dublin itself. The route winds through side streets and over tiny stone bridges, repeatedly doubles back on itself, and is marked with small, ambiguous signs. But eventually I arrived.

The K Club is the dream project of an Irish megamogul named Michael Smurfit, who in 1988 bought an ancient 330-acre estate and spared no expense in turning it into an almost absurdly luxurious resort. Among a great many other attractions, it has a golf course designed by Arnold Palmer and a clubhouse on a level with those of the snottiest American country clubs. The hotel—the only one in Ireland ever to be awarded five stars by the Automobile Association—occupies the magnificently renovated and expanded Straffan House, parts of which date to the sixth century. At the time of my visit, rooms in the hotel began at £145 a night and went up to £800 (for the Viceroy Suite). I could have lived comfortably for several weeks in just the bathroom of my single. It had a tub the size of a small swimming pool and a shower in which the water pressure was so ferocious that when I turned it on I feared for the safety of ships in Dublin Harbor. The bathrobes, towels, drinking glasses, ashtrays, and nearly every other item smaller than the bed was decorated with a three-color rendition of the K Club's attractive logo—an almost irresistible invitation to thievery.

After a quiet lunch in the clubhouse, I teed off by myself. I had been warned about the course by George, my playing partner at St. Margaret's. He had told me that the K Club's builders had wildly underestimated the amount of drainage they would need to keep the course dry. The river Liffey winds through the estate, and parts of the course are well below flood level. As I played, teams of workers were top-dressing muddy fairways with enormous loads of sand. Others were installing gravel-and-sand-filled slit drains on the mounds and tee boxes, which were especially mucky. I wore my rain pants just to keep the mud from soaking through to my skin, and after a few holes I was muddy up to my knees. (There was a shoe-cleaning contraption near the clubhouse, but you had to walk through thick mud going to and from it.) The greens were in better condition than those at St. Margaret's, but they still showed signs of immaturity and were annoyingly untrue. All things considered, the £70 green fee seemed audacious.

Despite the drainage problems, the K Club is a beautiful course, and I had it almost entirely to myself. Elements of the old estate—such as ancient walls, huge oaks, and tangled windrows—are skillfully incorporated into the design of several holes. My favorite hole was the seventh, a long double-dogleg par-five whose green is situated at one end of a wooded island in the Liffey. You cross to the green on a 150-year-old iron suspension bridge, while Straffan House and its gardens loom majestically behind you. My affection for the hole was not dampened by the fact that I put three balls into the stone-banked river before finally managing to land an approach shot on dry land, in a bunker behind the hole. Later on, I realized that I could see the green, the island, and the bridge from the window in my room, and as the sun set, I looked down on them with longing.

Only three of the hotel's forty-five rooms were occupied on the night I stayed there. Two of the four other guests had decided to eat dinner elsewhere, so the staff-to-guest ratio in the ornate dining room was uncomfortably high. I ordered venison, and it wasn't bad, but it didn't alter my opinion of Irish cooking. The only other diners were an elderly couple from Mississippi. The woman had spent the day watching birds, and the man had spent it shooting birds, so they had a common interest. Between big bites, the man entertained the waiter with information about the different types of quail to be found in the Southern United States. The waiter's only escape was to visit me frequently in order to top off my glass of water, which I sipped from only to give him something to do. For dessert, on the recommendation of the waiter, I had three tiny scoops of home-made ice cream. One was coffee-flavored, one was ginger, and one I couldn't identify. "It's asparagus," the waiter said, explaining that the chef liked to experiment. After dinner, I wandered around the hotel, which seemed as big as a castle and as dead as a mortuary.

There was a heavy frost on the grass the following morning. From the window in my room, I watched cows coldly grazing in a white pasture on the far side of the Liffey. I ate breakfast alone. An underoccupied bellman carried my bag to my car and meticulously de-iced the windows with an aerosol can of some potent solvent. On the road, I retraced most of my route of the morning before. My destination was a golf club called the Island, which is situated on a sandy peninsula just up the coast from Portmarnock. (My wildly inefficient itinerary was the work of the Irish Tourist Board.)

The Island was founded in 1890 by ten unmarried men, known in club lore as the Bachelors. They objected to what was then a ban on Sunday golf at Royal Dublin, and they chose as the site of their new club a forlorn stretch of nonarable dunesland known locally as the Hills. In a grainy photograph in the club history (which was published in 1990, on the occasion of the club's hundredth birthday), the Bachelors look jaunty and collegial. All are wearing jackets, ties, and caps, all but two have bushy mustaches, and several have inebriated-looking smiles. The Island is not, in fact, an island, but it looks like one from Malahide, the village across the inlet to the south. At first, the course was accessible only by boat from Malahide; now it's just a short car trip from Dublin. In the early years, the Bachelors leased the land from a local farmer for £10 a year. The fairways and greens were cleared by farmhands equipped with scythes. The use of caddies was discouraged (and banned outright on Sundays) "with a view to keeping the Links as private as possible," according to an early list of rules.

Of all the courses I played in Ireland, the Island is the one that seems to have rooted most firmly in my mind. It is by no means a better course than Portmarnock or Baltray, but it has powerful charms. The dunes flanking the fairways are enormous—one of the holes is called, appropriately, the Andes—and on several holes they create a supernatural sense of enclosure as you make your way from tee to green. Throughout the course, you can see evidence of earlier routings. (Both the course and the peninsula have changed dramatically over the last century.) There are blind shots, sheltered greens, and stirring views. There are also corrugationlike furrows in several areas—the remnants of old potato fields. Among other attractions, the course has several outstanding short par-fours. The most unusual is the 340-yard fourteenth. Its fairway is the narrowest

I have ever seen—just a few paces wide. The fairway is guarded on the left by tall grass and a ridge of dunes, and on the right by tall grass and the muck of the estuary. The green is no wider than the fairway. From the air, the hole would look like the back of your index finger. A member once made a hole in one there, but you could as easily get a ten. Standing on the teebox (which sits on the foundation of an abandoned early clubhouse), you can see the landing where, as late as the early seventies, members used to arrive by boat.

After a lengthy frost delay, I played eighteen holes with a middle-aged married couple who both worked in television. We played from winter tees, which had been set well forward of the regular members' tees, but by that point in my trip I was happy to play a shortened course. The Island's first hole is a wonderful starter, a medium-long par-four that rises gradually between high dunes to an elevated green. "Can a family of four live comfortably in America on thirty thousand dollars a year?" my male playing partner asked me. His wife showed me a spot near the seventh green that is known as Carron's Hollow, after an old hermit who once lived there in a sod hut and had to be chased off the course periodically by the greenkeeper. The Island's most notable hole is probably the thirteenth, called Broadmeadow, a two-hundred-plus-yard par-three that plays along the curving shoreline, with the rooftops of Malahide as a backdrop. When the tide is high and the wind is blowing, the tee shot is distinctly intimidating. Actually, it's distinctly intimidating at any time.

After my round with the married couple, I went out again, hoping to squeeze in as many more holes as possible on my last golfing day in Ireland. On the fourth hole, a nice, short par-four called Pot, I ran into an elderly man who was walking his dog, looking for balls, and hitting an occasional eight-iron. His name was Liam, and he had once been an officer of the club. We meandered from hole to hole, in no particular order, until it was too dark to follow the flight of a ball. At one point, he led me back to three, a long par-four that runs along the water, so that I could play it properly, from the medal tees. Inspired by this special treatment, I hit my best tee shot of the trip, so long that it would have been unfindable in the gloom if it hadn't stopped in the middle of the fairway. Liam told me about the history of the club and said that the members had always been protective of it, not wanting it to be overwhelmed by outsiders. It wasn't terribly well known, he said, and that was the way they liked it. The course's relatively inaccessible location had always kept the traffic down, even when the boat service ended. Some younger members complained about the quirky older holes, he said, but he hoped there would be no impetuous rush to change them. It was almost entirely dark by the time we finished. We shook hands in the parking lot, and I headed back to Dublin.

That night, I stayed at the Shelbourne Hotel, which is to Dublin what the Waldorf or the Plaza is to New York. It's across the street from St. Stephen's Green (from the depths of which a rooster crowed the following dawn), and three blocks away from Grafton Street, a lively shopping district that is off-limits to cars. On Friday evenings, the Shelbourne's lobby transforms into a tasteful pickup joint, filling past overflowing with what must be every young professional in Greater Dublin. I shouldered my way through this hormone-rich crush and made my way to Oísin's (pronounced something like "oceans"), a small restaurant that serves scrupulously authentic Irish fare and is recommended by several guidebooks. The food was—oh, well, never mind. Still, I enjoyed trying to make out the Gaelic on the menu, and I passed the time between courses by listening to the noisiest eater I have ever heard, an American tourist sitting at a table halfway across the room. Slurping his spinach-and-barley soup, he sounded like a man in heavy boots walking across a muddy field.

Before turning in that night, I studied my road map, planning my next trip to Ireland. Next time, I decided, my itinerary will be more ambitious. I'll play at Portmarnock, Baltray, and the Island again. I'll also go north, to Royal County Down and Royal Portrush; and northwest, to Rosses Point, in County Sligo; and southwest, to Lahinch, Ballybunion, and Waterville. (You can windowshop for places to play in John Redmond's *Great Golf Courses of Ireland,* a handsome coffee-table book that was published in the United States a couple of years ago by Random House.) I wouldn't mind traveling in November again. Ireland lies as far north as parts of Saskatchewan, but the Gulf Stream keeps the seaside courses playable year-round, offering a snowbound, golf-starved New Englander an interesting alternative to Myrtle Beach. Winter days are short near the top of the world, but the golf courses aren't crowded, and the roads aren't clogged with tourists. And if you get homesick for Jimi Hendrix, you can always take a daytrip into Dublin.

GROWN MEN ON
SPRING BREAK

IN TERMS OF OPTIMUM CLUBHEAD SPEED, THE LENGTH OF
the hosel and the apparent angle of the groove-to-punch-mark
declination, minus the reciprocal of the angle of the axis of the shaft
as it relates to the heel, must under no circumstances exceed the
distance in millimeters between the axis of the shaft or the neck or
socket and the back of the heel.

There. That ought to take care of my wife. I don't think she would
read this anyway, but she'll definitely never get past that paragraph.
We can now speak freely.

Why does my wife—and, by extension, virtually everyone else's
wife—hate golf? One reason, I suppose, is that Ethel (not her real
name) does not herself play golf. She doesn't get the point of competitive sports and, in fact, won't even play cards. She will occasionally play Scrabble, but if you get a big word in your first few turns
she will insist on starting a new game. (Why not simply press?) In
addition, she doesn't like anything that she isn't good at immediately—a character trait that rules out putting, chipping, pitching,
sand play, short irons, medium irons, long irons, fairway woods,
and driving.

I don't necessarily view any of this as a drawback; I'm glad Ethel doesn't play golf. I have several friends whose wives reluctantly took up the game in an effort to share their husbands' lives but ended up merely adding to their own already hefty burdens of resentment. They used to be angry at their husbands for spending so much time playing golf. Now they're angry at their husbands not only for that, but also for never wanting to play with them.

Obviously, not all golfing wives are like this. I have a zero-handicap friend who made it to the quarter-finals of the British Amateur a decade ago; when he plays with his wife, she gives him a stroke a side. They have what may be the perfect marriage—my concept of the ideal woman has changed in the last few years—but their relationship is very unusual. More typical of golfing wifedom are the four women my friend Jim and I encountered one day at our local nine-hole course. Jim and I were playing twenty-seven holes, and the women were playing nine, and we played through them three times. The problem wasn't so much that they were terrible golfers, although they were. The problem was that they approached the game with a baffling sort of lackadaisical vagueness that precluded, for instance, making any effort whatsoever to control the direction or speed of a putt. A round of golf, for them, was a social outing; it wasn't a round of golf.

Everything I've said so far is pigheaded and unfair, but it is positively enlightened in comparison with the things that Ethel says about golf. In her view, the game is beneath contempt, like vivisection. When I say, "I'm going to play golf," she looks at me as if I had said, "I think I'd like to start dating our daughter." She approves of flower arranging, liposuction, psychotherapy, hair dye, and aimless, irrational driving—but a nine-hundred-year-old game played by the president of the United States she can't stand.

The paradox, I suppose, is that Ethel's feelings about golf seem to increase my enjoyment of the game. It may be that men are chromosomally predisposed toward doing virtually anything their wives don't want them to do. (My literary agent, an enlightened woman, provides ironic support for this hypothesis. For many years, she has tried to persuade her husband to take up golf—"I *want* to be a golf widow," she says—but he has refused.) This innate contrariness must have given our humanoid ancestors some powerful evolutionary advantage. A possible scenario: Female cave people implored their mates to spend more time around the cave, picking up woolly-mammoth bones and entertaining the children; those who complied watched their families slowly starve to death, while those who ignored their mates and went hunting instead survived. In such beneficent behavior we may be seeing evidence of the forerunner of the modern golfing gene.

Whether or not our intention was to infuriate our wives, my brother, John, my friends Jim and Mike, and I spent a good bit of the fall and winter planning an early-spring golfing trip to Myrtle Beach, South Carolina. We sent away for catalogs listing courses and motels, then spent several happy weeks poring over them, like sorority sisters dreaming of the perfect honeymoon. In and around Myrtle Beach are dozens of motels and hotels that offer inexpensive golf packages. Some include a room, breakfast, and a round of golf for less than thirty dollars a day, depending on the season. The rates are so low that locals will sometimes make phantom motel reservations to take advantage of a package rate that is lower than green fees alone.

After much heated but essentially ignorant deliberation, we settled on a motel in North Myrtle Beach that, for legal reasons, I will refer to as the Bates Motel. We called the proprietor to tell her when and where we wanted to play, and that was that. She made all our golf reservations for us. All we had to do was survive two more months of snow.

On a golf-hole-per-square-mile basis, Myrtle Beach is far and away the springtime golf capital of eastern North America. There are something like eighty courses on the strip of Carolina seaside known as the Grand Strand, and so many more are under construction that the maps on the placemats in the restaurants are invariably out of date. During the peak spring season—which runs roughly from the middle of March until the first of June—the area fills with men from the North whose veins are throbbing with resurgent golf

hormones. During the two months before our late-February departure date, I remembered what it felt like to be a child waiting for
Christmas. By the time the great day arrived, my partners and I were
so excited that we could scarcely make intelligent conversation
with our wives, who were no longer speaking to us anyway.

We were nearly an hour late in taking off from Charlotte, North
Carolina, for the final leg of our journey. Bad weather elsewhere in
the country had played havoc with connecting flights, and ours was
the last plane bound for Myrtle Beach that night. The plane by that
point was filled almost entirely with Myrtle Beach golfers, of which
there are two broad species: Golf-Dependent Personalities and Ar-
rested Development Cases. These species are easily distinguish-
able. The GDPs go to bed early, play thirty-six holes a day, and lose
sleep worrying about frost delays. The ADCs are former high school
bad boys who haven't quite surrendered to the constraints of married life. They smoke cigars, cruise the strip joints at night, play only
one round a day, and never have a morning tee time. Members of
both species are exclusively male and closing in on middle age.
None would remember to call home if his wife didn't give him a
Post-it reminder to stick to the telephone in his motel room.

On the plane, the GDPs were wearing golf hats, reading golf
magazines, and debating the merits of penal versus strategic course
architecture. The ADCs were angrily complaining that they hadn't
been allowed to sit out the delay in the terminal cocktail lounge. A
linebacker-sized ADC sitting behind me grumbled, "We're going to
miss our tee time at the Doll House," referring to a well-known
Myrtle Beach strip joint. The stewardesses, who had been forced by
the collapse of the Soviet Union to take early retirement from Aeroflot, were surly and unapologetic. Through my window I anxiously
watched cadaver-shaped golf bags ride the dark conveyor belt into
the belly of our plane. Was that one mine? Finally, just as the last
liter of oxygen in the cabin had been converted to man breath, we
took off.

Like most GDPs, my partners and I rented a minivan when we
arrived in Myrtle Beach. (ADCs rent, and often wreck, Lincoln
Town Cars.) A Grand Voyager is exactly the right size to hold four

tubby men, four golf bags, and four poorly packed suitcases. Plus, it has drink holders, and you can dry two pairs of golf shoes at a time by wedging them between the windshield and the defroster. In the nation at large, the minivan is an icon of family values; on the Grand Strand, it's just an oversized, all-weather golf cart. We called ours the Man Van.

It was close to midnight when, after approximately an hour and a half of being hopelessly lost, we pulled into the parking lot of the Bates Motel. A cold, stinging wind was blowing off the Atlantic, causing sand, newspapers, plastic foam cups, and a big garbage can to tumble around the swimming pool, which had been covered with a flapping tarp. Rain, if not snow, seemed imminent. Ghostly breakers slammed into the beach. The motel's office was dark, empty, and locked. Taped to the door was an envelope that turned out to contain our golf vouchers and a note explaining that our room keys could be found under the mats in front of our doors. We lugged our bags up to our rooms—two tenement-quality two-bedroom suites, each with a minimalist living room and kitchenette—turned on the rasping wall-mounted heaters, and fell into bed. Comfortingly, just as I was about to doze off, I heard a golf ball bounce and roll on the floor of the room above. I got up half an hour later to look for an extra blanket, but couldn't find one, and ended up unpacking my suitcase on top of my bedspread in an effort to raise the R-value of my bed.

A little over four hours later, when my alarm went off, an icy rain was lashing the broken window at my head. Stumbling out of bed, I discovered with sorrow that I had packed too many golf shirts and not enough Arctic-weight down-filled Gore-Tex jumpsuits. Our first tee time was seven-sixteen, at the Legends, a three-course complex virtually all the way back to the airport, some forty-five minutes away. On our way south, we stopped at one of Myrtle Beach's ubiquitous pancake houses to choke down bacon, eggs, and Advil. Two men who didn't look like golfers were the only other diners. They eyed us coldly as we pestered the waitress for additional coffee. Then, back into the Man Van. As we drove, I kept the windshield wipers on intermittent speed, even though I could barely make out the car ahead of me, because I didn't want to encourage the rain by seeming to give in to it. "I think the clouds are breaking up," Jim said hopefully, as thunderheads collided above us.

Myrtle Beach is the sociological equivalent of the inside of a single man's refrigerator. Driving to the course from our motel, I got an inkling of what the world would be like if wives did not exist. There were gas stations, cheap motels, a topless karaoke bar, liquor stores, pawn shops, hangar-sized fried-food restaurants, golf-equipment stores that stayed open until ten, and very little else. A white frame bungalow that looked like a farmer's vegetable stand turned out to be a used-golf-ball store. You can find anything you need in Myrtle Beach, as long as it isn't broccoli or a diaper.

Myrtle Beach's history as a low-cost golf destination stretches back about a quarter-century. The first golf package was offered in 1959 by the Dunes Club and the Caravelle Hotel. Golfers could stay at the Caravelle and play at the Dunes, which had opened a decade earlier (and is still one of the prime courses in the region). At that time, there were only three eighteen-hole golf courses in the Myrtle Beach area. The antifeminist spectacle that the Grand Strand would later become was yet undreamed of. But the Dunes package was a hit, and it inspired imitators. By 1979, there were more than thirty courses operating, and many packages. Truly explosive growth came in the eighties, when more than forty new courses were built. By 1990, there wasn't a compulsive golfer in America who didn't know about Myrtle Beach. The Grand Strand was the place to go for a quick, cheap fix.

Myrtle Beach's reputation for high-quality golf was slower to develop, but—surprisingly, given the distinctly seedy atmosphere—it is deserved. In recent years especially, a large number of excellent courses have been built, making it possible for diehard GDPs to get their daily fixes on courses that are actually quite decent. The courses tend to be crowded, but the crowds have their positive side: They generate the revenues that make premium-course construction possible.

The three courses that make up the Legends—Heathland, Moorland, and Parkland—are among those frequently cited as being tops. Heathland, which opened in 1990, was designed by Tom Doak, who is one of the most interesting young American course designers. Doak majored in golf-course architecture at Cornell and spent a fellowship year in Britain, where he visited 172 different courses. He also worked as a caddy at the Old Course. After graduation, Doak served his design apprenticeship with Pete Dye. He came away from these experiences with a firm grounding in classical design coupled with more than a touch of Dye-esque inventiveness. Ben Crenshaw, who has a reputation for being the PGA Tour's resident keeper of the flame, views Doak as a kindred spirit and has called him "a *real* lover of the game."

Heathland represents one of Doak's highly satisfactory efforts to build a linkslike course in the United States. We certainly had Scottish-style conditions. The rain fluctuated in intensity but never entirely disappeared, and the wind picked up. After wavering briefly in the pro shop, we decided to cough up an additional twenty bucks for plastic covers for our carts. These provided a certain amount of protection from the gusty, twenty-five-mile-per-hour wind and the steady, enervating rain. Curiously, though, I think the carts made the weather seem even nastier than it was. I had played in worse weather in Ireland but minded it less—mostly, I think because walking kept my muscles warm and my blood circulating. At Heathland we were constantly climbing in and out of our absurd vehicles, zipping and unzipping the plastic covers, sitting in chilly puddles, and rolling back or tying together the dripping flaps that covered our clubs. The roofs of the carts amplified the sound of the rain, making a drizzle seem like a downpour. The windshields were merely translucent. The runoff from the roofs drained directly into our golf bags. All day long, I felt *encumbered*. Worse, a cart makes it very hard to get a sense of what a course is actually like. A hole doesn't unfold to you the way it does when you are on foot—especially if you can't see out the windshield.

Still, Heathland is a very good golf course. It doesn't make you think you are in Scotland, but it wears its influences very well.

Several holes were directly inspired by favorite holes of Doak's in Britain (the fifteenth is modeled after the third at Royal St. George's; the eighteenth is Doak's tribute to the eighteenth at Royal Lytham and St. Annes). Once or twice I was reminded of Carnoustie. Someday I would like to go back.

My hands were so numb by the end of our first round that I could scarcely grip the hotdog that I didn't have time to eat as we raced around the back of the clubhouse to sign in for our second round. The proprietor of the Bates Motel had scheduled our two rounds just five hours and four minutes apart, an overoptimistic spacing considering the glacial pace of play at most Myrtle Beach golf courses. We played our second round on the Parkland course, which is the newest of the three Legends. It was designed by Larry Young, who owns the entire complex and is responsible for several of the more distinguished courses on the Grand Strand. (Moorland was designed by P. B. Dye, who is the son of Pete.) Unfortunately, my memories of Parkland are few and indistinct. The forecast we had checked at five that morning had said the rain would end by midday, but it did not. There were many occasions when the clouds seemed to be breaking up, or when the splashes on the ponds seemed to be thinning, and there was a moment when we actually took off our rain jackets, thinking the sun was about to break through. But the weather never really changed. We were cold and wet, and we had trouble paying attention.

To help pass the time during our second five-hour round of the day, we played a game that I had learned in Phoenix during a round at Moon Valley with a couple of Karsten employees. The game is played with six animal headcovers—a beaver, a camel, a duck, a gorilla, a pig, and a snake. The headcovers are awarded for particular kinds of bad shots. If you hit a tree, you win the beaver, and have to place it on the head of one of your clubs until someone else hits a tree. The camel is for a shot into a bunker, the duck is for water, the gorilla is for a shot out of bounds, the pig is for a shot that the other three players agree is the worst so far, and the snake is for a three-putt. At the end of nine holes, you pay the other players a dollar for each headcover in your possession; you pay double if you have four or more, and triple if you have all. Then the game begins again. This is a good pastime for slow golf courses, because it takes forever to play. No one is ever allowed to pick up, no matter how desperate his situation, because his next shot might hit a tree or go in the water, or he might three-putt once he eventually reaches the green. At Moon Valley, my playing companions had been quite ruthless. On one hole, my drive came to rest about three feet from a wrought-iron fence behind which two snarling Doberman pinschers eyed me hungrily. I couldn't take a proper stance over my ball without placing my butt in chomping range. I ended up topping my shot and squirting it into a small tree—exactly the outcome my companions had been hoping for. On the final hole, two of the other players intentionally played short of the green, even though doing so virtually guaranteed they would lose the nassau (which we were playing simultaneously), because they figured that chipping on would reduce their likelihood of three-putting and thus being stuck with the snake.

The animal game wasn't quite as much fun in the rain as it had been in Arizona. Constantly fussing with the sopping animals (which I had brought with me in a little black bag) got to be a nuisance very quickly, and we were playing so poorly that covers changed hands after virtually every shot. After half a dozen holes, we abandoned the game for good. At about the same time, I dropped my last dry towel into a puddle and stepped on it. I had been carefully hoarding that towel—the only dry one in our foursome—and had come to view it as a sort of lifeline. Now I no longer had a way to blot water out of my neoprene gloves, and I began to check my fingers for signs of frostbite.

Shortly after five o'clock, we drained our last four feeble putts and staggered into the nice, big bar in the clubhouse. Silently, we drank beer, ate potato chips, and stared at the two huge television sets, one of which was showing a tape of the 1992 U.S. Open, and the other of which was tuned to the Weather Channel. Obsessive viewing of the Weather Channel is the closest thing in Myrtle Beach to an organized religion. The guys at the bar were all gazing at the radar map and arguing about the significance of the shifting pattern of green and orange splotches, which signified rain. The forecast for the next day seemed to be better. Or maybe it wasn't.

Shortly afterward, we stowed our soggy equipment in the back of the Man Van and headed north again. We stopped for dinner at a Myrtle Beach institution called Dick's Last Resort, where we drank Big Ass Beers (from glasses so labeled) and ate buckets of fried and barbecued food. Dick's is a sort of human feedlot with long, greasy tables in it. Our waiter gave us matchbooks with pictures of naked women on them and promised us free drinks if we could figure out which one of the naked women was now a (fully clothed) waitress in the restaurant. Every few minutes, a quartet of weary golfers would stumble through the front door and ask for a table. (In Myrtle Beach, the basic social unit is not the couple or the family but the foursome. Every hour or so, at least one member of every foursome will grin smugly at his mates and say, "It just doesn't get any better than this," usually at a moment when the statement is obviously and even poignantly not true.) As we waited for our check, a tall man surrounded by half a dozen beautiful young women strolled into the bar. He wore a hat that looked like a condom. A golfer at the next table said, in a hushed voice, "That's Dick."

On our way home after dinner, we spotted a brightly illuminated after-dark executive golf course on the main drag. John and I wanted to stop for a few bonus holes under the halogen lights, but Jim and Mike were still emotionally distraught from our day at the Legends, and they insisted on returning to the Bates Motel. John and I dropped them off, then drove back downtown and stopped at Martin's, a massive golf-equipment store that's open till ten o'clock five nights a week. We bought Jim and Mike each two bags containing twenty-four sepia-colored used balls, for $4.95 a bag (Jim and Mike had each lost at least a couple of dozen balls that day). For myself, I bought a dozen new balls, several pairs of socks, a map of Myrtle Beach, and some tees. John and I tried out various putters. Then we went home.

Jim and Mike were semicomatose when we returned, but John and I still hadn't had quite enough golf, so we putted on the floor of our living room, then used nine-irons to hit nickels from the carpet into the heavy curtains covering the front window. John had learned this trick while staying in motels during various away matches with his golf team in college. If you keep your head fairly still, you can pick a coin cleanly off a rug that has a decent pile, and the big double curtains protect the windows. When we got tired of hitting money, we switched to balls and laid out a short but challenging course that wound through the three and a half rooms of our suite. We got into quite an analytical discussion concerning the difference between hitting off our beds and hitting off the couch, and whether it was better to putt or chip from the linoleum floor of the kitchenette onto the carpeted floor of the living room. All in all, we made only a few dark marks in the popcornlike acoustical finish on the ceilings, mostly with overenthusiastic follow-throughs.

Not every hotel or motel room is ideally suited to golf. In most rooms, there's a big window (with the requisite heavy curtains) at one end, a big bed or two on one side, and a bureau, desk, and so forth on the other side. If you are a right-handed golfer and the beds are on the left as you face the window, you have plenty of room to take a full swing without unduly damaging furniture. If the beds are on the right, however, you run the risk of smashing the TV at the top of your backswing. In such a room, a golfer is limited to putts, chips, and three-quarter knockdown shots. The wisest course is probably to specify the type of room you need when you make your reservation: "I'd like a nonsmoking single for a right-handed golfer, please." Of course, the ideal room also has a big mirror on the wall over the bureau, so that you can stand on your bed and check your takeaway from three different angles. The mattress makes any weight-shift errors instantly obvious, but only in the older, more luxurious hotels—those with high ceilings—is it possible to take a full swing while standing on the bed.

While John and I were playing, we were also drying our equipment. We had removed all our clubs from our bags and leaned them against the walls, so the grips could dry. I had Velcroed my five sopping golf gloves to a wire hanger and dangled them in front of the heater. We had already discovered that we could dry our shoes in about an hour by placing them upside down on top of the shades of our bedside lamps. When my gloves were dry, I draped my wet towel (which I had stepped on at the Legends and stuffed into the bottom of my bag) over the vents of the heater and promptly forgot about it. While John and I chipped from chair to couch, the towel slowly turned to the consistency of tree bark, while gradually humidifying and odorizing our room.

A world-class drunk can cheerfully hop out of bed without a trace of a hangover the morning after downing a couple of quarts of gin. Similarly, a Golf-Dependent Personality can cheerfully whistle while screwing new spikes into his golf shoes the morning after playing two rounds of dreary, life-threatening golf. Although all of us had suffered mightily in the wind and rain the previous day, all of us were smiling and eager to begin again when our alarms went off at five-thirty on the second morning. All of us, that is, except Mike, who kept us waiting for twenty minutes while he sulked in the bathroom, covering virtually his entire epidermis with Band-Aids. "Would you like some of my Advil?" asked my brother, who was playing with two broken ribs, the result of a skiing accident. "I don't need Advil," Mike said gloomily. "I need Prozac." Fortunately, the Weather Channel at that very moment was promising that the rain would not return.

Our first round of the day was at Marsh Harbour, a wonderful course that wanders among the salt marshes along the Intracoastal Waterway. Marsh Harbour was designed by Dan Maples and by Larry Young, who owns and built this course in addition to the Legends. The signature hole is the seventeenth, a lengthy par-five with intimidating carries over marsh for both the second and third shots. I managed to par that hole while my brother got a bogey— one of the few holes on which I bested him, despite his broken bones. Jim and Mike launched perhaps a dozen balls into various portions of the marsh before retiring glumly to their cart. (That morning, they had dumped their bags of used balls into the wire-mesh baskets on the back of their cart, and they dipped into these stores frequently, as though the baskets were bowls of peanuts.) The entire course was challenging and thought-provoking, and it

was full of photo opportunities. We saw several herons, a pair of
eaglelike birds called oslos, and a woodpecker the size of a ptero-
dactyl. Once again, the day began chilly and got cooler, but there
was no rain, and the intermittently bright sun provided the occasional illusion of warmth.

We played our second round, after a real and relatively unhurried
lunch, on the other side of the waterway, at a course called Ocean
Harbour. (Both courses straddle the border between the Carolinas,
making it possible to hit shots from one state to the other.) None of
us liked Ocean Harbour very much, even though the staff was
extremely solicitous. "If you have any trouble with this cart, let me
know and we'll get you another," a friendly attendant said as we set
out. Six holes later, we found out why he had been so friendly. The
cart stopped dead. Jim got out and pushed it for a while, trying to
reinspire it. Mike sat morosely in the seat, nursing blisters that made
it difficult for him to limp even from one greenside bunker to
another. Finally, we managed to flag down a ranger, and traded
carts with him. The ranger's cart had a jagged, ball-sized hole in the
middle of the windshield, but it moved along quite briskly.

The groups ahead of us for as far as we could see were playing
at the pace of weary tortoises, and darkness began to fall long
before we were finished. We played the fifteenth, a 140-yard par-
three, without being able to see the flag, but all miraculously hit the
green. By the time we reached the eighteenth, a par-four that is
edged along its entire right side by the Calabash River, we could see
nothing except the clubhouse lights. We fired all of Jim and Mike's
remaining balls out toward the fairway, hoping to find at least four
in play. We turned up six, and fired all of them toward what we
presumed to be the green. One of the shots was followed at a
suspect interval by the sound of crunching metal—the roof of a car
in the parking lot?—but we never saw any of those six balls again,
on the green or anywhere else.

That night, we ate dinner at a restaurant whose name, if memory
serves, was Homer Simpson's Calabash Deep-Fat Aortic Aneurysm.
The blue-roofed barn was brightly lit, and it was filled with senior
citizens plus a sprinkling of foursomes. Our waitress was young

and cute. Giving her our orders was as close as we had come so far to having any sort of sexual adventure in Myrtle Beach (no lap dancing for us). Jim, John, and I ordered the seafood special: lobster tail, fried shrimp, fried oysters, fried clams, fried scallops, fried "fish," a basket of hush puppies. Mike ordered something called, I believe, Hoof and Brine: a steak and various fried seafood items. John suddenly felt queasy and ate only one hush puppy, which, he said, instantly expanded to a size slightly greater than that of his stomach. We were all entitled to eat all we wanted at the seafood bar, which consisted mostly of teeny shrimp that appeared to have spent less time in the sea than in a can. We all left feeling ill, especially John. On the way back, we stopped at Revco (to buy Band-Aids, moleskin, and Advil) and at a fairly tony golf-equipment store (to buy more balls for Jim and Mike). Back at the Bates, we all went straight to bed—John and I didn't even putt—after our customary evening devotional with the Weather Channel. The forecast: sort of good.

We were all a little poky in the mornings, but none of us was slower than Mike. After the first night, Jim had set his alarm clock half an hour ahead, to trick Mike into thinking he had less time to gird himself for battle than he did. This ruse worked pretty well, and Mike never caught on. On the third morning, Mike told Jim that the mornings were his favorite part of the trip, an astonishing statement that Jim initially took to be a joke. But it turned out that Mike was serious. "I can't believe how cheerful and optimistic I feel each morning," he said, "given what the reality is."

The third day of our trip was Mike's tenth wedding anniversary. His wife had assured him that she didn't mind his being away on the big day, but a friend of his wife's had been appalled, and she had been trying to make trouble. As we drove to breakfast (with two pairs of damp golf shoes drying on the dashboard), we debated what to do. "Maybe we should call your wife's friend tonight and have it out with her," I suggested. Mike didn't think that was such a good idea. "I keep telling my wife that she ought to take a trip by herself sometime, too," Mike said, "but she never does it." He professed not to be bothered, but he was clearly brooding. We let the matter drop when we reached the Pearl.

The Pearl is a two-course complex in Calabash, North Carolina, not far from Marsh Harbour. There was quite a bit of frost on the greens and fairways when we arrived, but we were allowed to tee off at our scheduled time anyway. (I've always wondered about frost delays. Is there a scientific basis for them, or are they the golf equivalent of my mother's prohibition against swimming after a meal? At the Island, in Ireland, a member told me that, several years before, the club's trustees had decided to find out once and for all, by walking around on a frost-covered practice green. At the last moment, though, they had all chickened out.) We played Pearl East first. It's a decent layout, but at the time we played it, it was in very ragged condition. Many years had passed since the old golfing rituals of replacing divots and repairing ball marks had been observed. In the afternoon, after an unexplained sixty-minute delay, that had apparently been caused by overbooking, we played Pearl West, which was even rattier, beginning with the back nine. The group ahead of us—four hatless, beer-swilling hillbillies who had apparently taken up golf that morning—insisted on playing from the rearmost tees, from which the course measured more than seven thousand yards. They had their worst trouble immediately, at the tenth, a medium-sized par-four with a small pond directly in front of the tee. Although the carry to dry land was less than a hundred yards, the water constituted an insurmountable psychological barrier, and none of the hillbillies found the fairway. One sliced his ball so dramatically that it nearly returned to his feet, like a boomerang. Another hit a banana that made it over the water, though barely, and burrowed deep into the scrub, perhaps a hundred and twenty yards to the right of the fairway. He slashed through the undergrowth with a golf club and searched for his ball as intently as I would search for a lost child, though not in the right place. "He's looking too far to the left," John said. At that moment and for minutes following, the hole was essentially open; no member of the foursome was within a pitching wedge of the fairway. If we had had any sense, we would have teed off then, while all four golfers were distracted. But we didn't know what lay ahead.

When we reached the twelfth or thirteenth hole, all progress on the course ground to a halt. John said he had suspected we were in trouble when he noticed that no one in the foursome ahead of us was wearing a hat. One member of that group was playing the course twenty yards at a time: slice, duck hook, slice, duck hook, slice, duck hook. Looking off through the woods in another direction, we saw one tee that had seven or eight groups backed up on it—possibly the members of a Rotary outing, or the participants in a work-release program from some nearby penitentiary. In the woods alongside an adjoining fairway, four tubby slicers wandered aimlessly near their golf carts, waiting for the group ahead of them to advance so they could attempt to slice their balls back into play. They didn't even begin to look for their balls until the group ahead of them was out of sight. Each of them needed four or five shots just to reach the bend of the dogleg.

When two holes had opened up in front of the foursome ahead of us, we gestured impatiently in their direction, then sent an emissary forward to request permission to play through. Permission denied. The fattest member of the group, who was wearing either plus-fours or sweatpants pulled up to his knees, said that playing through was "not allowed" at the Pearl. We contemplated simply hitting our balls over their heads and then racing past them in our golf carts, but Mike said he wasn't certain he could carry the guy in the knickers. We ended up practicing our chipping, and waiting for the clot to move on.

The most memorable hole of the day for us was a par-five where Mike's scalded second shot traveled fifty yards at an altitude of two or three inches before striking two of my clubs, which I had left lying in the fairway near my ball. (Mike was moving so slowly by that point that the rest of us had taken to reconnoitering our own shots while he limped up to his.) Mike's ball cleanly severed the shaft of my seven-wood, while merely bending double the shaft of my five-wood. Pieces of both clubs glinted in the sunlight as they flew three feet into the air. Mike offered to split the cost of having them reshafted—a gesture that I considered insufficiently contrite and rejected out of hand. On the next hole, Mike hit a similar shot, which missed all of my equipment but struck Jim in the left instep. After that, we adjusted our pace to Mike's.

It was quite dark when we finished. We bought two six packs of Heineken in the clubhouse, put a can in every cup holder in the Man Van, and headed for Barefoot Landing, a sort of shopping center alongside the main drag. That night, we ate our first unfried meal, at a terrific Italian restaurant called Umberto's. The restaurant was busy, and we had to wait for half an hour in the bar. The owner dropped by to chat, and he made what I interpreted as a half-hearted attempt to hire us as waiters. The man-to-woman ratio in Umberto's, as in Myrtle Beach itself, was roughly twenty-five to three, including waitresses and a couple of women who might have been off-duty strippers. The food, however, was very good.

That night, we faced the strangely sad chore of packing. I used my unworn golf shirts to wrap my sodden socks, then gave my shoes a final drying on a lamp. Our room by that point had developed a dank sort of ambience that no amount of airing seemed to affect. I gave the grooves of my irons a final cleaning and putted for a while with John. And so to bed.

The morning of our fourth and final day in Myrtle Beach dawned beautiful and clear, though still a bit chilly. There was a thirty-minute frost delay at Carolina Shores, a forgettable course that had been added to our itinerary by the proprietor of the Bates Motel. John, Jim, and I hung around the pro shop, drinking coffee and worrying in a vague way that other foursomes were somehow going to get ahead of us. Mike stayed in the Man Van, alternately reading *USA Today* and snoozing. Our van was one of eight or nine parked in a row, and more vans arrived as we waited. At last, the frost was deemed to have melted, and we were allowed to tee off.

Carolina Shores had hundreds of sand traps and thousands of rakes, but no rakers. We devised a local rule that permitted us to rake the sand under any bunkered ball before hitting it. Mike had no sand wedge, and so made frequent use of Jim's. Shoulder-deep in one bunker, he swung mightily, causing the ball to bury itself deep in the earth's core and the lower half of the sand wedge to fly high in the air, landing near the pin, while the grip and a few inches of the shaft remained in his hands. Jim laughed heartily, then realized what had actually happened and shouted, "Hey, that was my club!"

Many of the fairways at Carolina Shores are closely flanked by rows of houses. The houses were so close that I was periodically tempted to slip inside one to check out the fridge or use the bathroom. Bathrooms were in my thoughts because there weren't many likely peeing spots on the course itself; the houses were so close that the only bushes tended to be in people's yards. In a philosophical moment, my brother said, "Maybe the reason women don't like golf is that it's so hard for them to go to the bathroom while they play." I thought about this for a moment, then said, "Maybe the reason there are so few bathrooms on golf courses is that women don't like to play without them."

Hoping to cram in as much golf as possible, we ran from the eighteenth green to the Man Van, and raced to Heather Glen Golf Links for our farewell round. Our haste turned out to be unnecessary. Heather Glen had had a two-and-a-half-hour frost delay that morning, and our tee times were meaningless. In an effort to secure special treatment, I more or less claimed to be the editor of *Golf Digest,* but the starter was unimpressed. We moped around the clubhouse, ate a leisurely lunch, practiced putting, and moped around some more. When we were finally allowed to tee off, at around three-thirty, we quickly calculated that we would still be able to make our six-thirty flight if we played no more than six holes and changed our clothes in the parking lot. I had taken the precaution of wearing a pair of nice pants underneath my now grubby golf pants, so I would merely have to peel off my outer layer in order to make myself presentable to the women from Aeroflot.

As it turned out, leaving Heather Glen was heartbreakingly difficult. Of all the courses we played, we liked it the best. It consists of three separate nines, which can be played in different combinations; we played just two-thirds of the second nine, but the course made a deep impression. The holes were varied and beautiful and stunningly maintained, and the effect was heightened by the splendor of the day. As we floored our carts back to the clubhouse after holing out on the sixth, we gazed longingly at the holes we had not reached. If we hadn't had wives, children, and jobs, we might have torn up our plane tickets and stayed.

We made it to the airport by five-fifteen. John said, "You know, I think we could have played two more holes." That idea plunged us both into lousy moods. Sitting in gloomy silence as we waited to board our plane, I had thoughts of a religious nature. Never before had I been able to understand the appeal of the monastic life. What could possibly cause a man to forsake the pleasures of the world and become a monk? Now, though, I understood. "Oh, I get it," I said to myself. "Monks feel about God the way I feel about golf." The two words are even almost spelled the same. I suddenly had a vision of a sort of ideal community of golfers: a golfing monastery, or golfastery. Men who worship golf living humbly with other men who worship golf. Simple food. Lots of putting practice. A big driving range with well-spaced target greens. Excellent video-taping facilities. Careful study of the rules. Pilgrimages to the great courses of the world. Beer making in the evenings.

Who wouldn't want to live like that?

8

PLAYING ON THE
PARTNERS TOUR

THE THIRTEENTH HOLE ON PETE DYE'S STADIUM COURSE at the Tournament Players Club at Sawgrass is a straightforward par-three that measures 150 yards from the blue trees. The hole is nowhere near as famous or as frightening as the island-green seventeenth, but it's a good, solid hole, with water both in front and on the left. Despite the dangers, I was briskly confident as I stepped up to the tee. The day before, during my practice round, I had chipped in from the fringe for a birdie, and I had birdied the following hole as well, and (because golf is an easy game) I had parred the hole after that. Now, waggling my eight-iron and visualizing a soaring draw, I glanced one last time at the flag and half-shanked my ball into the trees on the right.

"I'd better hit a provisional," I said, not feeling particularly concerned. I teed up another ball and, with a swing grooved through long and patient repetition, half-shanked it into the same stand of trees.

"I see the second ball," someone shouted. Five minutes of crawling through dense undergrowth failed to turn up the first. I crouched in a bush to survey my prospects. To put my second ball on the green, I calculated, I would need to hit a crisp thirty-yard smother-hooked four-iron through a window-sized gap in the branches, applying enough backspin to keep the ball from skidding off the green into low earth orbit. I declared the ball unplayable and returned to the tee. Taking a deep breath, I swung again. My third ball found the water on the left.

An eerie hush fell over my playing partners. I felt my consciousness rise slowly out of my body and gaze down, with ineffable pity, at my golf hat. I dropped a fourth ball at the front of the teeing area and, with my pitching wedge, yanked it safely onto the far left corner of the green, perhaps fifty feet from the pin. Three putts later, I had my ten.

From that point forward, my memories of my round are indistinct. I had been playing pretty well before my disaster, but I ended up with a 102, including double or triple bogeys on all the remaining holes except the celebrated seventeenth, on which I had a seven. (First ball into the water over the green; second ball into deep rough next to a piling at the rear of the green after bouncing hard and high off a piling at the front; chunky chip; three putts.) As I watched an official inscribe my score on the big board near the clubhouse, I wondered whether I ought not to give up golf altogether, for the good of the game.

The tournament in which I was playing was not, quite obviously, the Players Championship, which is held at the Stadium Course each spring. It was an amateur tournament conducted by the PGA Tour Partners, a sort of professional-golf fan club. You may have seen commercials for the Partners on TV: Jack Nicklaus explains that joining the Partners will enable the average hacker to help troubled youths, secure jobs for disabled people, provide specialized care for heart patients, and so forth. Members receive goodies of the bag-tag and window-sticker variety, along with a monthly magazine called *On Tour* and a chance to participate in a sort of betting pool based on the tour's money list. Curiously, the commercials don't mention the program's best feature, a schedule of amateur tournaments known as the Partners Tour. Several such tournaments are held each year, at some of the country's best courses, including Pebble Beach. The tournament in which I took part was one of two four-day events held at Sawgrass, near Ponte Vedre, Florida. For my $1,275 entrance fee—the price has since gone up—I got one practice round (on the Stadium Course), three tournament rounds (one on the Stadium Course, one on the adjacent Valley Course, and one at Jacksonville Country Club), unlimited extra golf on the Stadium and Valley courses, four nights at the Marriott at Sawgrass, three breakfasts, three lunches, two dinners, and a money clip made of goldium.

Unlike certain other mediocre golfers of my acquaintance, I do not seriously expect to be invited to join the Senior PGA Tour when I turn fifty, in 2005. But I do enjoy playing competitive golf. Tournaments force you to keep your mind on your game, and they inject some adrenaline into your swing. They also enable you to entertain Walter Mittyish fantasies. (Come to think of it, I *do* expect to be invited to join the Senior PGA Tour when I turn fifty.) To make the fantasizing easier, my fellow Partners and I were given lockers with our names on them in the TPC's inner locker room, which is ordinarily reserved for tour players and VIP members of the club. (Among these special people are the club's founding members, a bunch of local rich guys known as the Munchkins.) My locker was next to that of Deane Beman, who at the time was the commissioner of the PGA Tour. I didn't see Beman, but I did get a pretty good look at his shoe trees and a pair of his socks. One night when no one was around, I snuck into the very innermost locker room, which is reserved for Arnold Palmer, Jack Nicklaus, Ben Crenshaw, Fred Couples, and other winners of the Players Championship. My heart pounding, I tiptoed up the carpeted stairs. In the solemn hush of the sanctum sanctorum, I saw a guy vacuuming the rug.

Sawgrass seemed a far cry from the first competitive golf event I ever played in, a weekend scramble at my local club. In a scramble, every player on a given team tees off, then every player plays his second shot from the team's best drive, then every player plays his third shot from the team's best second shot, and so on, until the ball is holed out. This scramble was held toward the end of my first summer as a born-again golfer—the first time I felt confident enough to go public with my feeble, untutored slice. My handicap at the time, twenty-five, was the highest on our five-man team. In the interests of squaring things up somewhat and keeping the bad players interested, the pro had decided that the A and B players would play from the farthest tees, the C and D players would play from the regular men's tees, and the E players—among them, me—would play from the ladies' tees. Our team's first hole was a par-five with a difficult tee shot, over a pond. The shot was especially difficult for the A through D players, who had to shoot down through a claustrophobic tunnel of trees. While they trudged up the hill to hit their drives, I sat on my bag on the ladies' tee and waited. A few minutes later, a ball splashed into the pond. Then another. Then I saw a ball soar over my head and over the pond and into thick rough on a scrubby hill, far to the right of the fairway. Then I saw the fourth ball land near some trees to the left of the fairway. Four bad shots.

It was my turn to hit. I teed my ball quickly so I could play my shot while my teammates were still out of sight. The ladies' tee was situated on the near shore of the pond, 140 yards ahead of the farthest men's tees. If I could somehow manage to propel my ball just fifty yards straight ahead, I would clear the water and reach the fairway and have the longest drive of the team.

Saying a silent prayer, I took my usual over-the-top flail with my five-wood (the longest club I dared to swing in those days) and hit my usual 170-yard slice. In and of itself, this shot was dreadful; under the circumstances, it was breathtakingly brilliant. My ball ended up in the fairway some 310 yards from the farthest tees. When my teammates trudged down from the hill and saw what I had done, they slapped me on the back and made numerous flattering comments. Buoyed by their approval, I swung from then on without fear. We ended up using my drive on fourteen of the eighteen holes.

Since then, I have played in many competitions. I have sometimes played well, and often played poorly, and mostly played somewhere in between. No matter how well or poorly I have played, I have always had fun, and I have come to view competitive golf as the best part of the game. Indeed, there are times when I view it as the best part of life—excluding religious visions, stuff with my kids, and so on. The combination of anxiety, adrenaline, terror, confidence, despair, and exhilaration is hard to match in ordinary existence—at least in my ordinary existence, which so far has been, well, pretty ordinary. A good golf match turns up the amperage in your nervous system in an interesting way. Like roller coasters or caffeine, it temporarily boosts you to an elevated plane of experience.

I would now like to describe in minute detail every great shot that I have ever hit in competition—every drive, every gorgeous drawing six-iron, every pitch shot, every twelve-foot birdie putt. That's what I would like to do. Instead, after talking things over with my editor, I have decided to describe only a small handful of particularly memorable playing experiences—some good, some bad—that have at least a remote bearing on my narrative. Will these experiences be as fascinating to the reader as they are to me? The reader must be the judge. Still, I personally find them so compelling that I don't see why a disinterested but thoughtful outsider shouldn't be spellbound as well. Here they are:

• The first serious head-to-head match I ever played was in the chump flight of my club's men's championship a few years ago. In the first round I was paired with a guy who was approximately my father's age. My handicap at the time (fourteen) was four strokes lower than his, but this was a championship tournament, so we were playing even—a significant advantage for me. I was a brilliant overachiever on the front nine, shooting a thirty-seven that included birdies on the fourth and fifth holes. "How ya doin'?" the assistant pro asked when we made the turn. "I'm two over and four up," I whispered, winking, not wanting to rub my score in my opponent's face. As the assistant pro looked on, I took a nice, easy swing on the tenth tee and sliced my ball into the woods. I didn't feel any different—at least, I didn't think I did—but all of a sudden I couldn't find my game. I lost one hole, then another. Everything seemed to go wrong. To make matters worse, I began to worry about how humiliated I would feel if I somehow managed to lose my match after being four holes ahead. People would say that I had choked, and that thought constricted my breathing and shortened my backswing. With considerable help from me, my opponent managed to claw his way back to all square after eighteen.

At that point, the pressure began to affect him as well. On our nineteenth hole, a teeny par-four, we both took four strokes to reach the green. "I'll tell you one thing," my opponent said, "whichever one of us wins this match doesn't deserve it." I got a seven, and he got a six. I had followed my thirty-seven with a forty-eight—playing exactly to my handicap, incidentally—and I had had my first experience of the competitive gag reflex.

Lesson: Holding a big lead in a golf match can be a terrifying experience. The key is to remain patient, stick to one's game plan, and play one hole at a time. Conversely, a player facing a big deficit should not necessarily despair. Even the pros sometimes tremble when they have a lead that looks too big to lose.

• A year later, in the final round of an annual two-day match between my club and a neighboring one—a tournament that some people consider to be the Ryder Cup of southwestern Litchfield County—I was one-up when my match reached the eighteenth tee. I pushed my drive a bit; my opponent pulled his. As I surveyed my second shot, I happened to glance up at the clubhouse, where I saw that several hundred people were crowded onto the porch and looking back at me. No, wait, it was only about a dozen people, and most of them were drinking beers and looking the other way. Still, I had an audience. I didn't know it at the time, but my match was crucial. If I won or tied, we would win the competition; if I lost, we wouldn't. Because I was one-up, I could do no worse than tie, but I didn't know how things stood. I sensed that my match was important, and I very much wanted to win. My opponent was away; he topped his shot, and it dribbled about twenty yards. Figuring that I could now halve the hole with a five (and in doing so win my match),

I decided to play my own approach shot conservatively, to the left of the green, away from a yawning bunker. My heart pounding in my throat, I managed to do this more or less successfully. We both ended up with bogeys, meaning that I had won. As I strode up the clubhouse steps to accept a beer from my ebullient teammates, I felt just about as good as I have ever felt.

Lesson: Don't take a long-odds stab at a birdie if a bogey will win you the match. There's nothing wrong with a three-putt if a four-putt would have given you a tie.

- In the first round of a handicapped tournament at the larger of the two clubs I belong to, I played a guy whose handicap was about the same as mine. On the first hole, a par-five, I hit a good drive up the middle, and he hit a bad one into the right rough. Then I hit a very long second shot up the right side, and he hit a mediocre one in the same direction. As we walked up the fairway, I felt great. He was away. He hit a decent nine-iron onto the green, in two-putt range. My ball was thirty yards farther ahead, and I had a perfect line to the pin. I'll nail this to the stick and tap in for my birdie, I thought as I strolled along. When I got to my ball, though, I saw to my horror that it was lying in a deep divot hole. The easy pitch I had been envisioning was no longer possible. I managed to get my ball onto the green—by slamming my lob wedge steeply into the dirt behind it—but I was above the pin and far away, and in my agitation I plowed my first putt roughly twenty feet past the hole, then left the come-backer six feet short. My opponent made his par, and I never got back on my feet. I lost the next two holes to pars, then halved the fourth by missing an easy putt. My confidence was in tatters, and so was my putting stroke. If my second shot on the first hole had ended up in a decent lie, I think I would have gone on to win the match, but as it was I lost, three and two. My entire mental outlook had turned 180 degrees in a fraction of a second. I never got my bearings back. I knew that I was a jerk.

  Lesson: Have a lobotomy.

- In a nine-hole mixed foursome at my local club, I played with a friend whose handicap is forty. (In a mixed foursome, each team consists of a man and a woman, who alternate hitting the shots. In this tournament, as in most mixed foursomes, both teammates hit from each tee, then chose one of the balls to play from there.) Through some miraculous dispensation from the golfing gods, my partner and I managed to par each of the first five holes. Sometimes we used her drive, sometimes we used mine. We both putted well. On the sixth, a longish par-four with a tricky green, we chose her drive. I hit my seven-wood to about twelve feet from the pin, but just to the right of the green, in some thick rough near the lip of a bunker. She bladed her chip, and I flubbed the next one, and we ended up with a double-bogey. But then we parred the next two holes, and I chipped in for a birdie on the ninth. Our gross score (without handicap) was thirty-six, or one over par; our net score was twenty-three. We won gross by seven strokes and net by ten, and the pro said that he couldn't remember anyone ever coming close to either number in all the years the tournament had been played. Tantalizingly, if my second shot on six had ended up two feet farther to the left, our gross score might very well have been one or two under par—an unheard-of score for players with our handicaps. It was the most otherworldly nine holes I have ever had anything to do with. It was the luckiest I have ever felt for two hours at a stretch.

Lesson: When you have a lucky day, enjoy it. When you have a lucky opponent, forget it. In either case, don't take it personally.

- In a recent men's championship at my local club, my friend Art caddied for my friend Jim in the third-flight final. Jim's opponent in that final match was a guy I'll call Herbie. When Jim and Herbie ran into each other at the driving range before their match, Herbie said, "Why is Art here?" Jim said, "He's my caddy." Herbie said, "You can't have a caddy. It isn't fair." Jim said, "What do you mean I can't have a caddy? This is golf." Herbie demanded a ruling from the tournament chairman, who said, "Of course he can have a caddy. This is golf." Herbie became extremely agitated and said he thought the whole thing was a travesty and Jim should have warned him the night before that he was going to have a caddy. On the first tee, as Herbie set up to his ball, he snapped at Jim, "Tell your caddy not to look at me while I swing." Art turned his back. Herbie sliced his ball into the woods. While Jim and Herbie went into the woods to look for Herbie's ball, Art walked up the center of the fairway. "I can't help you look," he hollered good-naturedly, "because I didn't see the shot." Jim closed out the match with many holes left to play, and Herbie still grumbles about the time he had to play the guy who had a caddy.

Lesson: Watch enough golf on TV to understand how the game is played.

I could go on like this for pages and pages, of course; any golfer could. Maybe the thing to do is post this stuff on the Internet. You could rush home from a great round and download adjective-filled descriptions of all your wonderful shots. I personally wouldn't be interested in reading anyone else's messages, but I would very much enjoy sending my own.

My point, at any rate, is that competitive golf is nearly as different from ordinary golf as ordinary golf is from bowling. It is golf on a higher plane, and it can be learned only through experience. Playing on the Partner's Tour was one of my first real lessons in the dark side of competitive golf. I looked into my golfing soul, and I didn't necessarily like what I saw.

There were surprisingly many women at the opening cocktail party at Sawgrass. Partners tournaments are not restricted to men—the long-drive contest at a recent one was won by the mother of touring pro Robert Gamez—but no women had signed up to play in our event. The women present were the wives and girlfriends of participants. At the cocktail party, these women looked astonishingly cheerful, considering that the conversation consisted solely of stroke-by-stroke recountings of memorable recent rounds. There were a few tense moments. As we were eating dessert, a man at my table said bitterly, "At one time, I owned more than five hundred golf shirts. But one day when I was out of town, my wife took a hundred and fifty of them and gave them . . ." here he paused for dramatic effect ". . . *to the poor.*"

While the men played golf, most of the women hung out by the pool, explored the Ponte Vedre area, or watched TV. A few accompanied their husbands on the course. One of these was Anne, the wife of a man named Sy who was paired with me during my practice round. Anne had never been on a golf course before, and she was fascinated by everything she saw. "*How* do you make the ball curve like that?" she marveled at one point, after Sy had just hit his customary screaming banana into a waste area far to the right of the fairway. Sy could only smile weakly and shrug. I said, "It comes from years and years of taking lessons, and never doing anything the pro tells you to do." Anne also enjoyed driving the cart.

The following morning—the first day of the real competition—it was almost unbelievably hot, as might be expected of Florida in June. (Ponte Vedre is just far enough north to have seasons, sort of; they count it as a white Christmas if there's a frost delay on December 25.) The weather didn't bother one of my playing partners, a salesman from Chicago named Ron. "Ever since Vietnam, I haven't been able to get warm enough," he said as we waited to tee off. Ron's handicap was eighteen. He wore very short shorts, and he had a little gizmo with a grip on it that swung around to loosen up his muscles. Encouragingly—though futilely, it turned out—I began with a par.

Tour players hated the Stadium Course when it opened, in 1980. They had loved the Sawgrass Country Club, across the street, where the predecessor of the Players Championship had been played for many years, and they hated Pete Dye's greens, which were terrifyingly contoured. Dye was eventually prevailed upon to skim off the scarier humps, and most of the pros now like the place. Thanks in part to the quality of the course, the Players Championship has produced some great contests over the years, and it now attracts a heady multinational field that is commonly referred to as the best in professional golf. In fact, the Players Championship is sometimes called the fifth major, after the Masters, the U.S. Open, the British

Open, and the PGA. Both the course and the tournament have long been popular with fans, fifty thousand of whom can sit comfortably on the strategically situated grassy berms that give the course its name. The seventeenth is one of the best-known golf holes in the world, and there are few golfers who don't yearn to test their nerve against it—even if they think an island green is a gimmick. Incidentally, the seventeenth green was not an island in Dye's original design. It began as a nubby peninsula flanked by a small lake, which grew inexorably during construction as more and more underlying sand was removed for use elsewhere on the course.

Deane Beman, who was the tour's commissioner at the time, conceived of the Stadium Course as a sort of home course for the PGA Tour. The tour's headquarters are on the property—a 415-acre tract that was purchased from a local developer for a dollar—and there are plans for a golf museum. Strategically situated near the course is a pyramid-shaped clubhouse, which has terrific views of several holes and of Ponte Vedre's stunning sunsets. The Players Championship is a great tournament, and the Stadium Course is one of the best courses in the country that just anybody can play. (It's one of a very few more-or-less public courses in *Golf Digest*'s 100 Greatest ranking.)

I played poorly in the first round, so I was demoted to the old-guy flight for the second round, which we played at TPC's Valley Course. The Valley Course, which is adjacent to the Stadium Course, is very different from the Stadium Course—it was designed by Dye and Bobby Weed—but it's still a good, challenging course. (The NAIA championship had been played there two days earlier.) I was grouped with an old guy from Texas named John, an old guy from South Carolina named Glen, and a regular guy from Florida named Gerry. Like me, Gerry had had a terrible round the day before. (A seven-handicap, he had shot a ninety-five.)

I started out quadruple bogey, double bogey, double bogey—a string of trouble that began when I decided to hit a big tee shot in front of Holly, a nice woman from the Tour office who was sitting at a table by the first tee. This triple disaster was doubly annoying because, the evening before, I had parred all three holes in a quick nine-hole practice round with a fellow competitor and a photographer from *Golf Digest*.

One thing that makes me nervous on a golf course is wondering when disaster is going to strike. Once disaster has actually struck, I often feel a sense of relief: Now I know. Finding myself eight over par after three holes, I gave up hope, settled down, and began to make pars. I eased up on my swing, and my shots became longer and straighter. I no longer cared so much about my putts, and they began to drop. I even made a couple of birdies. Part of the credit belongs to my playing partners. John (whose golf shirt had a picture of an oil derrick on it) and Glen made flattering noises every time Gerry or I hit a ball more than 150 yards. Under their benevolent, calming gaze on one hole, I unwound a mighty two-wood—my fraidy-cat driver—for what turned out to be the longest drive of the day. Gerry played well, too. Meanwhile, John and Glen gave each other shortish putts and provided a steady stream of cracker dialogue:

"The way I'm playing, I got no business being on a golf course. I ought to be in an insane asylum instead."

"There's people in there for less."

"Yeah, but they're short-term."

"Say, this Coca-Cola is gooder than snuff."

On one hole, John bladed a chip far past the hole, to the most distant corner of the green, and Glen asked, "You got family back there?"

After shooting eight over on the first three holes, I shot just four over on the remaining fifteen, giving me a very respectable score of eighty-four. Gerry did even better, with an eighty-one. Substituting my three opening pars from the day before would have given me a seventy-six.

After we finished our round, I went out to play again. I was joined by Rich, a divorced pharmacist from Georgia, and Gust, a low-handicap employee of the Tour. This was Rich's fifth Partners tournament. He had been in my group during the practice round, his handicap was about the same as mine, and we had taken to hanging around together. Playing with Gust, we developed a theory of the golf swing whose central premise is that the difference between a slice and a draw is a certain number of beers. The Beer Draw Hypothesis—as we came to call it—is based on the well-known fact that tension in the arm muscles ruins golf swings, most often promoting a slice. Almost anything that causes a golfer to squeeze his club harder will harm his game; conversely, almost anything that causes a golfer to ease up on his death grip will improve his accuracy and length. Hence, beer. A moderate infusion of alcohol can have the same effect on the muscles of golfers that it is said to have on the inhibitions of attractive strangers in bars. This is why golfers sometimes refer to alcoholic beverages as "swing oil"—yet another instance in which an ancient folk remedy has been proven by modern scientists to be medically valid.

As scientists, Rich and I were interested in determining the exact level of intoxication required to cause our tee shots to move consistently from right to left. As is well known, excessive consumption of alcohol can be every bit as bad for one's game as clenched biceps are. A golfer who is too loose tends to hit a mixture of big hooks, big slices, and impotent sky balls, and he may also fall over while lining up putts. This is why company golf outings have such a bad reputation. Furthermore, golfers who have eliminated too much tension from their golf swings will sometimes drive their carts right onto the greens. How can a golfer secure for himself the maximum advantages of the beer draw without making it hard for everyone else to putt?

After careful study and much learned debate, Rich and I concluded that the ideal swing-oil dosage is one and a half beers, or the equivalent, administered fifteen minutes before teeing off and then carefully maintained throughout the round. Not surprisingly, it is the maintenance that poses the difficulty. A golfer who has drunk one and a half beers before teeing off is seldom willing to wait until reaching, say, the third hole before taking another swig. Ideally, of course, the beer would be administered steadily and intravenously, perhaps under the supervision of a registered nurse also serving as a caddy. In the real world, though, the average golfer is forced to rely on his own sense of restraint, which the very treatment has a well-known tendency to impair.

Given recent advances in psychopharmacology, reliance on beer to encourage an inside-to-outside club path may seem comically old-fashioned. My question, in brief, was: "Would Prozac make me a better putter?" Rich, though trained as a pharmacist, said he felt unqualified to answer: The necessary research simply has not been done. But the new generation of antidepressant drugs would seem to offer tantalizing possibilities for golfers. Nervousness and obsessive fear of failure are among the principal enemies of smooth putting strokes. Mightn't Prozac help? Curiously, my own physician later declined to write me a prescription, saying that a tendency to jab at the ball under pressure was not among Prozac's published indications. Needless to say, he is not a golfer.

Of course, beer and Prozac are mere palliatives. The real problem is that human evolution over the last few million years has followed a course that is decidedly inimical to golf. Neurologically speaking, the human brain is way too big. All those folds and creases and networks of neurons are a hopelessly fertile breeding ground for golfing disasters. The ideal golfing brain would be mostly spinal cord, probably about the size of a clenched fist. There would be enough synapses to enable you to move your putter back on line but not enough to leave you torn between a hard six and a smooth five. An added bonus: Play would move faster, because there would be no distracting conversation.

Intoxicated not only by Budweiser but also by the thrill of scientific inquiry, Rich, Gust, and I played skins. After a few holes, the sky suddenly opened, and it rained hard for several minutes—the sort of storm that ends just as soon as you've struggled into your rainsuit and opened your umbrella. With characteristic poor timing, I shot a thirty-eight, my best nine holes of the week. Gust was one shot worse but still managed to win virtually all the skins. Rich had a forty-one. Rich and I wanted to play a second nine, but Gust said he felt uncomfortable on a golf course when it was too dark to make out his shoes while standing over his ball.

We played our final round the next day, at Jacksonville Country Club, a course I didn't like very much. On every hole, it seemed, there was water to the right, out-of-bounds to the left, a ravine in front, and (just behind you) a fat guy in bathing trunks hosing down his patio and smoking a cigar while you teed off. New houses were being built at a furious pace alongside nearly every fairway, so that you had to be careful to swing between hammer blows. One of my playing partners actually hit a ball into one of the new houses; there were no boundary markers near the construction site, so he climbed through the rough opening for a picture window and hit it back out again. I began more or less as I had begun the day before, with an eleven on our first hole, a par-five—once again steadying my nerves by beginning with an insurmountable disaster.

To make matters worse, the day was supernaturally hot. Before the round, virtually everyone had congregated in the pro shop, which was air-conditioned, and pretended to be deeply interested in buying shirts. Out on the course, we drove fast and aimlessly in our golf carts, trying to generate breeze. (My playing partner warned me not to let one foot dangle out of the cart, as I am accustomed to doing, saying that an acquaintance of his had once hit a railroad tie while doing the same thing and had wrenched off his foot at the ankle.) I drank water and Gatorade almost constantly, but never had to pee. The Texans and Vietnam veterans looked reasonably comfortable, but most of the rest of us were miserable. My opening sextuple-bogey didn't help.

After the round, Rich and I raced back to the TPC and commandeered a cart and a cooler. We wanted one last dose of the Stadium Course before that evening's awards banquet. At the thirteenth, the site of my septuple-bogey during the opening round, I naturally hit my tee shot to seven feet, then stroked the putt into the back of the cup for a two. At the sixteenth we ran into one of the locker room attendants, who was practicing. ("*Playing* by yourself is too easy," he explained.) The three of us played the seventeenth from the pro tees, from which it measures 132 yards. The hole looks shorter in person than it does on television, but the green, when you stand on it, seems horrifyingly smaller. I pulled my first ball into the water on the left. I pushed my second ball, but it landed on the front right of the green, where they put the pin on Sunday. Unfortunately, the pin was way over to the left, where they put it on Thursday. The locker-room attendant told us that every year scuba divers retrieve more than 200,000 balls from the lake, which is patrolled by alligators.

An even bigger peril on the Stadium Course is the St. Augustine grass that grows alongside a number of the holes. This is a thick, vinyl-like ground cover that digests golf balls, like something from an old *Star Trek* episode. During the first round, one of my playing partners slightly pulled his approach shot, and his ball disappeared into the side of a mound that was covered with the stuff. We all saw the ball land, and we all knew exactly where it was within a radius of a foot or so, but for several minutes we couldn't find it. Finally, I searched the little plot inch by inch, carefully pressing my hands into the rubbery grass until I detected a small, hard lump under one thumb. Digging down among the roots with our fingers, we finally caught a glimpse of the top of a ball, and the golfer it belonged to took an unplayable lie.

Rich and I got back to the clubhouse just in time for the awards dinner. I won an attaché case with a PGA Tour logo on it for my long drive on the second day, and a sleeve of balls for playing more rounds than anybody else. Ron, the Vietnam veteran from Chicago, and Sy, whose wife had been bowled over by his slice, tied for low net, and won Waterford crystal trophies. When the banquet was over, about fifteen of us moved over to the bar at the Marriott, where we carried on until three in the morning, ultimately deciding that we would all travel to Scotland together, taking both the bartenders with us.

I now correspond semiregularly with Rich, my fellow beerologist. Not long ago, he sent me a visor and a score card from Pebble Beach, where he had just earned his sixth Partners money clip. I was almost terminally jealous when I opened the package and saw what was inside. If I had enough money and could figure out something to do with my wife and kids, I might join the Partners Tour full-time myself.

9

A COUNTRY FOR OLD MEN

COREY PAVIN STRUCK THE FIRST SHOT IN THE 1993 RYDER Cup matches. When his name was called, his hands were trembling so much that he had trouble getting his ball to sit on its tee. Paul Azinger couldn't eat his breakfast and was afraid that he was going to be sick. Davis Love III carried a bottle of drinking water in his golf bag, because anxiety had made the inside of his mouth as dry as a sock. The Ryder Cup's effect on the nerves of its competitors is so legendary that golfers begin to worry long before there's anything to worry about. As Lee Janzen walked off the final green of the 1993 United States Open, which he had just won in a stirring display of nerves and concentration, his attention shifted three months into the future. "I thought to myself, 'If there's any more pressure than this at the Ryder Cup, I might be in trouble.' "

The pressure of the Ryder Cup—which is contested every other year by teams of a dozen golfers from the United States and Europe, and which in 1993 was held at the Belfry, in Sutton Coldfield, England—has several sources. One is the format. The Ryder Cup is one of the last remaining match-play tournaments in professional golf. The players play not for an overall score but head-to-head, one hole at a time. Match play has its own psychology, and it requires its own kind of cunning. The best match players have an ability to get inside the heads of their opponents and turn their weaknesses against them. In stroke play you play the course; in match play you play the guy walking beside you, and you play him not only with your golf clubs but also with your wits.

A second source of pressure in the Ryder Cup is that the players are not competing primarily for themselves. (Nor are they competing for money. Each player receives an enormous golf bag, some swell clothes, and a few thousand dollars for expenses, but there is no purse.) To blow a lead in the Masters is devastating, but the disappointment is contained. To blow a crucial match in the Ryder Cup, in contrast, is to let down not only oneself but also one's teammates, one's country, and even, in the case of Europe, one's land mass. When Mark Calcavecchia failed to beat Colin Montgomerie in his 1991 Ryder Cup singles match after being four holes up with four holes to play—a situation in which a single tied hole would have given him a victory—he was so shaken that his career seemed to disintegrate. That same year, the outcome was not decided until the final putt on the final hole of the final match, between Hale Irwin of the United States and Bernhard Langer of Germany. On the eighteenth green, Langer missed a six-footer that would have beaten Irwin and retained the cup for Europe, which had held it since 1985. The consensus among golfers since then has been that Langer's putt, given the circumstances, was literally impossible. "No player should ever have to shoulder such pressure," said Langer's teammate Seve Ballesteros. "No one could have holed that putt."

The closeness and excitement of recent Ryder Cup matches has helped to create a third source of pressure: the overwhelming level of interest among golf fans. As Irwin and Langer walked up the final fairway in 1991, thousands of roaring spectators closed in behind them, and Irwin found that he could scarcely breathe. At the Belfry in 1993, every hole was surrounded from tee to green, often by fans standing five and six deep. At the end of each section of the competition, when there were only one or two matches remaining on the

course, the crowds became so dense that those fans standing nearest the ropes were unable to move, and those standing farthest
away could do no more than try to interpret the cheers, roars, and
groans.

For all the hooplah and commotion, though, the greatest source
of pressure in Ryder Cup competition comes from the players themselves. Increasingly, the biennial match has become the forum in
which American and European golfers at the highest level measure
themselves both against one another and against the game's immortals. On the final day, nearly every match has the potential to turn
into one of the defining confrontations of the sport. To play in the
Ryder Cup is to play for "a place in the history books," in the words
of Tom Watson, the 1993 American captain. The best competitors
feed on the pressure and use it to elevate their play to a level
beyond that even of the final pairings in most major tournaments.
As a result, the Ryder Cup is in some ways the most private of golf
tournaments. A spectator is reminded again and again of how small
and feeble his own game is, and how unearthly the great pros can
be when they are truly inspired. There is nothing for the humbled
fan to do except wave his little flag and try to stay out of the way.

Like many Americans bound for the Ryder Cup, I flew to England
early so that I could squeeze in a little golf myself. Sutton Coldfield
is a suburb of Birmingham, one of the least prepossessing cities in
the British Isles. I drove past it as fast as I could, heading straight for
Liverpool, which lies a couple of hours to the north and is a good
jumping-off place for some of the best golf in England. Beginning
just west of the city and working north, one finds the Royal Liverpool Golf Club, better known as Hoylake; the Formby Golf Club,
which lies perhaps forty-five minutes to the north; Royal Birkdale,
which is just twenty minutes north of Formby; the Southport and
Ainsdale Golf Club, which is virtually next door to Birkdale; and
Royal Lytham and St. Annes, another hour up the coast. Hoylake,
Birkdale, and Lytham between them have hosted twenty-five British Opens; Southport, Birkdale, and Lytham have hosted the Ryder
Cup two times each. You could play in the vicinity of Liverpool for

a couple of weeks without either stooping very low or repeating yourself. And if you somehow got tired of England, you could take the car ferry to Northern Ireland and squeeze in a few rounds at Royal Belfast, Royal Portrush, and Royal County Down.

I played Formby, Hoylake, and Lytham. (I had also hoped to play Birkdale, but a number of its greens were undergoing major surgery, so I skipped it.) All three are links courses, although the sea is not much in evidence at Formby and not at all at Lytham, which is enclosed entirely by the town. I began at Formby. It is a very good course—the British Amateur has been played there three times, most recently in 1984—but it is not especially frightening, at least when the wind isn't blowing hard. I played it twice, and loved it. The course begins mundanely, with a flat, straight first hole that is reminiscent of the first at Royal Dublin, but after a few holes it heads off into dunes and pine trees, which isolate the holes from one another and make golfers feel that they have wandered many miles from the clubhouse by the time they make the turn. From the tee of the tenth, a windswept over-two-hundred-yard par-three, you can see the remains of three holes that were abandoned when the members got tired of shoveling the beach off the greens. I played two rounds and had the course almost entirely to myself. The conditions were exactly opposite those of a Ryder Cup match. With no one watching and nothing at stake, I swung smoothly, hit far, and never had a three-putt. If I could always play by myself and phone in my scores, there's no telling what I could accomplish.

The next day I headed south, to Hoylake. On the way there, I drove through the docklands of Liverpool. Down-at-heels for decades, the once-great seaport has lately been undergoing something of a renaissance. I passed several enormous old warehouses that either had been or were being transformed into luxury apartment buildings. I passed the Liver Hotel. Then I took a tunnel under the Mersey and made my way to the charming suburb of Hoylake. The club is just off the main road. The pro shop and the courtyard outside it were thickly populated by American tourists killing time before the Ryder Cup. Like most of my countrymen, I entertained myself by buying things. After a wait of about an hour, I teed off with two nice women from New Jersey.

"At Hoylake," Bernard Darwin wrote in *Golf Courses of the British Isles,* "the golfing pilgrim is emphatically on classic ground." It is the second oldest seaside course in England, having been founded, as a scrappy nine-holer, in 1869, five years after the founding of Westward Ho! The British Amateur championship was born there, in 1885. The gutta-percha ball died one of its several deaths there, in 1902, when Alex Herd won the Open with a rubber-cored ball. And the first organized tournament between British and American amateurs was played there, in 1921. That competition led directly, in 1922, to the founding of the Walker Cup, and helped to inspire the founding, five years later, of its professional equivalent, the Ryder Cup. Like the Old Course at St. Andrews, Hoylake looks placid but runs deep.

I got off to a great start at Hoylake, with a par on the difficult first hole—a dogleg that curves tightly to the right around the practice area, which is surrounded by a low, grassy bank and is out of bounds—but then reverted to form. One of my playing partners was a travel agent. She had organized a Ryder Cup trip for four clients, who were playing one hole ahead of us, and their plans had sounded like so much fun that she had decided to tag along and bring a friend. Her caddy was a member of a group of local trades-men who had long ago been granted limited memberships in the club in exchange for doing things like carrying golf bags and paint-ing fences. He pointed out his group's clubhouse, a low green shed at the far end of a field in a distant corner of the course. Many years ago, he said, the tradesmen's group had had 250 members; now its roster had been cut back to 30, to make room for more dues-paying regular members. He knew every twist and bump of the course, and he got my swing more or less back on track at one point by gently asking, "Have you ever heard of the expression 'low and slow'?"

That night I stayed in a nice hotel in Southport, a little over an hour to the north. Southport would make a good base camp for a golfing expedition, because it is situated near the midpoint of the region's imposing chain of eminent courses. It has a broad main drag lined with shops and restaurants, and, one block to the west, an attractive seaside promenade. I didn't see much else, because I arrived after dark and left shortly after dawn, bound for Lytham.

The Royal Lytham and St. Annes Golf Club is hard to find, both because the town closely surrounds it and because it is not announced by any sign. I found it only after receiving cryptic directions from a man at a Texaco station, and I might have missed it still if I hadn't happened to glimpse a golf bag lying near an unmarked building that I had taken for a school. Lytham is hard to find, I suspect, because its members are not eager to share it. It's one of the truly great competitive courses in the world, with a treacherous back nine that makes for gripping tournament finishes. The course also has an unnerving beginning. The first hole is a 206-yard par-three whose undulating green is surrounded by bunkers.

I played with an American businessman and his adult son. The son got into virtually every one of the course's two hundred bunkers and had enormous difficulty getting out. Our caddies privately fretted about this, at first individually and then together. Finally, one of them could bear it no longer and approached the father. In a tone of polite alarm he said, "Begging your pardon, sir. The gentleman is not opening the blade of his sand iron."

Lytham first hosted the British Open in 1926. The winner was Bobby Jones, who had decided to play only at the last minute and had then qualified with a round, at Sunningdale, that at the time was viewed as virtually untoppable: He shot thirty-three on the front and thirty-three on the back, took thirty-three swings, and had thirty-three putts. There were no twos or fives on his card, and he was on every green but one in regulation or better. In the Open itself, his game was a bit more earthly, but he still played well enough to win. The crucial hole on the final day was the seventeenth, a longish, left-turning par-four whose entire left side is pressed by bunkers, bushes, and scrub. The farther you hit the ball from the tee, the narrower the landing area becomes; the only safe play is well to the right. Jones's playing partner was a fellow American, Al Watrous, who had begun the day leading by two strokes but by now had fallen even with Jones. Watrous hit a perfect drive up the right side; Jones hooked his drive into the sand on the left, a position from which he could not see the pin. Watrous hit a mashie to the edge of the green. Jones's situation appeared to be hopeless, but he calmly took his own mashie and, from a hundred and seventy yards or so, put his ball well inside Watrous's. "There goes a hundred thousand bucks," Watrous is supposed to have said at the time. Unhinged by Jones's shot, he took three putts to get down, while Jones made his par. Watrous then put his final drive into a fairway bunker and was as good as done for. Jones ended up winning by two strokes. Today there is a plaque near the spot on seventeen from which he made his heart-stopping shot to the green.

In my own round at Lytham, I serendipitously managed to replicate all of the crucial bad shots of both players on those final two holes. Like Jones, I hooked my drive on the seventeenth, ending up in the sandy scrub not far from the plaque. Then, like Watrous, I hit a five-iron (the approximate modern equivalent of a mashie) to the right front edge of the green and, also like Watrous, three-putted for a bogey. On the eighteenth, I put my drive into Watrous's bunker. (There is no plaque.) I came out sideways, hit the green with my next shot, and two-putted for a bogey—shoulder to shoulder with the titans of golf.

Lytham's two Ryder Cups were only mildly notable. The first, in 1961, was the first of six in which Arnold Palmer competed; he won three and tied one of his four matches, laying the foundation for what remains the best lifetime Ryder Cup record. The second, in 1977, was the last before the British side was expanded to include all of Europe. (Ireland had been added in 1973, in the hope of squaring things up slightly, but the contest had remained an American walkover.) Inviting the rest of Europe was Jack Nicklaus's idea, and it would eventually turn the tournament into the epic contest that it is today. The effect was not immediate, however. The Americans continued to post decisive victories until 1983, when they squeaked through by a single point. Then, in 1985, they lost the cup, and didn't get it back until 1991, at Kiawah Island. The European victories in 1985 and 1987, followed by a tie in 1989, were the best thing that could have happened to the Ryder Cup. They made it a genuine contest, in a way that it hadn't been since the competition's first decade.

The exact origin of the Ryder Cup matches is disputed by golf historians; like most great ideas, it seems to have popped up in several places at the same time. Then, as now, the United States and Britain were natural golfing rivals, and by the early twenties the American game had progressed to the point where competition on equal footing was more plausible. Informal matches were played in 1921, at Gleneagles, and in 1926, during the week before the British Open, at Wentworth. (The American team was creamed both times.) Intrigued by the 1926 contest, an English seed merchant and fledgling golf nut named Samuel Ryder agreed to provide a gold trophy and expense money for a formal competition to be held the following year. Ryder ought to be the patron saint of all late-blooming hackers. He took up the game at fifty, employed the British professional Abe Mitchell as his personal teacher, and methodically worked his handicap down to six in little more than a year. (The stiff-legged, forward-leaning golfer on top of the trophy is Mitchell.) When Ryder died, in 1936, his beloved mashie was buried with him.

The first official Ryder Cup was held in 1927 at the Worcester Country Club in Worcester, Massachusetts. The American team included Leo Diegel, Johnny Farrell, Walter Hagen, and Gene Sarazen, who was then a hot young touring pro. (Bobby Jones, the best American golfer by far, couldn't be on the team, because he was an amateur, as he remained throughout his brief, brilliant career.) The British side included Archie Compston, George Duncan, Arthur Havers, and Ted Ray. Playing on native soil, the Americans won by a hefty margin. Britain won the next time, America the next, Britain the next, America the next. America repeated in 1937; then the competition was suspended for the duration of the Second World War. When play resumed, in 1947, the advantage had settled decisively on the American side, and Britain did not win again until 1957. Two years later, the Cup returned to the United States, and there it remained until 1985, by which time the inclusion of the rest of Europe on the British side had restored both balance and suspense. The only close contest before 1985 came in 1969, when the two sides tied for the first time ever. The tie was secured on the final hole of the final match, when Jack Nicklaus conceded a short putt to Tony Jacklin, halving the hole, halving the match, and halving the Cup. After picking up Jacklin's marker, Nicklaus said, "I don't think you would have missed it, but I wasn't going to give you the chance, either." Ever since, Nicklaus's gesture has been celebrated as one of the greatest acts of sportsmanship in the history of competition.

On the other hand, the conceded putt could also be viewed as one of the greatest acts of gamesmanship. By giving Jacklin the putt, Nicklaus made the half look less like a British triumph than like an American act of charity, and forever left hanging the possibility that the reigning British Open champion might have gagged over his eighteen-incher. That's one of the cool things about match play.

I arrived at the Belfry on Thursday afternoon, the day before the competition was to begin. The golfers had just finished their final practice rounds, and many of them were hitting balls on the driving range, which was thronged with spectators and had its own large grandstand.* I saw swing guru David Leadbetter working with his star pupil, Nick Faldo. Faldo would take half a backswing and freeze his position; Leadbetter would move Faldo's hands about an inch; Faldo would swing again. Toward midafternoon, the players went back to their rooms to put on jackets and ties for the flag-raising ceremony, which was held on the eighteenth green. The crowds around the green were so thick that it was impossible to see

---

*The American team for the 1993 Ryder Cup consisted of Tom Watson (captain), Paul Azinger, Chip Beck, John Cook, Fred Couples, Raymond Floyd, Jim Gallagher, Jr., Lee Janzen, Tom Kite, Davis Love III, Corey Pavin, Payne Stewart, and Lanny Wadkins. The European team consisted of Bernard Gallacher (captain), Peter Baker, Seve Ballesteros, Nick Faldo, Joakim Haeggman, Mark James, Barry Lane, Bernhard Langer, Colin Montgomerie, José Maria Olazabal, Constantino Rocca, Sam Torrance, and Ian Woosnam.

what was going on, or even to hear what was being said. I stood on my tiptoes for about two minutes, then wandered off to have a look at the course.

There are two courses at the Belfry: the Brabazon and the Derby. Neither is distinguished; the Derby is often described as being "even" less interesting than the Brabazon. During the Ryder Cup, big tents were pitched on parts of the Derby, rendering it mostly invisible, but it is known primarily for being characterless and boring—two adjectives that are also frequently applied to the Brabazon, which was used for the Ryder Cup. In a nation of legendary courses, the Brabazon is a faceless newcomer. Scraped out of an old potato field, it looks like a minor Florida resort course, and indeed, it was built by the European PGA with the express purpose of giving European golfers a place to practice for the American tour. The nicest thing *Golf Digest* could find to say about it, in Ron Whitten's Ryder Cup preview in 1993, was that its very blandness would prevent it from intruding on the golf—perhaps the faintest praise imaginable for a championship layout. The Brabazon has an important place in the hearts of Europeans, however. The epochal European victory, in 1985, occurred there, as did the Cup-preserving tie in 1989.

The Brabazon is often described as being a two-hole golf course. Those two holes are the tenth and the eighteenth—the shortest and the longest par-fours on the course. The tenth, which is only about 260 yards long as the pros play it—you and I play it as a wimpy but genuine two-shooter, from twenty or thirty yards farther away—is in many ways an ideal Ryder Cup hole. It is short enough to tempt players into recklessness, but it is laid out in such a way that reaching the green from the tee is possible only with a nerveless, perfect shot. Making a par is a no-brainer; making a birdie is fairly easy; making an eagle is always an enticing possibility. The eighteenth is a tremendous finishing hole. It measures 474 yards on the card but can be made considerably shorter depending on how closely a player is willing to flirt from the tee with a sprawling lake shaped like a gastrointestinal tract. The second shot is also intimidating, and also over water. The green is spread like wallpaper across the side of a big hill, is flanked by cavernous bunkers, is sixty yards deep, and has three treacherous levels. The hole's only flaw, in terms of Ryder Cup play, is that matches don't always last long enough to reach it.

As I walked around, the weather was slightly crummy—about standard for Britain at that or, indeed, any other time of year. There had been some rain, and there was supposed to be more. Despite the moisture level, though, the footing was pretty good. Wood chips and gravel had been spread in the wetter spots. Big slabs of plastic honeycomb had been sunk into muddy walkways, making them passable. The parking areas, which were laid out in a number of neighboring pastures, were crisscrossed by temporary roadways made of corrugated steel. "The British can flat do mud," an American spectator said, with genuine admiration. I didn't even need to wipe my feet when I took a shortcut through the meandering lobby of the hotel on my way back to the press tent.

Earlier that afternoon, Tom Watson and Bernard Gallacher—respectively, the American and European captains—had come to the press tent to announce their pairings for the opening matches, which would be played the following morning. The Ryder Cup has had a number of different formats over the years, with minor and major adjustments made from time to time. In the current configuration, which has been used since 1987, there are four foursome matches followed by four four-ball matches on each of the first two days, and twelve singles matches on the final day. A foursome, as the British use the term, is a match in which two pairs of golfers compete, with each pair playing a single ball. One member of each team drives on all the even holes, the other drives on all the odd holes, and they take turns hitting the other shots. This fast-moving game is little known in the United States, except in so-called Scotch foursomes. But it is popular at a number of British clubs, particularly on crowded weekends. From a spectator's point of view, it's a neat game, because it adds an extra layer of psychodrama: If one player makes a mistake, his partner is the one who pays. In a four-ball match—a game that in America is usually referred to as best-ball—each golfer plays his own ball, and each pair's better score on a hole is the only one that counts. The singles matches, on the final day, are plain old head-to-head match play.

It is possible to be a member of a Ryder Cup team and not play a single hole until the final day. (Actually, for reasons that will be explained later, it is possible to be a member of a Ryder Cup team and not play a single hole at all.) Each side has twelve players, but only eight at a time compete in the foursomes and four-balls. Benching some of the players served to even the odds slightly during the early years. Now that the teams are roughly equal in depth, the arrangement is mostly vestigial, but it does have interesting strategic consequences. The captains can lean on players who they think are stronger, and rest players who are weary or injured. But they are also sometimes forced to make difficult and unpopular decisions, and they have to be careful not to erode the confidence of the players they ask to sit out.

During Watson's visit to the press tent that afternoon, most of the questions had to do not with the pairings or even with golf but with an incident that had taken place the night before, at the players' Gala Ball. Sam Torrance, a veteran member of the European team, had asked Watson to autograph his menu, and Watson had declined. Torrance had been hurt and embarrassed, and the tabloids had said nasty things about Watson the following morning. (Among the headlines: YANKS FOR NOTHING and FORK OFF.) Torrance had said he was too angry to speak about it, the European team was supposedly feeling riled up, and someone asked Watson what had happened. "It was an unfortunate incident," he said, somewhat testily. "I have to apologize to Sam Torrance for not making it very clear about not signing autographs. But the reason was that last night, with eight hundred people there, I thought that if we started signing autographs it would spoil the fun for my players." Watson said that he had once timed himself signing autographs; he had been able to sign his name 320 times in an hour. At that rate, he said, it would have taken nearly three hours to sign dinner menus for all eight hundred people present. He had later told the Europeans that if they wanted to send some menus over to the American team room, he would have his players sign them there.

Discussion of the Menu Incident went on for quite a while, and it resumed when Gallacher dropped by for an interview shortly afterward. "Sam talked about it last night," he said. "He was embarrassed, because he had walked across the stage. I know Tom Watson's signature quite well, though, so I gave it to him, and he's quite happy." Someone asked whether other members of the European team had been affected as well. "Seve struggled with his fromage at the end," he said, "but he made it through."

The Menu Incident was dumb and trivial, and the aggressive dissection of it in the press tent was typical of the mindless wheel-spinning that takes place when reporters have nothing genuinely interesting to write or think about. But it also provided a glimpse into the very different personalities of the two captains. Watson is earnest and stubborn, and in public at least, he doesn't have much of a sense of humor. He also is mildly but openly disdainful of the press. In forums like press conferences and television interviews he often manages to seem simultaneously smug, stilted, and ill at ease. His comments curiously made the Menu Incident seem more rather than less significant. He sounded (with his autographs-per-hour arithmetic) like a legalistic stick-in-the-mud, and although he apologized to Torrance, he implied that he thought he didn't really need to.

Gallacher, in contrast, dismissed the whole thing with a couple of pretty good jokes while nonetheless managing to get in half a dozen digs at Watson. One was left with the impression that Gallacher knew how to work a crowd, and Watson didn't. Not that it matters. On the other hand, working the crowd is probably one of the captain's jobs. And in the view of a number of people I talked to, snubbing Sam Torrance had merely been Watson's most recent error of judgment. A far more important lapse, some people said, had been choosing Raymond Floyd and Lanny Wadkins for the American team.* Floyd and Wadkins are fierce competitors, but

---

*Ten of the twelve places on American Ryder Cup teams are filled automatically, based on performance in tournaments during the two years since the previous competition; the final two players are picked by the captain. On the European side, the first nine spots go to the top nine players on the European money list, and the last three are picked by the captain.

neither had been playing particularly well at the time Watson chose them, and both seemed long in the tooth, even by the lenient standard of golf. Floyd was fifty-one, and Wadkins was forty-three, just a year younger than Watson himself. Floyd played in his first Ryder Cup in 1969, when Joakim Haeggman, a member of the European Team, was three weeks old. Watson's choices were thought by some to betray a faded star's prejudice for the players of his own generation. What about John Daly?

Of course, second-guessing the experts is part of what being a fan is all about. Someone even asked Gallacher whether the Menu Incident would give the Europeans the psychological boost they needed to win the cup—as though a dozen of the world's best golfers could have felt insufficiently motivated to play well until Watson inadvertently slighted one of them over dessert. It was almost enough to make you wish that they would actually start playing golf.

Friday morning was cold, wet, and gross. Rain during the night had by dawn become a thick, all-smothering fog. The players came to the practice tee to hit balls into the soup, then one by one gave up and went back into the hotel. The first tee time, at eight o'clock, came and went: no golfers. Then all the other tee times came and went. Chilly spectators wandered around the tented village, sipping coffee, eating Egg McMuffins, and trying to keep warm. I walked past the betting tent and saw about a dozen people lined up near the door, waiting for it to open. The group was more or less evenly divided between well-to-do American men and scruffy-looking English thugs. On a practice green near the hotel, a few of the pros' caddies killed time with an informal putting contest. From behind, I saw a man wearing a tweed jacket with a sign pinned to it that said, ARM IN SLING—TREAD WITH CARE! Standing near him were two men and two women wearing golf shoes.

Why do so many spectators at golf tournaments wear golf shoes? I didn't make a scientific survey, but I would guess that something like ten percent of the fans had spikes on. I saw, for example, an American couple sitting on a wet curb, exchanging their sneakers for Foot-Joys. They were dressed entirely in red, white, and blue, including cowboy hats. I asked them why they reckoned they needed golf shoes, and the man said, "Better traction." But that's not the reason; it's just the excuse. For a spectator, wearing spikes is a way of claiming a connection to the action—the way my son used to put on his ninja mask to watch the Power Rangers. The people in golf shoes were like the eager, grinning fans who squirm up to Jack Nicklaus behind the practice tee at a golf tournament and say, "Jack, I'm originally from Ohio, and we met in 1986 in the pro shop at Muirfield Village, and I just wanted to introduce you to my wife, Mary, and wish you good luck." The pros have powerful auras, and we mortals like to stand in their glow.

Finally, around ten-thirty, the fog was officially deemed to have lifted. You still couldn't see the first green from the first tee, but you could make out the fairway bunkers, which had been invisible an hour before. The crowd around the tee was so dense that there was no point in trying to get close. Somewhere up there, I knew, was the first foursome: Corey Pavin and Lanny Wadkins, for the United States, and Sam Torrance and Mark James, for Europe. Pavin and Torrance would tee off, and then Wadkins and James would play the second shots. Pavin was first. I caught a brief glimpse of his face and of the blurred head of his driver, then heard a *thwack*. There was silence for what seemed like forever, then applause. Now it was Torrance's turn. I saw his caddy's head, and then, after a long time, I heard another thwack. Then silence. Silence. Silence.

No one cheered, no one booed. Finally, the crowd began to break up and move in the general direction of the first green. For Torrance—whose drive, I later learned, had ended up in the left-hand fairway bunker—the hush must have been excruciating. He had blown his first shot in the 1993 Ryder Cup, and now it would be up to James to get them out of trouble.

As it turned out, James couldn't get them out of trouble. Pavin and Wadkins won the hole with a par, and from that point forward they were never behind. I followed them but had trouble seeing much. The Brabazon is the opposite of a stadium course. There were no hillsides or mounds to stand on, and the trees were too small to climb. During the first two days, there were never more (and often fewer) than four matches going on at a time—not a lot of action, considering that thirty thousand people were trying to watch. Most holes were surrounded from tee to green by fans jostling for a glimpse of the players, many of them waving flimsy souvenir periscopes that looked like gift boxes of Johnny Walker scotch. (Johnny Walker was the principal sponsor.) I saw one man standing on a paint can, which he had somehow smuggled past the guards at the gate, and I saw many people standing on small stools, also smuggled. "We'll have to buy the video when we get home," one Englishman said to another. Grandstands had been erected in a few key places, but there wasn't much to see from them. The most coveted seats, initially, had been those behind the eighteenth green, but they turned out to be some of the worst seats on the course: Only one match made it to the eighteenth during the entire first day. The grandstand also had a view of the ninth green, but that wasn't much of a consolation. You could have sat in those seats from dawn to dusk and still seen nothing but about thirty minutes' worth of chipping and putting.

Because the viewing opportunities on the course were so meager, there were crowds around the few available television sets. There was a TV in the Lloyd's pharmacy tent, and one in the exhibition tent, and one in a rowdy refreshment tent near the tenth fairway. There were also about a hundred sets in the press tent, and that's where most reporters hung out for the duration. Unfortunately for couch potatoes, though, the BBC's coverage was dreadful. Tom Kite would be putting for eagle somewhere, but on the screen you would see Colin Montgomerie practicing a putt he had just missed, or Nick Faldo standing by his golf bag, chatting with his caddy. The camera operators couldn't track balls in the air and had trouble finding them when they were on the ground. The director would suddenly cut to Barry Lane, picking him up in mid-follow-through. The BBC's sound equipment looked like Second World War surplus. The British announcers treated taped shots as though they were live, and as a result often tripped themselves up, as when they would announce that a team was putting for a birdie

that would put them two-up, when in fact they had sunk the putt
several minutes before, and that was how they had got to one-up.
The coverage was so wretched that for a moment I found myself
feeling sentimental about—please forgive me—Brent Musberger.
(The American Ryder Cup broadcasts, which Musberger had nothing to do with, were significantly better than the British—as I discovered when I got home and watched some tapes made by a
friend—because NBC and USA Network, which between them
were on the air for close to twenty hours, used their own camera-
work in addition to the BBC's. They also had Johnny Miller, who is
far and away the best golf commentator on TV, and who could
probably make a golf tournament seem interesting even on radio.)

The only wholly satisfactory way to watch the Ryder Cup was
from inside the ropes. That privilege was restricted to wives and
other guests of the players, certain officials and volunteers, various
dignitaries, members of television crews, and a limited number of
reporters and photographers. To step under the ropes, you needed
an armband, and those were in short supply. After about an hour of
aimless wandering along the edges of the churning crowds, I went
back to the press tent and, after pledging my wallet as security,
managed to borrow one from a daily-newspaper reporter who was
typing frantically.

Back on the course a little later, I followed Tom Kite and Davis
Love III, who were playing Seve Ballesteros and José Maria Olazabal. Love was the only rookie in the morning lineup. In the words
of the British sportswriters, he was being "blooded" by Kite, who
was playing in his seventh Ryder Cup. Ballesteros and Olazabal
may be the greatest pair in Ryder Cup history. Coming into the
Belfry, their Ryder Cup record together was nine wins, one loss,
and two ties, and they were undefeated in foursomes. They are
known as the Spanish Armada, and in foursomes and four-balls
during the three previous Ryder Cups they had beaten many of the
best players in the world: Paul Azinger, Chip Beck, Fred Couples,
Mark Calcavecchia, Ben Crenshaw, Raymond Floyd, Ken Green,
Tom Kite, Mark O'Meara, Larry Nelson, Payne Stewart, Curtis
Strange, Tom Watson. Neither Ballesteros nor Olazabal had been

playing well enough to make the European team on points, but no one had doubted that Gallacher would pick them. (His third selection was Haeggman, a rising young Swedish player.) The consensus prediction in the press tent the night before had been that Kite and his young pupil would be sunk by the Armada.

I picked up the foursome at the tenth, the dinky par-four with the theoretically drivable green. All four golfers had been playing extremely well; Kite and Love had never been behind, and were now leading by a hole, but the tenth is the kind of hole that can turn a match on its head. It runs downhill for a couple of hundred yards, then takes a slight bend to the right, across a creek. The creek runs along the right-hand side of the fairway and the left-hand side of the green, which is very long and very narrow. Big trees overhang the right side of the green. The creek, a steep hillock, and more big trees guard the left. The hole was playing even shorter than its posted length of approximately 260 yards, because it was both downhill and downwind. Still, going for the green from the tee was by no means an easy choice. Because of the creek crossing in front of the green, the shot was all carry. Because of the narrowness of the green and the perils on either side, the shot had to be laser precise. Because of the overhanging trees on the right, the shot had to either fade slightly or be dead straight. As a result of these difficulties, most players were sensibly choosing to lay up. Playing first, Ballesteros hit a solid nine-iron down the center of the fairway, leaving Olazabal a sand wedge to the pin. Now it was Kite's turn. Without a moment's hesitation he pulled his driver from his bag, made a swing entirely unruffled by doubt, and put the American ball five and a half feet from the cup—a gutsy shot under any circumstances, but doubly so considering that because of the format he and Love would have had to play his ball no matter where it ended up. I was sitting on the little hillock to the left of the green when Kite hit the shot, and for a moment I almost believed that the ball was going to go in the hole. Kite said later that he had never even considered laying up; he had been swinging well all morning, he said, and he had never doubted that he was going to put the ball on the green. Olazabal pitched the European ball to ten feet, and

Ballesteros made the putt, for a birdie, but Love completed his mentor's lesson by sinking the eagle putt, and the Americans were two-up with eight holes left to play.

Psychologically, the American eagle on ten was worth more than just a single hole. To make a birdie and halve a hole in match play is frustrating; to make a birdie and lose can cause a player to sink into despair. Ballesteros and Olazabal were two under par after ten holes, but they were nonetheless two holes down. The eagle on ten made Kite and Love feel invincible, and left the Spaniards wondering what they were up against.

It took me awhile to learn how to decipher the sounds of the crowd. I would be standing near one green and hear a deafening roar coming from the direction of another green, and I would figure that one of the Europeans must have just holed out from 250 yards. But it would turn out that what had really happened was that one of the Europeans had just hit a sand wedge only ten yards over the green and now had a chance to chip in for par. Similarly, I would hear restrained applause and assume either that nothing had happened or that the crowd was politely acknowledging a mediocre tee shot. But it would turn out that one of the Americans had just made an endless, snaking birdie putt to go three-up. The teenagers working the manual scoreboards would add to the confusion by playfully pretending to register an American victory on some hole, and then at the last moment sliding in a red European card instead. That trick—played over and over during the tournament—never failed to produce a joyful crowd reaction that was easy to confuse for a greenside celebration of some masterful European shot. Anyone who paid attention only to the roars of the crowd would have assumed that the Europeans were pummeling the Americans everywhere, all at once.

Despite the clear and understandable partisanship of the predominantly European gallery, though, the crowd was extremely civil—almost superhumanly so when measured against the low standard set by the beer-chugging, flag-waving, camouflage-fatigue-wearing, "USA"-chanting American crowd two years before, when the Ryder Cup was held on the Ocean Course at

Kiawah Island, South Carolina. The European fans at the Belfry didn't applaud as enthusiastically for good American shots as they did for good European shots—and why should they?—but they did applaud. I didn't hear any fans shout or mutter anything nasty during anyone's backswing, and the players reported only isolated and minor incidents of rudeness (although one did prompt Paul Azinger to refer to someone in the gallery, in a loud voice, by an epithet too nasty to print). You never felt—as you often do at, say, a big American tennis tournament—that the spectators were just a bunch of fucking assholes (oops—that's the epithet Azinger used).

Among the large, inside-the-ropes collection of hangers-on following the Kite-Love-Ballesteros-Olazabal match were the mothers of Love and Olazabal. I walked with Love's mother at one point. On fourteen, her son lagged a long putt to about four feet, and she said, hopefully, "That's a gimme." The Spaniards, understandably, didn't concede the putt, but Kite made it, and the Americans halved the hole to remain three-up (they had gone to three-up the hole before, on a six-foot birdie putt of Love's). Kite and Love were playing so well, and appeared to be so perfectly in synch, that you figured they had the match in their pocket. In fact, if they could win the next hole, they would finish it off.

The fifteenth at the Belfry is a long, straight par-five. There's a creek running across the middle of it, but it doesn't come into play, even for hackers. Love and Olazabal both hit big drives. Ballesteros then laid up with a three-wood. Kite went for the green with the same club and ended up in a bunker on the front left. As Kite and Love walked up the fairway, Watson pulled up in a golf cart, congratulated them on their good match, and told them that they would be playing together again, in the afternoon's four-balls. They chatted for a moment. Olazabal pitched to eight feet. Then Love climbed into the bunker to extract the ball that Kite had put there. I was crouching not far behind him, with his mother. The shot was harder than average—green a bit elevated, pin fairly close—but not by much. Love dug in his feet and swung. The ball hopped weakly into the rough just over the lip of the bunker, short of the green. "Oh, dear," his mother whispered. "That's his first bad shot all morning." Kite chipped the ball fairly close. Then Ballesteros had an eight-foot putt to win the hole.

One of the things the Americans had worried about going into the Ryder Cup was that Ballesteros might suddenly click into his furious-Spaniard mode, playing Batman to Olazabal's Robin, awakening the crowds, and inspiring the entire European side. Standing on the fifteenth tee, he had looked distant and bummed-out. Lining up his eight-footer now, though, he looked like the Seve of myth: all black hair and eyebrows. I wondered later whether Watson had inadvertantly upset the chemistry of the match by being premature in congratulating Love and Kite. Before Watson's visit, the Americans had been calmly devouring the Europeans. Now they seemed off-balance. For fourteen and a half holes, they had been on offense; now, suddenly, they appeared to be on defense. At the same time, Ballesteros had apparently decided that the match was not over. He stroked his putt. It caught the lip. It didn't go in.

Both sides ended up with pars. The Americans could now do no worse than tie the match. Or, to look at it a different way, the Europeans could still get a half. Despite the setback, Ballesteros was once again transforming himself into the golfer that other golfers are afraid of. On sixteen, he had another putt to win a hole, a twenty-eight-footer. This time, he drained it. Two down with two to play. On seventeen, he had a fifty-foot birdie putt. The ball looked in from the moment it left his putter. It curled up the slope of the green, bent toward the hole, and, once again, just missed. Both sides ended up with pars. The hole was halved, and the Americans had won the match. In truth, they had probably never been in very much danger. Then again, who knows? If that eight-foot putt had fallen on fifteen, the Europeans would have come to seventeen just one hole down with two to play, and the adrenaline would have been dripping from Seve's pores. It didn't happen, but you could see why other golfers worry about Ballesteros.

During the four-balls later in the afternoon, I followed Paul Azinger and Fred Couples in their match with Nick Faldo and Colin Montgomerie. Azinger and Couples had both had lousy mornings. Azinger and Payne Stewart had lost, seven and five, to Ian Woosnam and Bernhard Langer, and Couples and Raymond Floyd had lost, four and three, to Faldo and Montgomerie. Both losses had been surprises for the Americans. Azinger and Stewart had been the premier American pairing, and Couples and Floyd had looked like a sure thing, since the two had been magical together at Kiawah Island in 1991. For the afternoon, Watson decided to break up what had turned out to be losing combinations.

One thing you can't really appreciate while watching golf on television is how incredibly well pros hit the ball. Viewed from up close, their drives look nothing like the drives that you and I hit. I don't mean only that they go farther, although they do. I mean that they look like an entirely different kind of golf shot, as different from an ordinary drive as an ordinary drive is from an iron shot. People talk about Couples playing a fade, or working the ball from left to right, but his fades don't look anything like the shots that you and I refer to as fades. They are not miniature slices. A trademark Couples drive takes off dead straight and rising at what seems like the speed of sound. About 250 yards out, it levels off and bends perhaps one degree to the right. It returns to earth at roughly the 300-yard mark, and rolls another twenty or thirty yards down the middle of the fairway. It is not a banana.

Azinger and Couples had clearly found whatever pieces of their games had been missing during the morning. Faldo and Montgomerie were playing well, too. On the front side, seven of the nine holes were decided by birdies. One of the most exciting came on the sixth, a 396-yard par-four whose narrow fairway is bordered on the left by water and on the right by trees and water. During the entire tournament, no player hit a driver from the tee; in this group, all four players hit three-irons. Couples pushed his shot into the rough to the right of the fairway, leaving himself 175 yards or so from the elevated green, with a stand of small trees directly in his line. He brooded about his situation, then took a five-iron and, with roped-in spectators leaning practically in his face, hit a high fade that missed all the trees, soared high above the spectators to the left of the green, turned back toward the pin, and ended up twelve feet from the cup, well inside the other balls. It was a shot to take your breath away, and it won the hole. The Europeans both two-putted; Couples got his birdie; the Americans were one-up.

Couples has often been criticized for acting like a goofball on the golf course. He fiddles with his clothes and looks as though his mind is a thousand miles away. But if you watch him carefully, you begin to suspect that all his silly mannerisms are just a routine he uses to keep himself focused and calm. On the sixth green, while Azinger blasted from the sand and Faldo and Montgomerie tried futilely to sink their birdie putts, Couples picked at imaginary lint, looked at his fingernails, poked at a leaf with his putter, and tucked and retucked his shirt deep into his pants. He was settling himself before attempting a putt that he knew would be crucial. Couples isn't really a goofball; he just calms himself by preening. And it works.

On the short tenth, with the match all square, Montgomerie, hitting first, went for the green with a three-wood. There was no roar from the green, so it was obvious that the ball was in some kind of trouble, but no one on the tee (where I was crouching) could see where it had ended up. An American television announcer said he had heard over his headset that the ball was in the water. "Are you sure?" Faldo asked. He fretted for awhile but eventually decided to go for the green anyway. His own shot, hit with a three-wood, started right and went farther right, disappearing into the big trees, off to the side and short. Couples then hit a three-wood fade that didn't fade. It caromed off the bank to the left of the green and ended up in the water. With everyone else in trouble, Azinger laid up with a seven-iron, then hit a sand-wedge to eight feet.

It turned out that Montgomerie's ball had settled deep inside a sloping flowerbed between the front of the green and the water. He studied his predicament for a long time, then waded in and took a big swing with a sand-wedge. There was a major explosion of blossoms and loam, and his ball took off like a bottle rocket over the grandstands and the television tower at the rear of the green. Montgomerie laughed at the shot and at the mess he had made of the green, as did most of the spectators; it was a shot to warm a hacker's heart.

Then it was Faldo's turn. He was so far from the green and so deep in the trees that you couldn't see him from the bank on the left, where I was now sitting. Finally, his ball came squirting feebly through the trees and landed in a bunker just short of the green. Montgomerie waded into the crowd beyond the green, then returned. Had he given up? Faldo played a great bunker shot, leaving himself three feet for par. Azinger sank his birdie putt, and it was all over.

Or was it? Azinger and Couples left the green, but Faldo and Montgomerie didn't. The American television announcer said into his microphone, "Tommy, I don't think we're done at ten." Montgomerie was talking with John Paramour, the chief referee. I learned later that he was asking whether Azinger hadn't putted out of turn. Everyone had assumed that Montgomerie had picked up after skulling his ball from the flowerbed, but if he hadn't, then Azinger had indeed putted too soon; according to the rules of golf, he would have to replace his ball and putt again, without penalty, after Montgomerie had tried to hole out with a miracle pitch from behind the stands. This seemed like an altogether desperate tactic, given the impossible situation of Montgomerie's ball. "It's a stall," someone sitting near me sneered. But Faldo—who in addition to being a tremendous golfer is also a tremendous sportsman—said to Montgomerie, "Come on, we're out of this hole. Let's get on to the eleventh." And so they did.

On sixteen, in rapidly disappearing daylight, Azinger made his third consecutive birdie to take the Americans one hole ahead. The match had been wonderfully tense from the very beginning. Faldo and Montgomery between them had birdied seven holes; Azinger and Couples had birdied nine. The Americans had never been worse than all square, the Europeans never worse than one-down. Both sides were playing well enough to have been five- or six-up against lesser opponents. In fact, Faldo, Azinger, and Couples were all playing well enough to be running away with a major tournament. And Montgomerie wasn't playing too shabbily himself; his birdies on the first two holes had kept the Americans from snatching the match at the outset.

When the players reached the tee of the par-five seventeenth, it was arguably already too dark to play, and any one of the four players could have called for a postponement. The Americans understandably wanted to go on; Azinger's string of birdies had pumped them up. Gallacher told Faldo and Montgomerie that they ought to stop—figuring partly that a time-out at this point might deflect the American charge—but Faldo didn't want to quit, and so play continued.

Almost immediately, Faldo's decision looked dumb. Uncertain about what sort of shot he wanted to play (as he later explained), he skied his drive, advancing his ball perhaps 170 yards. Couples, meanwhile, had clobbered his tee shot and was in position to reach the green in two. A win here would take the Americans two-up with one to play, giving them the match.

But Faldo can never be counted out, even when he looks dead. He hit two seven-irons to the green, then sank a five-foot putt for a birdie; both the Americans made pars, and the match was back to all square. The golfers moved on to the eighteenth tee, but by then it was so dark that you could scarcely make out land on the far side of the water. Going on was really no longer an option. The golfers would finish their match—which was already being described as a Ryder Cup classic—in the morning.

In Ryder Cup scoring, a victory is worth a single point, and a tie is worth a half-point. By the end of the first day, with the one match still to be completed, the Europeans were leading by a score of four to three.* If Couples and Azinger should win the eighteenth hole outright the following morning, the tournament would be all square. If Faldo and Montgomerie should win, the Europeans would have a commanding two-point lead.

*In the morning foursomes, Wadkins and Pavin had beaten Torrance and James, four and three; Woosnam and Langer had beaten Azinger and Stewart, seven and five; Kite and Love had beaten Ballesteros and Olazabal, two and one; and Faldo and Montgomerie had beaten Floyd and Couples, four and three. In afternoon four-balls, Woosnam and Baker had beaten Gallagher and Janzen, one-up; Wadkins and Pavin had beaten Langer and Lane, four and two; and Ballesteros and Olazabal had beaten Love and Kite, four and three.

By eight o'clock the next morning, fans had surrounded the entire sprawling eighteenth hole. I squirmed my way into the crowd beside the green and found a spot from which I could occasionally glimpse the flag through a small, moving gap between the hip of a man standing on a stool and the shoulder of a man standing on the ground. I couldn't see the eighteenth tee from where I was standing, but I could see the fairway, which looks bigger from the green than it does from the tee. After what seemed like a wait of several hours, a ball came bouncing into view. It hadn't been hit particularly far, but it was right in the middle—probably Montgomerie's, I figured. Then a ball hit the water. Could it be Faldo's? Then a ball came soaring almost all the way to the edge of the water in front of the green. That must be Couples's. Everyone waited in silence for the final drive. But a fourth ball did not appear.

As it turned out, I had guessed wrong about all the shots. The first ball I had seen had been Faldo's. Invisible from the green, Montgomerie had hit next, and pushed his drive into a nasty lie through the fairway and to the right—out of view and, in effect, out of play. The splash had been Couples's. The boomer had been Azinger's. With Montgomerie in trouble and Couples in his pocket, the entire match had now come down to a shoot-out between Faldo and Azinger.

In many ways, that was exactly what one might have hoped for, since Faldo and Azinger had been the stars of the match so far. The pressure on both players must have been staggering. In four-ball you count on your partner to bail you out if you get into trouble. On this hole, though, Azinger had had to face the course's most demanding drive knowing that his partner was out of the hole. I was surprised that Couples hadn't taken a drop and played a second ball, if only to provide Azinger with the illusion of emotional support; there would always have been the chance that he would hole out from the fairway for a par. He might even conceivably have reached the green from his drop with a monster hook, depending on where he would have been allowed to drop his ball. But maybe he figured that Azinger's drive was so good that to play another ball would have been superfluous, or even insulting.

After the massive inside-the-ropes entourage had settled itself in the fairway, Montgomerie hit a five-iron into the water. Faldo played an indifferent six-iron to the front edge of the green, at least fifty feet below the cup. Then Azinger, the last to play, took a pure swing with an eight-iron and stuck his ball pin-high, perhaps twelve feet to the right of the hole.

The crowd now began to rearrange itself, and I lost my narrow window on the green. I followed the rest of the match by sound. When Faldo putted from below, there was silence followed by a few gasps. (He had left his putt where I might have left mine: twelve feet short and to the right.) Then Azinger tried for his birdie and the win: silence, a few anxious squeaks, then groans. (He had rolled his ball just around the top of the hole, leaving himself a gimme for par.) Then Faldo's putt for par, and the half. Everyone was squirming to see, and I momentarily caught sight of Faldo's caddy, Fanny. The crowd grew deathly still. Silence. Silence. Silence. Silence. Then joyous shouts and a sudden roar. (He had drained it, duh.) The match was halved, and Europe now led by a score of four and a half to three and a half.

Faldo and Montgomerie then went immediately to the first tee, where they were paired with Wadkins and Pavin in the morning's first foursome. I joined the large group inside the ropes, which included Deane Beman and his wife, and David Leadbetter, who was repeatedly blowing his big, Dickensian nose. An English spectator standing behind the ropes pointed an elbow at Leadbetter and said, "He's ruined this golfer, hasn't he?" He was referring, of course, to Faldo, who is Leadbetter's most distinguished pupil. And he was obviously wrong, given that under Leadbetter's tutelage Faldo had firmly established himself as the best player in the world. People often complain that Leadbetter has made Faldo "too mechanical." Given the results, though, it's difficult to see the problem. Besides, *mechanical* is really just a synonym for *consistent,* and what golfer in the world wouldn't choose to be more consistent? Furthermore, during the Ryder Cup, Faldo was not at all the icy automaton he has often seemed to be during tournaments. The first-day rumor was that Faldo and Montgomerie had been teamed together because none of the other Europeans had wanted to play with either of them. But they appeared to be a convivial couple—in part, perhaps, because Montgomerie looks like the separated-at-birth brother of Fanny. Faldo also smiled pretty often, and even did a fair amount of wisecracking. ("What's for breakfast?" he had asked after sinking his heart-stopping par putt on eighteen that morning.)

Later, as we walked along, I asked Leadbetter whether he had had any special instructions for Faldo the night before, in anticipation of his having to play the Belfry's hardest hole first thing in the morning. "I told him to work on visualizing the shot," he said. "That tee calls for a draw, which is not Nick's favorite shot. He has been working on making his swing a bit shallower, and that tee shot calls for that. To be perfectly truthful, I think he pulled his ball a little. He really wanted to be a little to the right of where he was." Leadbetter said that the match had been one of the greatest ever, and that he figured Faldo had shot something like a sixty-three on his own ball—a score that Azinger had at least matched.

A little while later, Leadbetter, commenting on the match at hand, said that Pavin was probably the game's best shaper of the ball. Pavin had certainly been putting on a show in the Ryder Cup. (Later in the day, playing with Gallagher, he would hole out on the fly with a nine-iron from 141 yards, a shot he makes so often that he has actually developed a set routine: As he explained later, he doesn't raise his arms in triumph until he has seen for certain that the ball has not bounced back out of the hole.) Pavin doesn't have a gigantic following among fans, but other players view his iron play and his putting with something like awe. They also view him as a tremendous match player, and indeed, the format seems to bring out the best in his game. At a press conference that evening, he explained that in match play he tries to adopt a "go-and-kill-them" attitude. "You can do things that your opponent does not expect you to do," he said. "Make great recoveries that are very deflating. If he holes out from ten feet, and then you put one in from eight, that can be very demoralizing. But, of course, it can work both ways." Naturally, I feel a special regard for Pavin, having become a close personal friend of his by playing a round with him in the pro-am at the Disney Open. (Only with a massive effort of will did I manage to overcome a temptation to walk up to him on the driving range and say, "Corey! How've you been since we last played together—was it Florida? Of course—it was Disney!") My sentimental attachment to him increased when I saw him search the crowd for his wife, Shannon, and hold out his ball for her to touch before he made his way to the next tee.

Something you don't pick up from watching golf on television is how avidly the pros try to figure out which clubs their opponents are hitting. On one hole I saw Couples lean so far to his right in an attempt to peer into Faldo's bag that he practically tipped over. The rules of golf prohibit a player from asking (or telling) an opponent which club he has hit (or from seeking or supplying any other kind of "advice"), but there's no rule against trying to figure things out for yourself. Of course, the players are fully aware of this, and they will sometimes intentionally try to throw off their opponents by asking loudly for one club but taking another, or by taking too much club and hitting it easy, or by ostentatiously pulling one club before an opponent hits and then exchanging it for a different one afterward. In addition, the pros have to be careful when they snoop, because many players modify their irons, for one reason or another—for example, by bending a two-iron to the loft of a one-iron, as John Daly does, or turning a four-iron into a three-and-a-half-iron, as Tom Kite does. Still, I suppose, it's human nature to want to know.

The Europeans may have been better spies that second morning, because they trounced the Americans in the foursomes. By lunchtime, the score stood at seven and a half to four and a half, and the Americans were looking gloomy.* In the afternoon four-balls, I decided to follow Chip Beck and John Cook, both of whom were playing for the first time. Keeping Cook on the bench until the

*In morning foursomes on the second day, Faldo and Montgomerie beat Wadkins and Pavin, three and two; Langer and Woosnam beat Couples and Azinger, two and one; Floyd and Stewart beat Baker and Lane, three and two; and Ballesteros and Olazabal beat Love and Kite, two and one.

second afternoon had been a fairly easy choice for Watson. Cook had earned his place on the team primarily by having a stellar year in 1992. His play in 1993 had been erratic, and he had been the shakiest of the twelve Americans during practice earlier in the week. He had obviously been disappointed not to be selected for the first three events, but he had been a good sport about it. I had seen him several times out on the course, cheering on his team-mates, and I had seen him on the driving range, trying to bang his game back into shape. Leaving out Beck must have been more difficult. Beck had one of the best Ryder Cup records on the team, with four wins and one tie in seven attempts during the two previous competitions. Like many people, I wondered whether Beck's globally reviled decision—five months before—to lay up on the par-five fifteenth during the final round of the Masters had tainted him in the eyes of his captain.* More likely, Watson was simply trying to figure out how to squeeze twelve first-string golfers into just eight playing positions. At any rate, he now called on Cook and Beck, and when he did, he told them, "We need your point."

Getting that point was a daunting proposition. They were playing in the lead match of the afternoon, and their opponents were Faldo

*Here was the situation: Beck was paired with Langer in the final round. When they got to fifteen, Langer was leading the tournament, with Beck two strokes back. Both players hit decent but shortish drives, into the wind. Langer, playing first, had 250 yards left to the green, which was protected in front by water. He sensibly laid up short. Now Beck. He was perhaps fifteen yards closer than Langer, with 235 to the front of the green and about 200 to dry land. He had a downhill lie, and the wind was in his face, and he, too, decided to lay up. The television commentators and virtually everyone watching immediately concluded that Beck had chickened out, drawing unflattering conclusions about his character, and Beck's own caddy later said that Beck had been protecting his score rather than playing for a win. All that aside, I think Beck made the right decision. In the Masters, a two-stroke lead with four holes to play can evaporate in a flash. Given the wind and the lie, Beck's chance of making eagle was about the same as his chance of winning the lottery. Realistically, therefore, the best result he could hope for, whether he went for the green or not, was a birdie. Also realistically—given the distinct danger of ending up in the water if he tried to go over—his best chance of making birdie was to lay up, pitch close, and sink the putt. As it turned out, Langer was the one who pitched close and got the birdie, while Beck ended up having to claw his way to a par, but that didn't retroactively make Beck's lay-up a dumb thing to have done. His dumb shot was his pitch.

and Montgomerie, who were playing together for the fourth time and had yet to lose a match. Cook rose to the occasion, matching crucial birdies with Faldo on the first and fourth holes, and making an unanswered birdie on seven. Beck played extremely well, too. The Americans went to the eighteenth tee leading by a hole, and Cook iced the win with a conceded birdie. It was a very important victory, and one whose progress the other American players had followed closely on the scoreboards while they were playing and in person after they had finished. Beck and Cook's win from the bench helped to inspire the other Americans. Pavin and Gallagher beat James and Constantino Rocca, five and four, and Floyd and Stewart beat Olazabal and Haeggmann, two and one. The only Americans to lose were Azinger and Couples, who were smothered by Ian Woosnam and Peter Baker, six and five. (Baker put on one of the great shows of the tournament, and beat Azinger and Couples pretty much on his own ball. He sank putts of forty-five and twenty-five feet, and drained twelve-footers as though they were tap-ins.) At lunchtime, the Europeans had had a tremendous lead. At the end of the four-balls, they were still ahead—by a score of eight and a half to seven and a half—but the emotional momentum had clearly now shifted to the American side. The smart second-guessing money settled the blame on Gallacher, who had permitted Ballesteros and Langer, his second and third best players, to sit out for the afternoon, claiming fatigue. Their replacements—Haeggman and Rocca—had both lost.

In the press tent that evening, Gallacher announced that Sam Torrance (who had not been in the European lineup since his disappointing performance in the opening match) was injured, and might not be able to play in the singles matches the following day. Torrance, he said, had a serious infection in the little toe on his left foot, and had had most of the toenail removed the night before, but was still in great pain and would require additional surgery during the week. In order to play at all, Gallacher said, Torrance would have to be fitted with a larger left shoe, and would need two pain-killing injections during the round. He would have a fitness test in the morning, and a decision would be made at that time.

Torrance's injury was bad news for the Americans. The Ryder Cup's rules include a provision for dealing with an injured player on the final day. If a player on one team can't compete, the captain of the opposing team must select one of his own players to sit out as well. The two sidelined players are then considered to have played each other and tied, and each team is awarded a half-point. This rule is actually the very model of fairness: It reduces the likelihood of the tournament being decided by an accident. But the Americans were still disappointed. Almost everyone had been expecting Torrance to lose his singles match—meaning that his statutory half-point would be a half-point more than he had been expected to earn on his own. Even more disappointing, for the American players, was the fact that Watson would now have to choose one of them to sit out.

The rule covering injured players is called the envelope rule, because in the old days each captain would write the name of one of his players on a piece of paper and seal it in an envelope before the tournament began. The envelope would be opened only if a player on the opposing team became injured; if the name wasn't needed, the envelope was destroyed. Nowadays, the "envelope" is a fiction, and a captain doesn't actually select a player unless the situation arises on the final day. (Since each team plays just eight players at a time on the first two days, the envelope rule is needed only for the singles matches.) But now the situation had arisen, and Watson would have to choose.

As soon as word of Torrance's injury became public, people began to speculate about whom Watson would pick. Janzen had lost both his matches, but he had actually played very well, and it was hard to believe that Watson would bench the reigning U.S. Open champion. Cook might have been an obvious choice the day before, but now he was a hero. Gallagher was a possibility only because he was the least well known of the American players—he, too, had been playing well, and had won his most recent match. Azinger and Couples had each managed to play four matches without winning any, but leaving either of them out was unthinkable; besides, their half with Faldo and Montgomerie had been the highlight of the tournament so far. In truth, there weren't any obviously weak players on the American side.

In the end, Watson didn't have to decide. When a tournament official approached him on Saturday evening to explain that Torrance might not be able to play the next day, Wadkins happened to be standing with him. "Put my name in the envelope," he said. He and Floyd had discussed this possibility earlier, and they had decided that since they had been captain's choices, one of them ought to be the one to sit out should the need arise. (Floyd was alone on the driving range when the official approached Watson. He was trying—successfully, it turned out—to straighten out a swing flaw he had noticed earlier in the day.) Watson didn't like this idea; he wanted both Wadkins and Floyd in his lineup for the final day. But Wadkins argued forcefully that he was the logical choice. To be picked for the envelope could be a crushing psychological blow for any of the younger players, he said. They all had wives and children and friends at the Belfry to watch them play, and they had all earned their spots on the team. He said that he had played in more than his share of Ryder Cups, and he had played in three matches during the first two days; he would be very sad not to play on Sunday, but he wouldn't be devastated. He and Watson talked for a long time in the dark. Finally, Watson, with tears in his eyes, accepted his offer.

Torrance came to the press tent later that evening. He was wearing ordinary shoes, and he was walking normally. "I think I would have faked a limp," someone whispered. But no one really doubted that his toe was a mess, and the next morning, a doctor determined that he could not possibly play; the toe was shown to Watson, who readily concurred. In the original Sunday pairings, which had been made public earlier in the evening, Wadkins had drawn Ballesteros, and Torrance had drawn Gallagher; now Wadkins and Gallagher would switch opponents, and Wadkins and Torrance would each be credited with a tie. Dan Jenkins, looking at the revised list, said, "Talk about bad luck. Gallagher was paired against a nobody with a bad toe, and now he's got to play a fucking immortal." Before play began, Ballesteros ran into Wadkins in the Belfry and said, "Sorry we didn't get to play." Wadkins, smiling, responded, "Sorry I didn't get to kick your ass."

Americans are often said to have an advantage in Ryder Cup singles play: Thanks to our frontier heritage, the thinking goes, we are loners, gunslingers, show-offs, and so forth. Our constitutional self-ishness makes us unpredictable partners in foursomes and four-balls, but helps us be ruthless when we're playing head to head. As a matter of fact, there may be some truth in this. Since the fifties, the American team had lost the singles competition only once, in 1985, during the first of Europe's two consecutive victories.

There's a good bit of strategy in preparing lineups for Ryder Cup play. Before every section of the competition, each captain makes a list of the players he's decided to use, in order. The lists are then matched, with the first team or player on one list playing the first team or player on the other. Placing strong players high on a list increases the likelihood of building an early lead but may leave gaps later on. Using novices in the morning foursomes is risky, since the format is inherently nerve-racking; first-timers are more likely to see action in the afternoons, when the veterans are worn out and need a rest. On the final day, captains typically save their strongest players or most nerveless veterans for the final pairings, but run the risk of making these matches irrelevant, since the con-test may be decided earlier.

In preparing their lineups for the final day, Watson and Gallacher had been guided by similar inclinations. Each had led off with a very strong player (Couples, Woosnam) and finished with his best player (Azinger, Faldo). In the ninth, tenth, and eleventh spots, Watson had placed his tough old closers: Wadkins (later replaced by Gallagher), Floyd, and Kite; in those same positions, Gallacher had used Ballesteros, Olazabal, and Langer. As often happens in Ryder Cup singles, the middle spots on both sides had been filled primarily with weaker players and novices, along with a sprinkling of aces.

Many people have suggested that the Ryder Cup's pairing system ought to be changed. Rather than making the captains submit their entire lineups blind, why not have them take turns naming one player or team at a time (as is done in the brand-new Presidents Cup)? That would add a new layer of strategy and eliminate some second-guessing. It would also make for five suspenseful pairing parties (at which, ideally, there would be a lot of drinking and vulgar shouting). On the other hand the blind-pairing system preserves the possibility of serendipity. Pavin versus Baker was a great matchup—perhaps the best pressure putter in the world versus the hottest putter of the tournament—that might not have happened if the captains had had to lay all their cards on the table.

The singles matches began shortly before lunchtime. It was cold and windy, the sky was churning, and leaves were blowing across the greens. The players and the spectators were all bundled up. I put on my rainsuit to keep the wind out and wandered around the front nine, checking in on the early matches. Things weren't going too well for the Americans. Couples started out with a winning birdie on the first hole, but fell to even on the second, and stayed there. Beck won the first hole from Barry Lane, but then began to slip, and was two-down by the turn. Janzen lost the first two holes to Colin Montgomerie. Pavin and Baker hovered around all square, as did Haeggman and Cook. And of course Wadkins, in the phantom sixth match, had already halved.

The early money definitely favored the Europeans, as did the general mood of the crowd. The Americans never seemed to be leading any matches when I looked up at a scoreboard. The European spectators grew increasingly confident, and their ebullience seemed to protect them from the icy winds. The American spectators, in contrast, looked cold. Their flags drooped, and they pulled their cowboy hats down over their ears. But something happened in the afternoon that turned the mood in the other direction. Thinking back on it later, I decided that the crucial moment came on the fifteenth green in the match between Beck and Lane.

After a seesaw battle over the first few holes, Beck had gone to three-down after thirteen, with just five holes left to play. His plight seemed hopeless at that point, and I'm sure virtually everyone wrote him off. Watson hadn't shown much confidence in him during the early matches, having benched him till the second after-noon. Now Beck seemed to be crumbling in a hurry—and against an opponent whom no one had figured to be very tough.

At the par-three fourteenth, though, Lane three-putted for a bogey, while Beck made par. Two down. On the par-five fifteenth, Beck hit a good drive, then reached the green with a three-wood. Lane's second shot, a two-iron, ended up in a bunker. He blasted to twelve feet. Beck coolly surveyed his putt, a thirty-footer, then drained it, for an eagle and the hole. It was a thrilling moment. Beck was so cool that he suddenly seemed unbeatable—from chicken-shit to chicken salad in the space of a couple of holes. Now, it was Lane who seemed to be crumbling. He missed the sixteenth green with a nine-iron, then two-putted from five feet, for bogey. All square. Both golfers parred the seventeenth. On eighteen, Lane drove into a fairway bunker, and dumped his second shot, a three-iron, into the water. Beck drove somewhat feebly, and hit beyond the green with his three-wood approach, but chipped close and was given the putt—for the par, the hole, and the match. It was an improbable victory, and several of Beck's teammates said later that it inspired them in their own matches. Indeed, as Beck was finish-ing off Lane, the Americans' prospects were beginning to look very different from the way they had looked earlier in the day.

In the bottom half of the lineup, the Americans seemed brilliant. Payne Stewart ate up Mark James. He was five-up at the turn, and held on to win by three and two. Jim Gallagher, Jr., made Seve Ballesteros look like an old man. Ballesteros played the first six holes in even fives, shooting forty-two on the front nine. Gallagher beat him by three and two. Kite decimated Langer. He was the only player all day to hit the green at ten—he used a three-wood—making eagle to Langer's par. The match ended at the fifteenth, where Langer conceded Kite's twenty-foot eagle putt after dumping his second shot into a bunker and two-putting from forty-five feet.

The other matches were nail-biters. The match between Davis Love and Constantino Rocca teetered back and forth. Rocca had been a relative nobody on the European tour before qualifying for the Ryder Cup. He was thirty-six years old; he had spent eight of his prime playing years working in a polystyrene factory, before becoming a teaching pro; he had needed four tries to win his tour card; he hadn't won a European tour event until 1993, when he won two; he was the first Italian ever to play in a Ryder Cup. Love had been expected to make short work of Rocca, but Rocca had the upper hand during most of the match. He was making putts, and Love wasn't, and it began to look as though Love might actually lose. The match didn't turn until it reached the seventeenth green. Rocca was one-up. He narrowly missed a twenty-five-foot putt for a birdie that would have forced Love to make his own putt from a similar distance just to stay alive. Love two-putted. Rocca now had to sink a three-footer to maintain his one-hole edge going into the final hole. Make the putt, and the worst he could do was tie. His stroke was uncertain, he looked up, and the putt lipped out. As Rocca walked forlornly to the eighteenth tee, Watson told Love to practice his putting, to force Rocca to think about his missed putt for a little longer. Love hit a great drive, Rocca launched a banana into the gallery, and Love won by smoothly draining a six-foot putt for par. "I almost threw up on myself," he said later. "I couldn't breathe. There was no saliva in my mouth."

Love's performance on the eighteenth hole was all the more impressive because the green was surrounded by members of both teams, and Love believed that his win was crucial.* As it happened, though, the match that clinched both the Cup and the victory for the Americans was that between Floyd and Olazabal. That was appropriate, because Floyd was one of the real heroes of the competition. Along with his fellow fossils Kite and Wadkins, he had provided exactly the sort of leadership and inspiration that Watson had promised he would. Olazabal never led in their match. Floyd was at his most frightening on the par-three fourteenth, where his five-iron tee shot ticked the pin, leaving him a tap-in for a birdie and a

---

*Rocca was later derided in the press, most notably in *Sports Illustrated,* for blowing Europe's chances, but the fact is that he played very well and was still in the match until the final exchange of putts. He gave Love a real scare, even after hitting a bad drive on eighteen. He missed winning the match by a total of maybe three quarters of an inch.

three-hole edge. Olazabal clawed his way back to one-down, but
he put his drive in the water on eighteen and conceded the match
before anyone had to putt. Floyd, who has trouble walking unless
he stretches the muscles in his feet for ten minutes before getting
out of bed in the morning, had won three of his four matches. He
was the oldest man ever to play in the sixty-six-year-old Ryder Cup,
and he was the only man on Sunday, out of a field of twenty-two,
who hadn't made a bogey.

In his speech at the closing ceremonies, Watson read a lengthy
quote from Teddy Roosevelt: "It is not the critic who counts," Watson said, "not the man who points out that the strong man stum-
bled, or the doer of deeds could have done them better. The credit
belongs to the man who is actually in the arena, whose face is
marred by dust, and sweat, and blood; who strives valiantly; who
errs and comes up short, again and again; who knows the great
enthusiasms, the great devotions, and spends himself in a worthy
cause; who at best knows in the end the triumph of high achievement, and who at worst, if he fails, at least fails while daring greatly,
so that his place shall never be with those cold and timid souls who
know neither defeat nor victory."

This is off-the-shelf victory-speech material, but it also has a slight
fuck-you quality, don't you think? There's a dig at the critics—the
dreaded "eight hundred media," as Watson contemptuously referred to the press throughout the matches—and there are distinctly
unfriendly jabs at golf fans in general. This is our victory, Watson
seemed to be saying; you guys who slice it into the woods can't
even begin to understand. True, true. But surprisingly frosty nonetheless. One of the great things about golf, I think, is that the fans
and even the eight hundred media can sort of guess what the game
must be like way up there where Faldo and Azinger play it. Furthermore, spectators are a part of golf, as they are of any sport. The real
game may reside in a place that is far out of our reach, but the Ryder
Cup wouldn't be the Ryder Cup if the pros played it in private,
without all us cold and timid souls leaning over the ropes, begging

for autographs, shouting "You the man!," and using up some of the oxygen.

One of the great things about golf is that it manages to be both these games at once. It is the Olympian ordeal as enacted by the game's immortals in the Ryder Cup every other year, and it is the joyful, futile obsession that captivates hackers like you and me. We occasionally get a whiff of the metaphor-rich ether of the upper slopes, perhaps while standing on tiptoe beside the eighteenth green at the Belfry; the guys at the top, meanwhile, never entirely forget that playing golf is really just goofing around. In the end, the words that stuck in my mind were not Watson's arm's-length public pronouncements but one of Pavin's private comments. As the closing ceremony was drawing to a close, Pavin turned to Love, who was sitting beside him, and said, with a big, happy smile, "You know, this is a pretty good golf course."

10

A M E R I C A ' S   B E S T

LIKE MOST GOLFERS, I PLAY MOST OF MY ROUNDS ON courses that are not among *Golf Digest*'s 100 Greatest in America. One course in particular comes to mind. During a business trip to Seattle a couple of years ago, I ran out of business and found myself with half a day to kill before my flight home. I checked out of my hotel, took a cab to a public golf course I had spotted from the plane while flying into town the day before, and spent the afternoon playing with regulars, first with three guys who had taken a sick day from the assembly line at Boeing, and then with a big tattooed guy who drove a dump truck.

The course had a number of interesting features. Four of the holes were essentially continuations of the main runway of Seattle-Tacoma International Airport. Two ran toward the airport, and two ran away, and their fairways were separated by sequoia-sized steel pylons that had flashing lights on top of them. The roar of the big jets was so loud that it seemed life-threatening, and the churning backwash from their engines—which was made visible by dust and pollen in the air—did unpredictable things to golf shots. Any ball that strayed into the vortex was slapped, despun, and knocked from its trajectory. The greens were wet and scrappy, and one of them had been recontoured by local juvenile delinquents, who had driven a car onto it and spun the tires, making deep ruts that promoted yips. Compounding my difficulties were my rental clubs, a mismatched assortment of orphans and rejects, among them an old Cary Middlecoff three-iron, which looked like a curtain rod with a very small butter knife lashed to one end.

Despite these difficulties, though, I had a great time. Any day spent on a golf course is a good day, even if the course is less than perfect. The key is to view butter knives, tire tracks, and low-flying airplanes not as indignities but as challenges in shot-making. Golf is an opportunistic game, and always has been. You could hold the U.S. Open at the foot of Sea-Tac Airport and have a legitimate contest. Wouldn't you enjoy watching Nick Price and Fred Couples hit nine-irons through the wakes of jumbo jets? There is no such thing as a bad golf course.

And yet, there is very definitely such a thing as a good one. I will cheerfully beat balls around the lamest municipal dog run on the planet, but if given the choice I'd take Cypress Point every time. Who wouldn't? Certain golf courses are simply better than others. They aren't all better for the same reasons—one of golf's greatest fascinations is the limitless variety of its circumstances—but they nevertheless have qualities that set them apart. Some are longer, some are slicker, some are sterner, some are lovelier, some are tighter, some are wetter, some are windier, some are fairer, some are simply somehow indescribably more numinous. Some bring out the best in those who play them, and some bring out the worst. People will argue forever about the order of the ranking, or about the very idea of ranking, but there isn't a course among the 100 Greatest that won't copiously reward a thoughtful player.

On assignment for *Golf Digest* not long ago, I had the enormous good fortune to play fifteen of the 100 Greatest, including all of the first dozen. My mission, as I saw it, was to sample the best of the best and see what sort of revelations they might inspire: golf's true spirit, meaning of life, cure for cancer, that sort of thing. My golfing odyssey was tremendously satisfying, as one might expect, but it did not make my life easier. My playing partners at home began to turn the other way when they saw me bounding up the clubhouse steps, a stack of exotic scorecards in my hand. Even my editor at *Golf Digest,* chained to his desk at the office, stopped taking my calls. My feeling is: who cares?

My tour of America's best golf courses began where it might logically have ended, at the course that has never seriously threatened to sink from the first position, Pine Valley. For many golfers, a round at Pine Valley is the game's Holy Grail. Jack Nicklaus famously played it on his honeymoon, leaving his new bride in the car. (Women are usually permitted on the course only on Sunday afternoons.) A teacher friend of mine once drove all night and skipped the first day of school after receiving an eleventh-hour invitation to fill out a short-handed foursome. I made my way in without signing away my soul—my boss at *Golf Digest* is a member—but I still appreciated the gravity of the invitation.

The approach to Pine Valley is unprepossessing. Instead of skirting the cliffs of Monterey as you draw near, you stagger from stoplight to stoplight in the anonymous strip-mall vastness of southern New Jersey. As you cross the railroad tracks and pass the gate, however, you enter a different world. The driveway to the clubhouse divides the eighteenth green from the eighteenth fairway, and first-time visitors crane their necks and veer into the oncoming lane, trying to take it all in. The grass is not littered with diamonds, as one had halfway been led to expect, but the hole nonetheless magnificently fails to disappoint. Even glimpsed through a windshield at five miles an hour, Pine Valley is way cool.

The idea for Pine Valley arose in 1912 among a group of Philadelphia businessmen who yearned for a handy course that they could play during months when their home courses were snowed-in. The site, among the rolling sand hills of the Pine Barrens, was selected by George Crump, who also designed most of the holes. (Crump had help—how much is a matter of debate—from Harry S. Colt, a distinguished British designer whose other credits include the New Course at Sunningdale and significant redesigns of Muirfield, Ly-

tham and St. Annes, Royal Dublin, and the Old Course at Sunningdale.) Crump liked to design holes by hitting shots into the scrub
and building greens where the good ones ended up. He died before
his masterpiece was completed, and ascended into heaven. Today,
even the caddies speak of him reverently. John Schmidt, who carried my bag the first day, entertained me between shots by reciting
poems he had written to celebrate each hole. His verse for the
eighteenth:

> The Shining Star of Inspiration
> Passing through and absorbing
> These great changes
> In nature and self,
> I feel at One
> With the incredible vision
> I now Behold
> Above this signature Hole.
> Thank you, George Crump.

For Schmidt, as for most golfers lucky enough to play there, a
round at Pine Valley has a theological dimension. Pine Valley has
a reputation for being not only America's best golf course but also
its toughest. As a matter of fact, many golfers use the two terms
interchangeably. (It is not unusual to hear the 100 Greatest referred
to as the 100 Hardest—and, in fact, that's how the list was originally
conceived.) But equating mere difficulty with quality misses the
point. It would be easy to build a golf course harder than Pine
Valley, and people have. But no one, if the panel of raters is to be
believed, has yet succeeded in building one better. As a matter of
fact, the course strikes some first-time players as disappointingly
"easy": Even from the back tees it measures just a little over 6,600
yards; only one hole—the chasm-spanning par-three fifth—requires a big, do-or-die shot from the tee; virtually every hole offers
a safe, accessible path to the green; many of the fairways are so
wide as to seem essentially unmissable. A golfer with a reasonably
reliable swing who is content to shoot a mediocre score can play
the course without coming close to cardiac arrest.

The essence of Pine Valley, though, is that for every notch above mediocrity to which a golfer aspires there is a seemingly exponential increase in danger. Working your way around the course is like crossing the Nile by skipping along the backs of hungry crocodiles. One day, I shot an 86 that might have been a 76 if I hadn't yanked a few drives and four-putted a couple of times; the next day, I shot a 102 that might have been a 204 if I had counted every stroke and finished every hole. The difference between the two rounds was perhaps a one-degree shift in swing plane, temperament, and ambition. It is easy to get into trouble at Pine Valley, and very, very hard to get out. The first hole sets the problem nicely. There is ball-hungry scrub in front of the tee, but the carry across it is less than 150 yards. The fairway is so wide that it looks like a football field turned sideways, but even a moderately long hitter has to be careful not to drive through it into the rough on the other side. The hole doglegs to the right, generating a powerful temptation to cheat the corner, but the elbow is protected by dead-end weeds and bunkers from which the green cannot be reached. The green is broad and flat, but drops off steeply in back and on both sides. The conservative player has every opportunity to chicken out; the ambitious player is tantalized by the prospect of glory. On paper, the first hole looks like a cakewalk; in practice, it has often been the club's hardest hole in relation to par.

Every hole at Pine Valley is distinct and memorable. The second looks short on the card but plays like a thousand miles, with an elevated green that is inevitably too high to be reached by whatever club is long enough to reach it. The sprawling unraked desert that interrupts the seventh fairway has such a fatal attraction for golf balls that you might as well surrender to your fate and aim for it. Members whose tee shots land in the tenth green's tiny pot bunker (called the Devil's Asshole) typically declare their balls unplayable and retee without even walking up to have a look. You can see the fifteenth green from the fifteenth tee—across a lake, up a hill, through a tightening throat of fairway carved from the forest, 600 yards away.

Pine Valley is one of the last unashamed strongholds of masculine privilege. There is no men's room in the clubhouse, because there is no women's room; there's just the bathroom, with a plate-glass window in the middle of the door. The ban against tipping is absolute, and members have been suspended for sponsoring guests who violated it. (When I heard this, I felt like the child who has been warned not to lick the frozen pump handle, and I walked the property in dread that I might uncontrollably plunge my hand into my pocket and thrust a bill into a waiter's hand.) Ernie Ransome, the club's revered immediate past president, lives near the seventh tee, and is said to scan the course with a telescope, looking for players who play slowly, throw clubs, or fail to replace divots, three other offenses for which rustication is a possible penalty.

During my long weekend at Pine Valley, I stayed, along with a dozen other *Golf Digest* retainers, in one of a number of houses owned by the club. There was a putting green in the yard. The bar in the paneled den was fully and imaginatively stocked, and in the mornings we were served breakfast in the lovely dining room. One evening, we had cocktails in the home of Jim Marshall, who is the club's secretary. Marshall's golf cart was parked in his driveway next to his car, and the entryway to his house was lined with golf shoes. A hundred or so wedges leaned against one wall of his living room, and a hundred or so putters leaned against another. There were spike marks on the floor of the dining room. Near the door was a blanket-sized square of Astroturf. Like all guests in Marshall's home, we were invited to chip Styrofoam balls from the Astroturf over a couch onto a small oriental rug. Sticking a ball to the rug on the first try is so hard that in fifteen years it has been accomplished only twice. (Nick Faldo needed twenty-six tries.) You might not choose to live as Marshall does. Play a few rounds at Pine Valley, though, and you will see how it could happen.

A couple of hours' commute from Pine Valley, but eons away in sensibility, is the West Course at Winged Foot, in Mamaroneck, New York. Like Pine Valley, Winged Foot is the creation of early-twentieth-century urban rich guys. (It was founded in the twenties by golf-crazed members of the New York Athletic Club, the logo of which provided the course's name.) But the two courses are very different. Where Pine Valley overwhelms you with a sense of omni-present peril, Winged Foot impresses you first with its scale. In-deed, the club's forefathers instructed their architect, A. W. Tillinghast, to design them "a man-sized course." The result is what might be viewed as the consummate American country-club course. The fairways are long, narrow, and lined with trees. The greens are smallish, elevated, and fast, and they are protected by bunkers that from the fairways look like enormous outfielders' mitts. Some of the bunkers are so steep that the sand on their sides seems to contradict important physical laws. Smoothing my foot-prints is one of them; I felt like a plasterer skimming a wall.

Golf is obviously a three-dimensional game—as distinct from, say, billiards. On the seaside courses of Scotland, where the game began, the third dimension is usually defined by the unrelenting wind, and Scottish golfers look down their noses at Americans, who tend not to know how to slap a low, hooking screamer under a gale. In relatively unblustery America, the third dimension is pro-vided, for the most part, by trees. Despite what Old Tom Morris might think, this is neither better nor worse—just different. So what? The game is big enough to accommodate all.

Trees are an extremely important part of Winged Foot, as they are of many great American courses. The club claims some fifty differ-ent species, examples of which are individually located and labeled in hole-by-hole diagrams in *Winged Foot Story,* the club's official history (which is subtitled *The Golf, the People, the Friendly Trees*). Because trees don't stand still, the course has evolved considerably during the seven decades it has existed. (When built it was virtually barren.) Shots that once sailed over now often have to be shaped around. This gradual, natural metamorphosis is one of the distin-guishing features of many of our great courses, and something that American golfers should celebrate and take pride in.

The clubhouse at Winged Foot—which was built using stones turned up in the construction of the course—looks like the country home of an English lord. Its principle amenities are a sprawling, two-story locker room, which in the early years was the source of an annual upstairs-versus-downstairs tournament, and a wonderfully dark and welcoming Grille. The specialty of the house is toast that has apparently been soaked for days, weeks, or years in vats of melted butter. Like the menu specialties at most great American clubs—the snapper soup at Pine Valley, the peach cobbler and golf-ball-sized olives at Augusta National—this toast is celebrated out of all proportion to its actual distinction. The members love it, I would guess, mostly because Winged Foot members have always loved it. It's like the Jell-O your mother made you when you had the sniffles.

History drips from the walls at Winged Foot the way cholesterol drips from the bread. (Or maybe that's testosterone. Women aren't banned at Winged Foot, as they are at Pine Valley, but the masculine weight of the very air diminishes them to the point of invisibility.) On display in the main hallway of the clubhouse are mementos from the club's storied past, among them a golf ball used by Bobby Jones, who won the U.S. Open at Winged Foot in 1929. The ball is lumpy and uneven, and looks like something your first-grader might have fashioned from salt dough. Jones set up his Open victory by draining a snaking twelve-foot putt for par on the eighteenth green—a putt that few visitors to the course can resist taking a stab at. Grantland Rice, who was in the gallery but couldn't bear to watch, called Jones's twelve-footer the greatest putt in history, and it still gives Winged Foot members the chills. (The putt put Jones in a tie with Al Espinosa, whom he beat the following day in a thirty-six-hole playoff—by twenty-three strokes.) Rice also credited the putt with sparking Jones's epochal Grand Slam the following year. If Jones had fallen to Espinosa, Rice figured, his competitive career might have ended in despondency then and there. Few first-timers at Winged Foot can resist adding their names to the ever-lengthening list of those who have tried and failed to make that putt, including me.

Winged Foot is most famous for its back nine. It begins with a 190-yard, par-three tenth whose steeply elevated green is guarded by a pair of bottomless, kidney-shaped bunkers. This is a hole that can pick your pockets if you've let your attention drift during a mid-round pitstop at the bar. The last five holes are an unrelenting

succession of long par-fours, the final three of which average 450
yards. (The members play one of these killers as a par-five.) After
stumbling my way through the first thirteen—beginning, as Bobby
Jones did, with a double-bogey on the first—I managed to play the
final five in even par. If Tom Watson had pulled off the same feat
in the final round of the U.S. Open in 1974, he'd have nine major
victories instead of eight. Why do people say golf is a difficult game?

A few hours' drive from Winged Foot is another great U.S. Open
course, but one that is as different from Winged Foot and Pine
Valley as those two are from each other. Shinnecock Hills, in eastern Long Island, is set among windswept dunes and potato fields of
Southampton. Like the Old Course at St. Andrews, it doesn't necessarily look like much as you survey it from the first tee. You can't
see the ocean (though if the breeze is up you can smell it), and the
fairways aren't flanked by wave-battered cliffs. There are trees in
the distance, but they might just as accurately be described as tallish
shrubs; they seldom affect strategy on the course. Many of the
stirring pictures of Shinnecock that you see in coffee-table books
are tributes to the power of backlighting and wide-angle lenses.

Still, like the great Scottish courses to which it continually alludes,
Shinnecock is the real thing. Not surprisingly, the course's original
designers (in the 1890s) were Scots, and Shinnecock served as an
important evolutionary link between the Scottish and American
games. You would never mistake Long Island Sound for the Firth of
Forth, but the rolling terrain is pleasantly reminiscent of linksland.
I played with a well-traveled Scottish friend whose handicap is
zero; Shinnecock was the first American course that he un-
reservedly loved. (He views Pine Valley as punitively monomania-
cal, and Winged Foot as sprawling and bland.)

When I visited Shinnecock, during the summer of 1994, the
USGA was already hard at work bringing the rough up to its fiend-
ish standard for the U.S. Open of 1995. The tall grass at Shinnecock
is thick and wiry under any circumstances, and is especially so
when the USGA is breathing down the neck of the greenkeeper.
This grass, which must draw its power from the salty air, is one of

the course's strongest suggestions of Scotland, and it's something you seldom find on courses farther inland. The stuff tends to grab a club by the hosel, closing the face and making the ball go left. Advancing the ball a significant distance is phenomenally difficult for anyone wimpier than Ernie Els; simply getting it back into play is often a tall order. On two holes, I drove into the left rough, aimed a wedge straight back at ninety degrees to the line of play, swung hard, and ended up farther left than I had begun. The cruellest hole is the ninth, a 411-yard par-four whose steeply elevated green sits at the top of what from the fairway appears to be a vertical wall covered with foot-long grass. Land your ball a half-club short of the pin and you won't find it unless you accidentally poke it with your ice axe as your caddy hoists you up the precipice.

Shinnecock has an air of timeless nonchalance that may be achievable only by a club whose membership consists of a small group of absentee kazillionaires. The club has just 250 members, roughly half of whom can be counted on not to show up in a given year. You don't get the feeling that they hold a lot of square dances in the clubhouse. There was only one other golfer in sight when my friend and I set out, and we asked our caddy if we should invite him to join us. "No," he said. The sense of aloofness may arise from the course itself, which is so direct and unpretentious that it virtually cries out for someone to screw it up; somewhat surprisingly, no one ever has. The clubhouse—the first in America, designed by Stanford White—looks big and imposing from a distance, but is in fact as unassuming as a beach cottage, complete with creaking porches and banging screen doors. There is a grill but no dining room. The lockers are not slathered with black walnut veneer. The bag drop is exactly that: a section of lawn where you drop your bag as you turn into the gravel parking lot. If Walker Evans had photographed his sharecroppers on the back steps of the clubhouse, you wouldn't have been bowled over by the incongruity of the background.

Let's not dwell on score. (Golfers are unattractively obsessed with numbers, don't you think?) When our round was all over, my Scottish friend and I wistfully shook hands with our excellent caddy, then took the ferry from Port Jefferson back to Connecticut, drinking beers on the fantail, watching the red sun sink into Long Island Sound, and wishing we were rich.

Of all the well-known disadvantages of *not* being rich, having little hope of playing the best golf courses in this country must be near the top of the list. Only two of the first ten are in any sense public courses, and these two—Pebble Beach and Pinehurst No. 2—are not the sort of places where you drop by for a quick nine holes on your way home from work. Playing a single round at Pebble Beach, including hiring a caddy, eating a couple of meals, and bankrolling the mandatory overnight stay at the Lodge or the Inn at Spanish Bay, costs more than the annual dues at my local golf club. Naturally, because someone else was paying my tab, I stayed for most of a week and managed not only to play Pebble Beach three times but also to play every other great course on the Monterey Peninsula. But that's just the nature of what I do for a living.

If American golf had a home field, though, Pebble Beach would be it. The course is to golf what Niagara Falls is to honeymoons: you know what it's for, even if you've never been. Tourists automatically reach for their disposable cameras when they spot the sign above the pro-shop door. So powerful is the aura of the place that nonplaying visitors often feel moved to rent clubs and—what the hey!—give the game a whack, with the result that the first tee at Pebble Beach has probably witnessed as many whiffed and topped drives as any other tee in the world.

The first hole at Pebble Beach looks nothing like what I had thought it would. It's a short, uphill, right-bending par-four that could have been transplanted intact from any of a hundred indistinguishable resort courses. The second is a short par-five that would be entirely in keeping on a third-string municipal course. The third is a short par-four that is bothersome only if you flush your two-iron tee shot through the fairway instead of drawing it into wedge range on the left. The fourth is a tiny par-four that's a nice hole in its own right, but in the context of the previous three it can make you wonder. The real course doesn't begin until at least the fifth, a tough, uphill par-three. The pros like to come to that point about twenty under par, so that they can get into trouble on the holes ahead without drifting too far into the black.

The holes on which the reputation of Pebble Beach is based are the ones that run along the water—the sixth through tenth, and the final two. Any one of these holes would be enough to carry a lesser course; played one after another in a single round, they make a deep and permanent impression. I had seen Pebble Beach on television many times, but I was still unprepared for the heroic scale of these holes. The most notable is probably the eighth, which is viewed by many (among them Jack Nicklaus) as the best par-four in the world. The tee shot is blind, up a hill to the top of a cliff. (A few years ago, a golfer reaching to pick up a ball toppled over the edge and fell eighty feet to the rocks below, miraculously landing more or less unhurt on a little pocket of sand no larger than a mattress.) The second shot has to cross a corner of Monterey Bay and find a smallish, steeply sloped green that is protected by bunkers, beach, thick vegetation, and a wall of rock. Even if you decide to be sensible and treat the hole as a par-five, you still have to figure out where on earth you are supposed to lay up. The eighth is followed by two endless par-fours that appear to be sliding sideways off the cliffs to the beach below. Any shot that bends to the right is in danger of skidding off the edge of the world. This is where the pros spend the birdies they hoarded on the first few holes. It is one of the hardest, most breathtaking stretches in tournament golf, and the challenge continues as the course turns back toward New York.

During my three rounds at Pebble Beach, I was accompanied by nine golfers, three caddies, and four nonplaying wives (none of them my own). One of my playing partners—a ten-handicap for whom every drive was a "poke," every course was a "track," and every club was a "stick"—turned to me at one point and said, "Golf is akin to suicide." When I said, "Aw, it's not that bad," he gripped my arm, narrowed his eyes, and hissed, "It is! It is!" Another playing partner bought a triple-tequila-and-Gatorade at the snack cart at the turn, and downed it before we had finished the next hole. He addressed his ball as "Bitch." My caddy the first day carried two bags on one shoulder and was briskly efficient, but after fifteen years on the job he knew so much about the course that he was more often a hindrance than a help. Just as I was about to hit a straightforward pitch shot on the thirteenth hole, he stopped me and said, "You have thirty-two to the front, forty-seven to the pin. It'll play like forty-two, but land it three feet on, nine feet to the right. It will break down the ridge but into the grain, so it won't be as fast as you think, but it will die hard to the left about two feet from the cup." Naturally, I chunked it. On the fourteenth tee each day, I gazed respectfully at the house of the only member of Pebble Beach Golf Links, a woman in her nineties who is the last surviving member of the old Del Monte golf club, which was folded into the modern resort during this century's front nine. I could see her television set flickering in her living room. She has her own golf cart and her own cart path leading to the course. She likes to play a couple of holes toward the Lodge to pick up her mail, and then play a couple of holes back home.

The only aspect of Pebble Beach that disappointed me was the greens. The relentless tide of heel-dragging, putter-leaning, ball-mark-ignoring humanity that washes over the course on a typical day takes a heavy toll on the short grass, and the grass itself compounds the problem: *Poa annua* grows unevenly and doesn't putt true unless it is mowed every few minutes, something that isn't possible on a course in constant use. On several long downhill putts, my ball hopped and bumped like a marble rolling down a flight of stairs. (That may not be all bad. Like most golfers, I probably score better when my putts don't go where I aim them.)

My three-round Pebble Beach ringer score (made up of my best score on each of the eighteen holes) was even par, 72, a number I'm very proud of. My favorite moment came on the final day on the final two holes. A couple of no-handicap hotdogs—the last group on the course that day—had been shooting easy pars and birdies behind us for quite a while, and on the seventeenth tee, as darkness rapidly sucked in around us, we invited them to join us, so that they would be able to finish, too. Within about thirty seconds of this

invitation, one of the two hotdogs managed to work into the conversation the phrase, "When I was playing in the qualifying tournament for the U.S. Open . . ." We let them hit first.

The seventeenth is a deadly par-three that plays 209 yards from
the U.S. Open tees, and twenty or thirty yards shorter from the
human tees. The wide, shallow green looks like a dark crewcut
growing on the rim of the gaping bunker that guards its front.
Directly behind the green are more bunkers, rocks, and crashing
waves. This is the hole where Tom Watson miraculously chipped in
for birdie to set up his defeat of Jack Nicklaus in the final round of
the U.S. Open in 1982. The two hotdogs hit good-looking shots,
and then the four of us hit reasonably good-looking shots. In fact,
I hit my Heaven Wood just about as well as I had hit any club all
week, and when I lost my ball in the darkness it seemed to be
heading right for the pin.

When we got closer, I saw that there were three balls on the
green. One of them was only about six feet from the hole. The
qualifying-tournament hotdog walked straight to that ball and bent
to mark it. "I think that's mine," I said, my voice squeaking a little.
He looked at it closely, said, "Oh," and put it back. He checked the
other balls on the green, then found his own ball in the front
bunker. He ended up with a four. Everybody else got either a three
or a four, and then it was finally my turn. My putt was downhill, and
it broke to the right. I gave my ball a little tap, and it tumbled and
hopped down the bumpy, spiky *Poa annua* and rolled right into
the middle of the hole for a birdie. As I retrieved my ball, I felt like
turning to the hotdog and saying, "When I was playing in the
qualifying tournament for the Why-Don't-You-Just-Go-to-Hell," but
instead I chatted in a friendly way as we walked to the final tee, a
little shelf of wave-hammered rock with grass growing on it. Both
the hotdogs got double-bogeys on the eighteenth; I hit three
Heaven Woods and two-putted and made par. We did not invite
them to join us for a beer in the Tap Room—which looks like Bing
Crosby's den and is one of the most seductive nineteenth holes in
golf.

While at Pebble Beach, I stayed not at the famous Lodge but a few miles away, at the newer Inn at Spanish Bay, which is part of the same operation and which the readers of *Condé Nast Traveler* recently voted the best resort in America. My room had, among many other drop-dead amenities, a working fireplace that you lit by flicking a lightswitch. My window looked out over the first and eighteenth fairways of the Links at Spanish Bay, a Scottish-style course designed by Robert Trent Jones, Jr., with help from Sandy Tatum and Tom Watson. When I first looked out the window, there were three foursomes on those two holes—eight golfers and four deer. Beyond the eighteenth fairway I could see dunes and beach and the Pacific Ocean. The sun was going down. The low angle of the light made the course look shadowy and complicated. The sky was blue and red and orange and pink. The waves were so bright in places that it hurt my eyes to look at them. I could see surfers in the water and people holding hands on the beach. I thought: I may not be rich, but if I were rich this is what I'd be doing. Then I went for a long walk before eating a terrific, expensive dinner.

I played Spanish Bay twice, both times late in the afternoon after playing elsewhere in the morning. The first time, I played by myself in near darkness and howling winds. I was the only golfer still on the course. A maintenance guy in a golf cart drove back and forth ahead of me, removing the flags. I trotted along with my bag on my shoulder, and managed to finish fourteen holes before I could no longer see what I was doing. The second time, the starter paired me with a big, disheveled man in his late forties or early fifties who played every hole from the farthest edge of the farthest teeing ground. Several parts of his shirttail were untucked, and the toes of his brown golf shoes were scuffed almost down to his socks. He had a slow, strangled way of speaking that sounded a little like a southern drawl and a little like the way a close relative would talk to you if he was trying to sound polite while choking back a nearly overwhelming urge to kill you. Before making a shot, he would tear off his rumpled bucket hat and fiercely stuff it into the back pocket of his pants, sometimes missing the pocket once or twice before finally jamming it in. He had a fast, wild, lashing swing full of rising heels, bobbing shoulders, and flying elbows. After hitting almost every shot, he would rear back, shake his club at the sky, and cry, "No! No! No!" Thrusting his hand into his pocket for another ball was almost a part of his follow-through. We rode in separate carts, and we talked about nothing except how far into the scrub on what side of the fairway his most recent shot might have gone. He had a big Nevada Bob's shopping bag full of golf balls on the seat of his cart, and he must have gone through two or three dozen. Even so, he paused after each hole to write a number on his scorecard. When we finished, he shook my hand and said, "I enjoyed that. I hope we get a chance to play again."

Spanish Bay is not among the 100 Greatest, although it might be if it were situated anywhere but on the Monterey Peninsula, a non-gigantic promontory that astonishingly is the home not only of it and Pebble Beach but also of Spyglass Hill and Cypress Point—not to mention Poppy Hills, Pacific Grove, Monterey Peninsula, and several others. I played Poppy Hills and hated it, and Spyglass Hill and loved it. But the course that really got me was Cypress. Toward the end of my round there I turned to my playing partners and said, "You know, if I had to choose one course to play for the rest of my life, I think I would choose this one." It was only later, while reading an exquisitely beautiful picture book called *The Golf Courses of the Monterey Peninsula* (San Francisco: Sports Images), that I learned that this is one of the hoariest clichés in the game. Among the many other golfers who have said they would pick Cypress if forced to choose just one: Deane Beman, Dave Marr, Bob Rosburg, Sandy Tatum, Ken Venturi, Tom Watson, and a couple of orthopedic surgeons I recently had dinner with in Georgia.

Cypress has been called the Sistine Chapel of golf. Bobby Jones was so taken with it that he hired its architect, a Brit-turned-Scot named Alister Mackenzie, to help him dream up Augusta National. The course is sometimes mildly criticized for certain eccentricities— back-to-back par-fives on the front nine, back-to-back par-threes on the back, an uncharacteristically wacky finishing hole—but no one has ever seriously suggested that the layout is anything less than divinely inspired. I usually find that I need to play a course at least three times before I can mentally walk all eighteen of its holes in order; Cypress Point, with the exception of a couple of holes on the front side, is clear in my mind after just one round.

Like Pine Valley, Cypress has a teensy-weensy parking lot. You don't see guys in sneakers standing around in it, drinking coffee and fiddling with the X-outs in their pockets. I had my choice of most of the handful of parking spaces. The starter paired me with two other nonmembers, wealthy out-of-towners in their fifties who after months of scheming had finally managed to wrangle an invitation from a friend of a friend, and were now smiling so broadly they were practically squinting. During our round we saw no one behind us, and no one ahead. As at Shinnecock, the club's members were notable mainly for their absence.

Cypress feels like several different golf courses. There are holes that wind through forests of pine and cypress, and holes that play around or over enormous sand dunes, and holes that seem to have been spread with a trowel on the tops of the seaside cliffs. The first shot at Cypress is simultaneously inviting and terrifying. You hit down a hill to a fairway you can't see, over a tall, thick hedge protecting 17 Mile Drive, and you are warned to keep your ball to the left of a score-annihilating clump of cypress trees that would otherwise look like something you might be supposed to aim for. I had woken up in a cold sweat at four that morning, worried about that tee shot. Miraculously, I hit a good one.

Alister Mackenzie's confident hand is evident everywhere. At the fifth hole, an uphill par-five in the woods, my caddy pointed out one of the architect's favorite visual tricks: from the tee the hole appears to be nothing but bunkers; looking back from the green you can see almost no sand at all. Every hole is memorable, but the ones on the cliffs are unforgettable. In fact, you know them before you see them, since along with the holes that constitute Augusta's Amen Corner (which of course are also Mackenzie's) they must be the most photographed holes in golf. The epiphany begins at fifteen, a shortish par-three that plays from the side of a cliff over a narrow inlet in which you are likely to spot sea otters splashing among the kelp. Playing this hole invariably takes a newcomer thirty minutes or so. First, snapshots must be taken. Then, wayward tee shots must be found and rescued—from the many large bunkers, from the cypress trees, from the lethal ice plant, from the rocks. (The sea and the cliffs are not considered hazards at Cypress. If you hit your ball over the edge, you have to either find it and play it or declare it lost or unplayable, take the penalty, and hit again.)

Sixteen is another par-three over water, but it's nearly a hundred yards longer than fifteen, and its inlet is bigger, and the waves are louder, and the cliffs are higher, and the pin looks so far away it might as well be in Tokyo. It's a hole that looks as though it might have been designed some cloudless summer evening by four guys sitting on the clubhouse verandah and working on their third gin-and-tonics. ("Hey, let's put a hole over *there*!") Going for the green requires a shot designed by the Jet Propulsion Laboratory; laying up is nearly as scary, since a well-struck iron played too far left of the green can soar over the bail-out zone and end up on the beach on the other side. My first ball, hit with my two-wood, bounced off the cliff like a BB. My second, a layup, landed in the last few inches of short grass, and from there I got up-and-up-and-down, for a gentleman's six. The seventeenth plays back to the mainland from the other side of the sixteenth green. I tried to shorten the hole by cutting off an extra wedge of ocean, and ended up on the rocks. When our round was over, I wished that I had played those three holes better, but I felt unspeakably lucky to have played them at all.

From Cypress, I traveled to Las Vegas, the unlikely home of Shadow Creek Golf Club, which was designed by Tom Fazio and completed in 1990, and which cracked the top ten in 1993, when it was scarcely out of diapers. The course is owned by the company that owns, among other things, the Mirage Hotel, a glitzy casino that is the headquarters of world-famous tiger-taming oddities Siegfried & Roy. Shadow Creek's patron (and codesigner, if various signs and the scorecard are to be believed) is Steve Wynn, who is the casino's chief executive and the sometime star of its television commercials. Estimates of the construction cost vary; $38 million is a figure I've heard a couple of times, but my own awestruck, uneducated guess would be higher. If you need proof of the irrationality of casino gambling, all you need to do is stand on the first tee and look around you. After they have paid off all the blackjack and slot-machine winners, after they have changed the water in the 20,000-gallon tropical-fish tank behind the hotel's front desk, after they have fed the five Atlantic bottlenose dolphins out past the beauty salon, after they have set off the volcano in front of the lobby, there is still enough money left over to do *this*.

My host was Ken Wynn, who is Steve's younger brother and an executive in the company. When I called to ask for driving directions, he told me to take the freeway to a certain exit north of town. "As you look toward the mountains," he said, "you'll see a forest rising out of the desert." We both laughed, but he was right. Shadow Creek is a shimmering, Oz-like quadrant of green surrounded by miles and miles and miles of sand. The entire compound is enclosed by a tall chain-link fence. At the gate, I spoke my name into a telephone, smiled at a closed-circuit television camera, and was admitted. Driving toward the clubhouse, I shared the road with a ring-necked pheasant, a chucker, and a long-eared rabbit—a small sampling of the numerous non-native species with which Wynn has ornamented his course. In the early days, there were also wallabies and African cranes, critter types that turned out to be too large to coexist safely with mishit golf balls.

Tom Fazio is my choice as the best golf-course architect working today, a judgment in which I have lots of company. Shadow Creek can probably be considered our best look into his designing soul, since he was given not only a blank check but also a blank canvas. When he took the job, there was nothing here but desert. Every hill, every pond, every bump, every dip, every bounce, every break is there because he put it there. There are no compromises, or at least no obvious ones. For all I know, the stones in the artificial creek that circulates through the property (and tumbles over an artificial waterfall before returning to its artificial headwaters) were individually glued in place by Fazio himself. The entire course is, in a way, an optical illusion. The pine trees that surround you don't run all the way to the snow-capped mountains in the distance; all those acres of rye grass would wither and die if the grounds crew ever stopped doing the equivalent of irrigating it with ground-up money. It's a virtual golf course—except that it's real.

My playing partners, in addition to Ken Wynn, were a professional from a nearby country club and his wife. These two were wearing more gold than I am used to seeing on a golf course, and they had arrived in a white Porsche Carrera. "Ah, the life of a Las Vegas club pro," the pro said, smiling. Our golf carts were equipped with built-in coolers, which were filled (and, at the turn, refilled) with ice and soft drinks. We were accompanied by an affable caddy/chauffeur, who paced yardages, filled divots, repaired ball marks, and read putts. No other group on the course ever entered my field of vision. When I took divots on the immaculate fairways, I felt as though I ought to apologize to someone.

I also feel as though I ought to apologize for loving Shadow Creek. How can you love a mirage? But I did. The course's only glaring deficiency is that it lacks a history. No professional tournament has ever been held there, or is likely to be. Heck, they won't even let you take pictures. Play on the course is limited mostly to friends of the Wynns, friends of the casino (i.e., bigtime losers), employees of the company, *Golf Digest* course raters, and celebrities—including, on the day I visited, Joe Pesci, whom I have never seen in a movie, but have run into on three different golf courses and have seen several times on television playing in various pro-ams. Does the guy ever work?

Shadow Creek's lack of historical scope is a genuine weakness. To be truly great, I think, a course needs to be at least an occasional venue for truly serious golf. This is not just because being chosen to host an important tournament certifies a course's stature. It's also because in golf, more than in any other sport, history is a living part of the game. When Chip Beck laid up in front of Rae's Creek on the fifteenth hole at Augusta National during the 1993 Masters, for example, he was playing short not only of the water but also of Gene Sarazen, who holed his four-wood second shot there while winning the Masters in 1935. (The bridge over the creek on that hole is dedicated to Sarazen and his shot.) What's more, Beck and nearly everyone watching him knew that at the time. For close to sixty years Sarazen's double eagle had been as much a part of that hole as the creek in front of the green—and ever since 1993 Beck's layup has been, too. Those two shots will forevermore affect the confidence, strategy, and club selection of every Masters contender. They almost have a physical reality. Great golf courses become greater by accumulating moments like those.

A course doesn't have to be especially old to have a history. Muirfield Village Golf Club, in Dublin, Ohio, is just a bit over twenty years old, but during its relatively brief existence it has fortified its considerable assets with any number of great moments. Probably the most stirring in recent years was Paul Azinger's holed bunker shot on the seventy-second hole to beat Corey Pavin by a stroke and Payne Stewart by two in the 1993 Memorial, a tournament that would like to be to Muirfield Village what the Masters is to Augusta National. Another indicator of Muirfield's stature is the list of golfers who have won the Memorial, among them Azinger, Floyd, Irwin, Norman, Strange, Watson, and of course Nicklaus himself.

Both the Memorial and Muirfield are fitting backdrops for great moments, since both are explicitly dedicated to the history of the game. The Memorial each year honors a great player from the past. And Muirfield Village is in every sense a monument to the game's most important single source of history: Jack Nicklaus, who conceived the club and designed the course (with help from Desmond Muirhead and Pete Dye), and is the presiding spirit not only of them but also of the surrounding residential area, which didn't exist before he came along. There is a statue of Jack, a bust of Jack, old clubs that used to belong to Jack, books about Jack, covers from magazines containing stories about Jack, awards won by Jack, letters received by Jack, clothes with Jack's name on them, pronouncements by everyone from the club chairman to the caddy master beginning "Jack says" or "Jack thinks"—the very air pulses with Jackness.

If I couldn't have Cypress for my only-course-for-the-rest-of-my-life, I might choose Muirfield Village. This choice surprises most of the people I mention it to. My reason is that I think playing Muirfield every day would be good for my golf game. The fairways are wide, promoting an easy swing. (Nicklaus designed the course with his own game in mind, and in the early seventies he could be scary off the tee.) The approach shots are all challenging, promoting thoughtful course management and inventiveness in shotmaking. The greens are fast, true, and carefully maintained, promoting a durable putting stroke. The course is big and solid, and it's not tricked up in any way; it looks as comfortable on its site as Winged Foot does—no small feat, considering how young it is. The big holes meander over the hills and among the trees. They don't knock you over, the way the finishing holes at Cypress do, but you could play them over and over for a very long time without feeling you had used them up.

One reason Muirfield's greens are so nice is that spikes are not allowed. The instant I walked into the clubhouse, a locker-room attendant whisked away my shoes and used an electric drill equipped with a special bit to replace my metal cleats with soft-spikes—little green plastic rosettes that provide good traction on tees and fairways but don't chew up greens. The benefits of this policy, which was strongly endorsed by Nicklaus himself, are instantly apparent. Even at five in the evening, Muirfield's greens are as smooth as felt. The pros may never give up their spikes (the no-spike rule will be suspended for the Memorial), but I would guess that for the rest of us softspikes will eventually be the norm. That change will be welcomed by a number of my playing partners at home. There's an older member at our club whom we call Slippers, because his beaten-up beige golf shoes look like bedroom slippers. He shuffles across the greens in them, raking deep furrows with his spikes. (Maybe what he really needs is cross-country skis.)

No course designer has had a greater impact on American golf than Donald Ross, who grew up in Dornoch, Scotland, served his golfing apprenticeship under Old Tom Morris, emigrated to America toward the end of the nineteenth century, and had a hand in the design of perhaps six hundred courses, the great majority of them in the United States. Ross's masterpiece is undoubtedly Pinehurst No. 2, which he designed when he was in his early twenties. Ross was tapped for the job by James W. Tufts, an eccentric, bearded Bostonian who had piled up a fortune in the soda-fountain business and was now building a health resort in the sand hills of North Carolina. Golf was almost an afterthought at Pinehurst; Tufts's game of choice was a variant of croquet called roque. Thanks mainly to Ross, though, when people think of Pinehurst today they think mainly of golf.

There are seven courses at Pinehurst, and an eighth is under construction. Ross designed the original versions, and several modifications, of numbers 1 through 4; Ellis Maples designed No. 5, Tom and George Fazio designed No. 6, Rees Jones designed No. 7, and Tom Fazio is designing No. 8. Ross fiddled with No. 2 off and on until he died, in 1948. He made several major improvements in 1935, after Bobby Jones angered him by choosing Alister Mackenzie instead of him to work on Augusta National. Other hands, including those of Tom Fazio and Jack Nicklaus, have fiddled here and there. Despite the changes and the passage of time, though, No. 2 remains true to Ross's original conception. The key to the course, now as then, is the greens, which are crowned, firm, and fast. The straightforward appearance of most of the holes and the generous fairways is deceiving. To score on No. 2 you need to be in the right place with the right club in your hand, and you need to be on top of your putting. Unless the course is sopping wet, the greens are hard to hold from any distance, and they are easy to putt right off, even for the pros. And if you do roll off, there are few easy up-and-downs coming back.

Golf at Pinehurst was made considerably more enjoyable for me by my caddies, two sons of a local legend called "Loose Tooth" McLaughlin. Jerry McLaughlin carried my bag the first day, and his brother Carl (a favorite caddy of Jay Sigel's) carried it the second, and we spotted Loose Tooth at one point working on an adjacent fairway. Pinehurst has one of the best caddy programs around, and more golfers should avail themselves of it. The first day, I played with three German tourists, who shared two carts. Because they had to keep their carts on the inconvenient paths, they walked many more miles than I did, most of them perpendicular to the line of play, as they trotted back and forth across the fairways to change clubs or retrieve their vehicles. What can they possibly remember of their rounds, except all that pointless hurrying?

After playing golf, I wandered around the little hamlet of Pinehurst, which was laid out by Frederick Law Olmstead, the designer of New York's Central Park. Conceived with Tufts's background in mind, the town looks like a New England village. For a few months in the very beginning, it was known as Tuftstown. Nowadays, it could be called Realtorville, after the principal local industry. Residents and regular visitors over the years have included Annie Oakley, John Philip Sousa, Eddie Rickenbacker, Gloria Swanson, Yogi Berra, Warren Harding, and Larry Bird. The premier off-course haunt in town is the Pine Crest Inn, a slightly dog-eared hotel just off the main drag which was owned and run for a number of years by Donald Ross. When hotshot sports guys like Michael Jordan and Don Meredith come to town, they often hang out at the Pine Crest, along with what appears to be everyone else within twenty miles who isn't asleep. There's a piano bar in the lobby, and a chipping target in the fireplace. The main attraction is Bill Jones, who runs the bar just off the lobby and is a sort of walking encyclopedia of opinions about sports. Jones has a loud voice and a photographic memory for bar tabs. He also has a loyal following that includes both locals and visitors across a broad range of ages. It's a great bar, and it's more crowded when Jones is there than when he's not. One evening, while watching a college football game on the TV set over the bar, I had a long conversation with a retired guy from Pennsylvania. He showed me his business card. It said:

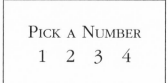

PICK A NUMBER

1   2   3   4

I picked 3. He flipped over the card and showed me what it said on the other side: ALL SEX MANIACS PICK 3. He let me keep the card, and I have tried it on about twenty people, all of whom have given the same answer.

Drowning my sorrows with retired Pennsylvania sex maniacs was something I actually felt like doing after visiting the next course on my tour, Oakmont Golf Club, just outside Pittsburgh. Of all the courses I played, Oakmont is the only one I would be just as happy never to play again. It was simply too hard for me. In the first place, it's miles long, and it played even longer when I was there. There had been a lot of rain over the past few days, causing a horrifying number of my drives to plug instead of roll a hundred yards, the way Ernie Els's did in the Open. In the second place, the greens were faster than the rate at which my brain is able to process information. On one hole, I faced a thirty-foot putt that ran almost imperceptibly downhill.

"Putt it like a three-footer," my caddy said.

I looked at it again. "An Oakmont three-footer or a normal three-footer?"

"An Oakmont three-footer."

I took my putter back perhaps an inch and gave the ball a gentle, indecisive tap. It rolled very slowly. I could read the name on the ball each time it turned: TITLEIST . . . TITLEIST . . . TITLEIST . . . TITLEIST. About ten feet short of the hole, it began to lose speed. Still slowing, it nicked the edge of the cup: TITLEIST . . . . TITLEIST . . . . TITLEIST. About three feet past the hole, it collided with a neutrino and veered off on a tangent. A lonely crow cried plaintively from a branch in a nearby tree. A good ten feet past the hole, my ball finally stopped. It was quivering when I picked it up.

"Good putt," my caddy said. (Lee Trevino: "Any time you two-putt at Oakmont, you're passing somebody by.")

I am prepared to think Oakmont is a swell course for people who have more moral fiber than I do. It is stirringly beautiful—something that doesn't come across on TV. And it is probably the ideal venue for the U.S. Open, since it permanently embodies in grotesque form every one of the harrowing qualities the USGA likes to see in a championship course: It is endless; its rough is deep, punishing, and slashed with vengeful ditches; its fairways are narrow to the point of inducing claustrophobia; it is one of the few courses in the world where pros don't shout at their balls, "Get in the bunker!"; and its greens are so fast that they actually had to be toned down for the Open. ("If they want to see Oakmont when it's really tough, they should play in the member-guest," a member told Larry Dorman, who covers golf for *The New York Times*.) It's easy to spot the members on the club's practice green, which is the rearmost quarter-acre of the ninth green: They're the guys with the facial twitches, trembling hands, and nervous, stabbing strokes. The club's guiding philosophy was succinctly stated by William Fownes, who with his father, Pittsburgh steel titan Henry Clay Fownes, designed the course in the early nineteen hundreds: "A shot poorly played should be a shot irrevocably lost." For someone who is prone on occasion to play a poor shot, a round at Oakmont can seem to last a very long time. In eighteen holes there, I didn't manage a single par (although I did make one birdie, on the short par-four seventeenth). *No mas!*

I had a very different experience on the other side of the state, at Merion Golf Club, just outside Philadelphia. Merion is to Oakmont as Philadelphia is to Pittsburgh. It is the all-time favorite course of many good golfers who have played it, and no wonder. It is beautiful to look at, perpetually (and deceptively) challenging to play, and thoroughly steeped in history. If I could choose *just one more* golf course to be the only one I would play for the rest of my life, it would be Merion.

Merion is tightly shoe-horned into the Main Line suburbs west of Philadelphia. Where Pine Valley floats in a world if not a universe of its own, Merion seems like the logical extension of the genteel neighborhoods that surround it. The course is bordered on the east by the Philadelphia & Western Railway, and it is bisected by Ardmore Avenue, a thoroughfare that players must cross twice in eighteen holes. As you hit from the first tee, you are intensely and sometimes fatally aware of being watched by members sitting on the clubhouse terrace, just a few paces behind you. No doubt they are checking to see if you will violate the sacred first commandment of the club's first tee: Thou shalt not take a mulligan. The clubhouse itself is a bit gone at the seams, like a favorite old jacket. Unlike the clubhouse at Augusta National, it doesn't give the impression of having been repainted fifteen minutes ago. Merion is so old that at the time of its founding one of its original members had recently lost an arm after standing too close to a cannon firing a salute at the funeral of Abraham Lincoln. It was a cricket club in those days; golf was first offered thirty years later, and the current course was built in 1912.

Merion shares a surprising trait with three other courses in the top ten: it was designed by a novice. Its principal architect was Hugh Wilson, an accomplished amateur golfer, who in 1910 was dispatched to Scotland and England by the Merion Cricket Club Golf Association to seek inspiration for a new course. (The distinctive wicker baskets that take the place of flags at Merion are a touch that Wilson discovered at Prestwick.) Like George Crump of Pine Valley, Jack Neville and Douglas Grant of Pebble Beach, and the Fowneses of Oakmont, Wilson had never designed a course before—although unlike the others he did move on to other design projects, including the four holes at Pine Valley that were still incomplete at Crump's death. Beginner's luck? Or maybe something to do with the nature of inspiration.

Whatever its source, Wilson's inspiration has inspired an awful lot of terrific golf. Merion's greatest single moment was probably Bobby Jones's victory in the 1930 U.S. Amateur—the title that completed his grand slam of the four major tournaments of that era. Jones closed out his match at the wonderful par-four eleventh, where an unspectacular par gave him an eight-and-seven victory over Eugene Homans. (The hole is a short par-four that plays downhill to a green protected in front and to the right by a moat-like creek.) Jones's feat is commemorated by a bronze plaque near the eleventh tee. Shortly before the plaque was unveiled, in 1960, someone noticed that it attributed the feat not to Robert Tyre Jones, Jr., the immortal amateur, but to Robert Trent Jones, Jr., the distinguished course architect. A narrow strip of bronze bearing the correct name was hastily produced and affixed to the face of the plaque, thus permanently memorializing not only one of the greatest triumphs in golf but also one of the silliest booboos.

Another great moment at Merion? How about Ben Hogan's unwavering one-iron to the eighteenth green during the final round of the 1950 U.S. Open? The shot set up a two-putt par that tied him with Floyd Mangrum and George Fazio, whom he beat in an eighteen-hole playoff the following day, just a year and a half after the terrible car accident that had come close to killing him and left him nearly unable to walk. If you follow golf at all, you know this shot, because Hogan's inimitably perfect follow-through was captured from behind by a photographer for *Life,* and the picture has been reproduced in coffee-table golf books ever since. Fazio called that one-iron the greatest golf shot he had ever seen.

Merion's most famous hole—and, for most players, its most horrifying—is the sixteenth, a long par-four known as the Quarry Hole. The quarry is an abandoned rock pit that figures in the design of seventeen and eighteen as well. On sixteen, it takes the form of two jagged bulwarks of stone, which stand, like Scylla and Charybdis, on either side of the weed-choked wall of sand that passes for an entrance to the green. In the 1950 U.S. Open, the quarry helped turn Cary Middlecoff from a contender into an also-ran. I managed to squeak a three-wood just over the abyss, where my ball nestled into some thick rough that by comparison with the rocks and sand seemed almost cozy. The next time I play the hole, I'll hit eight-iron, eight-iron, eight-iron, and say the heck with it.

And I desperately hope there is a next time. I wasn't quite on my game when I visited Merion, having undergone a radical swingectomy a couple of days before during a brief stopover at Sea Island's Golf Learning Center, the Mayo Clinic of my golf game. But I played well enough to catch occasional glimpses of the complex masterpiece that Lee Trevino called, on two different days during U.S. Open week in 1971, "a nice little course" and "the hardest course I've ever seen." Even as I was plucking my ball from the cup on the

short, wonderful, par-four first hole—which I parred, incidentally—I was already depressed by the thought that the day would
eventually come to an end.

The northeastern quadrant of the country is heavily represented on
the upper slopes of the 100 Greatest list, accounting for six of the
first ten spots. Is this a sign of some sort of regional bias among the
raters? Some people may think so. On the other hand, the Northeast
is where golf first took hold in the United States. The courses there
have had longer to settle into their sites and to put down layers of
history.

A course that suffers no shortage of historical layers is the Open
Course at the Country Club, in Brookline, Massachusetts, just outside of Boston. T.C.C. has hosted the U. S. Open three times, the
U. S. Amateur five times, and the Walker Cup twice, and it will host
the Ryder Cup in 1999. The club was the site of one of the great
watershed events in American golf: Francis Ouimet's astonishing
victory in the 1913 Open. Ouimet was a gangly twenty-year-old
amateur who had grown up in a house across the street from the
club. His parents weren't prosperous enough to be members, but
he had caddied there as a boy and had snuck rounds on the course
many times. With a caddy the size of a kindergartner, he tied British
golfing deities Harry Vardon and Ted Ray in regulation play, then
beat them in an eighteen-hole playoff. His victory amounted to a
don't-tread-on-me declaration that American golf was henceforth to
be taken seriously. Best of all, Ouimet was a perfect American hero:
an ordinary kid from a modest background who, through hard
work and indomitable courage, had brought a couple of smug
foreigners to their knees.

Like Merion, the Country Club had no connection with golf when
it began. The main interest of the founding members (whose last
names sound like a directory of Harvard dormitories) was horse
racing. You can still see the outline of parts of the track, which was
used until the early sixties, in the rough alongside the eighteenth
fairway and elsewhere. Even today, golf is only one of the club's
attractions. There are a curling rink, tennis courts, swimming pools,

a secluded pond that in the winter is maintained for ice skating, a skeet-shooting range, and an enormous, rambling clubhouse for launching debutantes. (Unlike the other clubs in the top ten, the Country Club is truly a country club.) The ancient paneled library is painted dark green, and its characteristically oddball selection of books includes a directory of Episcopal priests. The men's locker room is housed in an old brick building that from the outside looks like the administration building of a distinguished prep school. The lockers are massive steel vaults that are marked with mismatched lengths of plastic labeling tape—solid, practical, unpretentious furnishings that would seem equally at home in a fine old federal penitentiary.

The Country Club's Open Course is not the course that members play every day. It is pieced together from the best holes on the club's three nines, and it is too demanding for regular use by mere mortals. All three nines are worthy of celebration, however. The holes were conceived in the days when course architects bent their ideas to fit the landscape instead of the other way around. They have ragged edges and inexplicable dead ends and inconvenient outcroppings of rock. The sand in the bunkers looks like sand, not something you might stir into your coffee. The course is comfortable on its site, as Merion is, and it seems entirely unpretentious, like Shinnecock. May I pick a fourth course to be my one and only?

The most infuriating stop on my tour of America's greatest golf courses, in the view of the people I normally play golf with, was the final one, Augusta National.

"I don't want to hear about it," a friend of mine said.

"Did I mention that I'm going to be spending the night there, too?" I asked.

Angry silence; steam venting from ears.

No matter. I can make other friends. But there will never be another Augusta.

At some clubs, even the members must feel a little like guests— Cypress Point comes to mind, since most of the people who play there are just passing through. At Augusta National, in contrast, guests are made to feel almost like members. For me, this fantasy began at the front desk, where I was greeted by name, the news of my arrival having been forwarded by the guard at the gate. My caddy was magically waiting by my bag at the driving range when I strolled over to hit balls after lunch. The guy in the shoe room had my shoes in his hand before I could open my mouth to ask for them. I never locked the door to my bedroom, in the residential wing attached to the clubhouse, because why would I need to lock it? (They don't even give you a key.) This illusion of belonging is not entirely wholesome. Some of the members in the clubhouse bar look as though they are awaiting word of the outcome of the Civil War. The world that is preserved behind the fences at Augusta is a world whose passing was not widely mourned. But the place can be seductive nonetheless.

Augusta National is so isolated from the rest of the planet that it seems to have its own weather. Sleet could be falling on Washington Avenue, just outside the front gate, and a warm evening breeze would still be ruffling the green jackets of the members sipping bourbon on the terrace behind the clubhouse. The city of Augusta is gaudy and sprawling and filled with gas stations and crummy restaurants. (The best seafood place in town, according to a poll in a local magazine, is Red Lobster.) Inside the gates at the golf club, though, time stopped when Bobby Jones hung up his clubs.

Augusta National is the only place I have ever seen people sweeping grass. And the grass they were sweeping was not on the golf course. It was just a little triangle of lawn near the flagpole in front of the clubhouse. Even before it was swept, it looked better than any grass that *I* have ever had anything to do with. In fact, like all the other lawns at the club, it was indistinguishable from the fairways. And the fairways—did you know that at Augusta they cut the fairways in one direction only? The big mowers drive toward each green in formation, then lift their blades and return (in the rough) to where they started, then drop their blades and drive toward the green again. Monodirectional mowing reduces the chance that a misaligned blade of grass will accidentally bring the entire nine-hundred-year-old game of golf grinding to a standstill. Or something.

It's easy to laugh at such fetishistic care, but it's hard to laugh at the result, which is the Masters. Because the Masters is the only one of the four majors that is held year after year on the same course, it has a historical density that no other tournament can match. (The British Open has been held at the Old Course at St. Andrews ten times since 1934; the Masters, which began that year, has been held at Augusta National fifty-nine times.) Every year, the course embellishes itself with yet another layer of great shots, brilliant strategy, bad luck, undeserved disaster, heart-stopping heroics, lost opportunities, rescued fortune, and all the other highs and lows of competition at the highest level. Even for a bumbling hacker on a weekend pass, the place reverberates with all the transcendent golf that has been played there. Teeing off on the tenth hole is like walking into a dream. (By fiat of the club's executives, only the back nine is shown on television.) If you follow golf at all, you know these holes. You remember great rounds that have been made or broken at Amen Corner. You remember epochal putts that have dropped or lipped on every one of these greens. And when you hit two consecutive shots into Rae's Creek on twelve, you feel, in addition to the usual anger and disappointment, a powerful (if deluded) sense of kinship with all the great players who have done the very same thing.

It's almost a cliché to say that Augusta National is overrated as a golf course. (It's not very long! It has no rough!) But I think the Masters makes any such criticism virtually irrelevant. Besides, the course itself really is terrific. The 450-yard par-four tenth (which plays 485 yards in the tournament) may be my favorite hole anywhere. From the tee you look down into a deep, left-bending chasm that will tack an extra fifty yards onto a big smooth draw. The elevated green, which is protected in front by a bunker that from the fairway looks like the Gobi Desert, is hard to hit and harder to hold. It's a cool, cool hole—and you know as you play it that more cool holes lie ahead.

Leaving Augusta National at the end of my final round there, I felt like Cinderella at the stroke of midnight. My rented Taurus turned back into a pumpkin, leaving me with a lot of nice memories and a suitcase full of go-to-hell golf shirts. Naturally, I have devoted nearly every waking moment since then to figuring out how I can weasel my way back onto all those great courses—very possibly an insurmountable chore, since most of those courses are so private that from the point of view of the average golfer they might as well be on the moon. (This near-paranoid exclusivity is doubly annoying, because golf is in many ways ideally suited to being a sport of inclusion rather than exclusion. In fact, the game sets a noble example for society as a whole. Like all sports, it is perfectly meritocratic: If you shoot the best score, you win. At the same time, though, golf is the world's only welfare state that works: The handicapping system takes strokes from each according to his ability and gives them to each according to his need, and it does so in a way that functions smoothly enough to provide a framework for high-stakes gambling—communism with a human face. Unlike raw capitalism, golf has figured out how to foster individual achievement without smothering the hopes of those who can't keep up.)

The few friends I have who are still speaking to me sometimes ask me which of the top-ten courses I liked best, or how I would rank them myself. I never know how to answer. If I could snap my fingers and have a tee time at any of them tomorrow morning, I would probably pick Cypress, because of all ten it seems the most, well, ineffable. But that doesn't mean I think it's a better course than Pine Valley. In fact, the first ten courses are so different from one another that ranking them at all seems like a pointless exercise. However, I do sometimes fantasize about the perfect golf course. It would look pretty much exactly like Merion, although it would be set on the Monterey Peninsula. The Pinecrest Inn would stand beside the eighteenth green. The clubhouse would look a lot like Shinnecock's, with the men's locker room from the Country Club tacked on around in back. The greens would all be transplanted from Muirfield Village. I would live beside the first tee in a house like Jim Marshall's, at Pine Valley, except that I would probably just go ahead and park my golf cart in the living room. Most important of all, the perfect club would share a crucial characteristic with my little nine-hole course at home: Its membership would include me.

Oh, what the hell. It would include you, too.

ACKNOWLEDGMENTS

STANDING ON THE FIRST TEE AT PEBBLE BEACH OR Augusta National, I sometimes gaze contentedly at my playing partners and think, "Gee, I'm the only guy here who's working." For the past three years, playing golf and writing about it has been a big part of what I do for a living. Every couple of months, it seems, I find myself jetting off to Glasgow for a tour of British Open courses, or driving down to southern New Jersey for a long weekend at Pine Valley, or taking the ferry across Long Island Sound for an afternoon at Shinnecock. Lately, I have begun to wrestle with a thorny question: What will I do when I retire?

I am grateful to many people for helping me build the golf-based lifestyle from which this book arose. First, to Dave Johnson, the pro at Washington Golf Club, my first teacher. Dave taught me a good grip, repeatedly rescued my swing when I thought I had battered it past rehabilitation, and has above all been a good friend and golfing companion. During the past year, Dave has fought several heroic battles against cancer, remaining cheerful and brave even as his illness was ravaging his body and temporarily turning his steady fade into a slightly unpredictable draw. He is an inspiration to everyone who knows him.

I am also deeply grateful to: my direct golfing forebears, Loyd Owen, John Owen, and Bill Groner—respectively, my father, brother, and godfather; my wife, as previously mentioned; my ball-retrieving kids, John and Laura; my mother, Carol Owen, and my sister, Anne Owen, on general principles; Martha Fairbairn, who lured me onto the course again after twenty-three years; my usual playing partners, Jim Paisley, Art Peterson, Bill Fairbairn, George Auchincloss, and Mike Jackson; Dick Davis, Doug Heaven, and Ed Varley, the Fuckheads; Bob Witkoski, our scary greenkeeper; Mike Carney, Scott Davenport, Hank Johnson, Jack Lumpkin, Bill Murray, Gale Peterson, and Stan Thirsk, my teachers; Bob Hazen, Guy Morrone, and Red Teubner, my Thursday group; Howard Bascom, Rick O'Neill, and P. J. Johnson, the other members of my Wonder Years foursome; Ashley Farmen, my awesome Scotch foursome partner; Jerry Quinlan, my incomparable tour guide; my fellow compulsives, John Allen, Al Altorelli, Scott Anson, Peter Arturi, Gene Baslow, Mark Beebe, Dan Beller, Bruce Birenboim, Walter Bladstrom, George Blake, Jack Boyer, Bruce Bradshaw, Howard Bronson, John Bushka, Lyn Caceci, Paul Caceci, Bob Cantin, Graydon Carter, Alan Chapin, Charlie Chapin, Jean Chapin, Henry Childs, Bobby Clampett, Larry Colina, Jim Collins, Linc Cornell, Lyn Cornell, Mike Cornell, Steve Cornell, Fred Costello, Mel Crawford, Norm Cummings, Tim Daly, Tom Daniels, Denise DeVault, Bernie Dishy, Frank Dolen, Sean Donnelly, Peter Ebersol, Pam Emory, Tom Farmen, Jack Field, Allen Finkelson, Rob Fisher, Bob Fitterman, Gary Flood, Brendan Foulois, Spike Fowler, Bill Franklin, Joe Fredlund, Jim Fuchs, Larry Gendron, John Gillen, Ferris Gorra, Jim Graham, Doug Greene, Mary Anne Greene, Bob Hacker, Val Hastings, John Heinz, Scott Houldin, Spencer Houldin, Peter Houldin, William Houldin, Randy Hundley, Todd Hundley, Stan Jacoboski, Stan Jennings, D. J. Johnson, Bill Jones, Rick Jusko, Steve Kambanis, Buddy Kay, Nick Kearney, Pierce Kearney, Jim Kocsis, Peter Kostis, Gust Kouvaris, Alan Larrabure, Ivan Lendl, Phil Lengyel, Holly Lile, Henry Long, Rudy Mangels, Harry Mathews, Bob McDermott, Gerry

McDermott, Bob Mnuchin, Ted Morse, Ted Mygatt, Alan Newman, Colleen Newman, Marv Oonk, Rich Orr, Reese Owens, Jane Paisley, Joe Parrillo, Peter Pasch, Corey Pavin, Marion Pennell, Valerie Peterson, Jim Pickett, William Pickett, Rich Porri, Art Potter, Jean Potter, Ernie Ransome, Michael Rea, Nick Rimbocchi, Jim Robinson, Dick Sears, Greg Seeley, Chris Smith, Jim Solberg, Paul Spengler, Henry Steinman, Nancy Steinman, Lance Ten Broeck, Frances Tracey, Ray Underwood, Tom Watson, Ed White, Greg Wilson, Todd Wilson, Jan Wivestead, and many, many others; Diane Reverand and David Rosenthal, my editors; and Julia Coopersmith, my nongolfing agent.

At *Golf Digest* I am eternally grateful to Jerry Tarde, Roger Schiffman, Chris Hodenfield, John Huggan, Peter McCleery, Don Wade, John Barton, Peter Andrews, Michael Bamberger, Tom Callahan, Peter Dobereiner, Frank Hannigan, Dan Jenkins, Dave Kindred, Jim Moriarty, Bud Shrake, and all the other wonderful people there who have helped introduce me to the world's coolest job.

At *The New Yorker* I am grateful to Bob Gottlieb, who let me write about Karsten Solheim; to Chip McGrath, Nancy Franklin, and Roger Angell; and even to Tina Brown, who doesn't like golf and turned out to care not one bit about Karsten Solheim, but is still a nice person, and is, at any rate, my boss.

At *Esquire,* many thanks to Bill Tonelli, who packed me off to golf school.

At *The Atlantic Monthly* I am indebted to Bill Whitworth, Corby Kummer, Cullen Murphy, and Barbara Wallraff, who packed me off to Scotland.

At *Condé Nast Traveler* I am indebted to Peter Kaplan, even though he isn't there anymore.

Stop reading this, and go work on your short game.

DAVID OWEN was born in Kansas City, Missouri, in 1955, and had the same first-grade teacher Tom Watson did. He has been an editor of the *Harvard Lampoon,* a fact checker for *New York,* a frequent contributor to *Esquire,* a senior writer for *Harper's,* and a contributing editor of *The Atlantic Monthly.* He is now a staff writer for *The New Yorker* and a contributing editor of *Golf Digest.* He lives in Connecticut with his wife and their two children. At this very moment, he is probably playing golf.